MOONLIGHT EXPRESS

MONISHA RAJESH

MOONLIGHT EXPRESS

AROUND THE WORLD BY NIGHT TRAIN

BLOOMSBURY PUBLISHING

LONDON • OXFORD • NEW YORK • NEW DELHI • SYDNEY

BLOOMSBURY PUBLISHING
Bloomsbury Publishing Plc
50 Bedford Square, London, WC1B 3DP, UK
Bloomsbury Publishing Ireland Limited,
29 Earlsfort Terrace, Dublin 2, D02 AY28, Ireland

BLOOMSBURY, BLOOMSBURY PUBLISHING and the Diana logo are
trademarks of Bloomsbury Publishing Plc

First published in Great Britain 2025

A catalogue record for this book is available from the British Library

ISBN: HB: 978-1-5266-4412-1; TPB: 978-1-5266-4418-3; eBook: 978-1-5266-4413-8

2 4 6 8 10 9 7 5 3 1

Typeset by Siliconchips Services Ltd UK
Printed and bound in Great Britain by CPI Group (UK) Ltd, Croydon CR0 4YY

MIX
Paper | Supporting
responsible forestry
FSC
www.fsc.org   FSC® C013604

To find out more about our authors and books visit www.bloomsbury.com
and sign up for our newsletters
For product-safety-related questions contact productsafety@bloomsbury.com

For Maya, because my last book
was dedicated to your sister

Contents

CHAPTER 12

CHAPTER 7

Hamar

Oslo

Stockholm

Culloden

CHAPTER 9

Aberdeen

Dundee

Edinburgh

North
Sea

Baltic
Sea

Crewe

CHAPTER 8

Hamburg

The Hague

Amsterdam

Osnabrück

Berlin

London

Rotterdam

CHAPTER 11

Hanover

Antwerp

Göttingen

English Channel

Lille

Brussels

CHAPTER 16

Paris

Würzburg

Strasbourg

Regensburg

Stuttgart

CHAPTER 1

Linz

Munich

Vienna

A L P S

Budapest

CHAPTER 18

Milan

Venice

Genoa

Bologna

Marseille

Nice

Florence

Toulon

A P E N N I N E S

Rome

Mediterranean

CHAPTER 10

Naples

Sea

Strait of Messina

Palermo

Messina

Catania

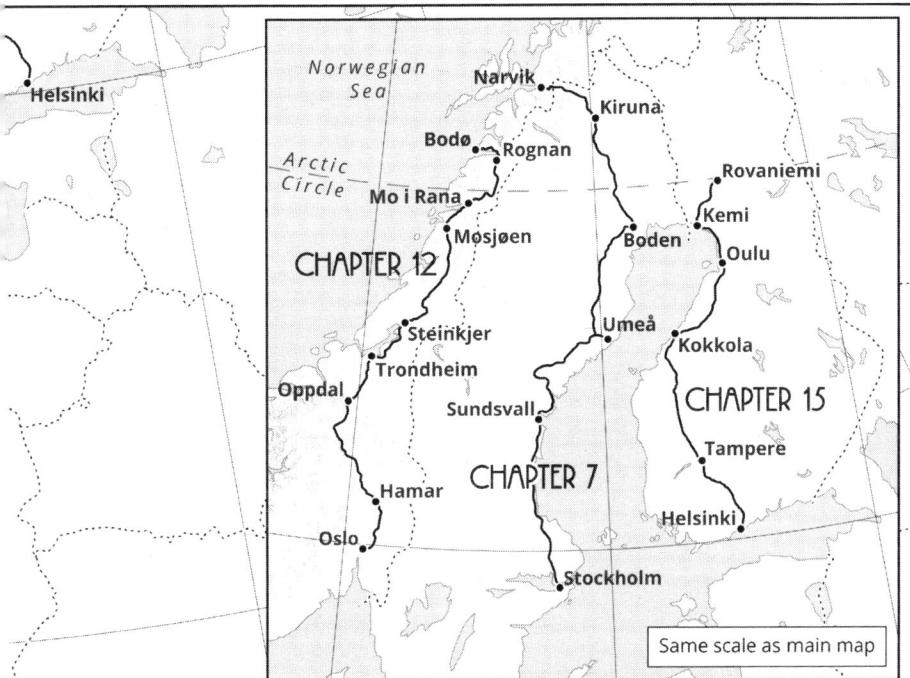

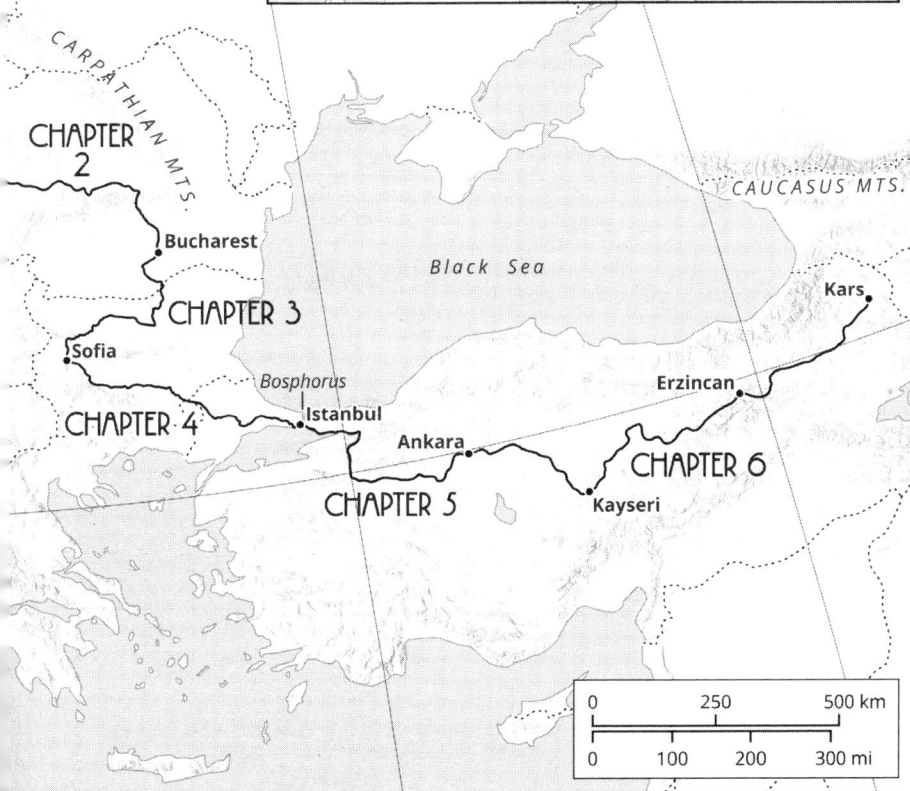

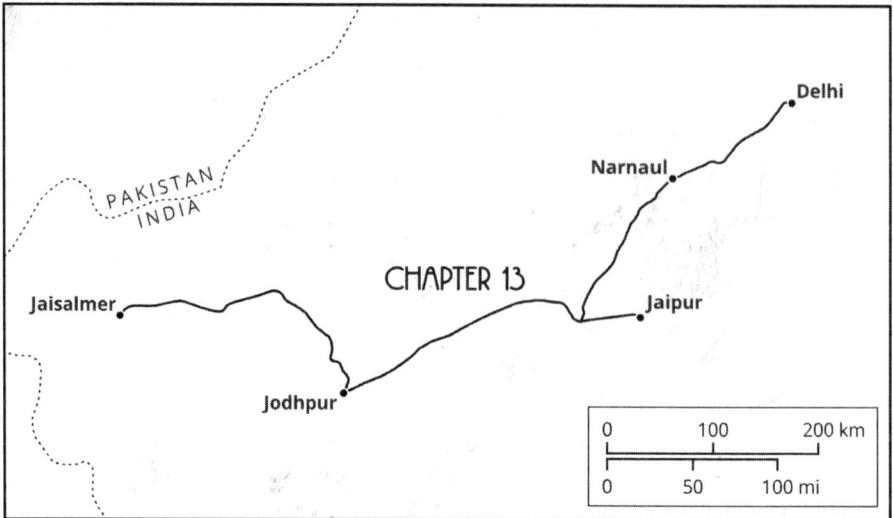

PAKISTAN
INDIA

Delhi

Narnaul

Jaipur

Jaisalmer

Jodhpur

CHAPTER 13

0   100   200 km

0   50   100 mi

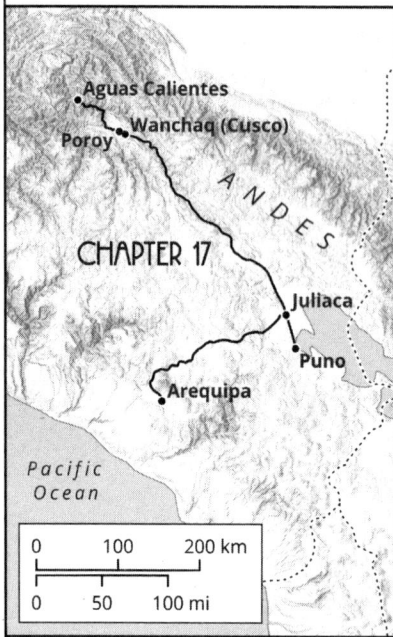

Aguas Calientes

Wanchaq (Cusco)

Poroy

A N D E S

CHAPTER 17

Juliaca

Puno

Arequipa

Pacific
Ocean

0   100   200 km

0   50   100 mi

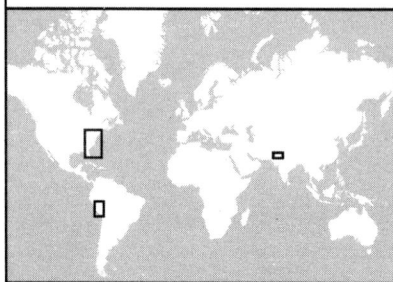

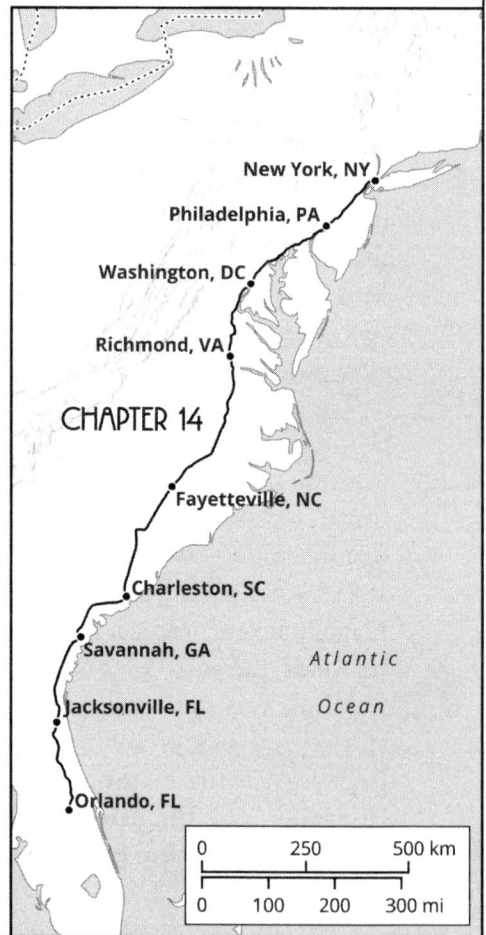

New York, NY

Philadelphia, PA

Washington, DC

Richmond, VA

CHAPTER 14

Fayetteville, NC

Charleston, SC

Savannah, GA

Jacksonville, FL

Orlando, FL

Atlantic

Ocean

0   250   500 km

0   100   200   300 mi

The Nightjet from Paris to Vienna

At 18.58 the Nightjet service from Paris to Vienna glides out from Gare de l'Est, embarking on a fifteen-hour journey through Strasbourg, Munich and Salzburg. On a Sunday night at the end of January, I should have been tucked up on board. Instead, I was shivering on a replacement TGV, eyeing a student watching porn on his phone. The high-speed train was crowded, the windows steaming up from the heat of compacted bodies. Those fortunate enough to bag a seat were sleeping face down on the tables or scrolling on their phones and sighing. Others were sitting on suitcases in the aisles, leaning against each other's shoulders and fidgeting in frustration as the train swept east past rows of Haussmannian apartments, attic rooms warmly lit. It was an inauspicious start to my grand adventure.

The Orient Express, the world's most famous train, was marking its 140th anniversary and it felt fitting to embark upon my journey into the world of sleeper trains by retracing its original route. Contrary to popular myth, the Express d'Orient – its original title – was far from a single luxury train. Launched in 1883 by a Belgian businessman, the fabulously named Georges Nagelmackers, it was a regular passenger service and for the first six years the journey between Paris and Constantinople (now Istanbul) was undertaken using a sequence of trains and ferries and several sets of rolling stock (or carriages). Trains departed Paris for Vienna via Strasbourg and Munich, then ran through Budapest and Bucharest to the southern Romanian city of Giurgiu. From there passengers were transported by ferry across the Danube to the Bulgarian city of Ruse, where a final train transferred them to Varna on the Black Sea coast, ending with a steamer to Istanbul. I felt tired just thinking about it. In 1889, however, the entire railway line was completed, and in June that year the first direct train departed Paris taking passengers all the way to Istanbul's Sirkeci station. Two years later the service was officially renamed the Orient Express.

That afternoon I'd arrived by Eurostar into Gare du Nord and, in the bright winter sun, walked the hour-long route towards the Left Bank, past pollarded plane trees, their flaking bark patched like camouflage. The aroma of caramelised almonds warmed the air around the burned-out beauty of Notre Dame, where I'd watched couples sharing macarons on benches, whippets in couture coats quivering at their feet. Vendors in fingerless gloves folded hot crêpes, and with one in hand, I'd picked my way between tourists cycling in the wrong direction and crossed over the road to the bookshop Shakespeare and Company, where I located a copy of *Murder on the Orient Express*. It had a striking cover featuring a vintage table lamp with the train running across a bridge at sunset. Now, two hours from Strasbourg, I thumbed through to where I'd left off in the story. For Hercule Poirot it had been a snowdrift that had disrupted his journey, bringing the Simplon-Orient-Express to a halt 'between Vincovi and Brod'. For me it had been an arson attack at Gare de l'Est. The fire had begun under an area of track by a signal point. No one was injured but the blaze had damaged around fifty cables and disrupted services in and out of the station. I'd turned up in good time, full of beans and eager to board, only to discover that the NJ 469 to Vienna was no longer departing from Paris, but five hours later from Strasbourg. At least the train wasn't cancelled and – on the upside – it had given me time to find a bistro for crisp confit de canard and a glass of Pinot noir. However, at 10 p.m., when I boarded the connection to Strasbourg, the wind had turned nasty, the air sharp with ice as we crowded onto the concourse, tensions high, moods low, limp toddlers hoisted over shoulders and everyone shoving to get on.

I remembered then how much of night-train travel involves killing time: reading in cafés; loitering in hotel bars and lobbies; praying for no delays. And yet, sleeper trains were well and truly enjoying a renaissance.

After the Covid lockdowns trains found their way back onto travellers' radars – much to my delight. Many people were nervous to fly, booking private compartments and taking the time to explore closer to home. In 2022 Interrail had a record year of sales – and then I saw it, one line at a time, sleeper trains inching back out of the darkness, headlamps ablaze. A decade ago, the romance of night-train journeys had fizzled out around Europe, a mass cull of sleeper trains giving way to budget airlines and high-speed rail. But who knew the world was going to shut down? The change of pace and perspectives, along with the added reality of climate change, was undeniable and passengers were increasingly concerned about their carbon footprints, keener than ever to rekindle the flames of night-time travel. Private companies like the Belgian–Dutch collective European Sleeper and the French start-up Midnight Trains were popping up with ambitious plans to launch new sleeper services across Europe, and existing operators like Sweden's Snälltåget wanted to extend routes, encouraged by campaign groups such as 'Back on Track' and 'Oui au train de Nuit!'

I placed a bookmark between the pages of my Agatha Christie and looked out to where a river gleamed like spilt ink beneath the street lights, feeling the thrill of being on the move again at night. Looking back over fifteen years of train travel – more than 200 journeys packed with everything from political chats and poker games to jam sessions, counselling sessions, history lessons, wonderful views, weirdos and copious cups of tea – I remembered how the sleeper trains were the ones that had enveloped me whole. Each departure seemed staged for a tryst: passengers boarded after sunset and left before sunrise, slipping in and out of compartments unseen. Others were there for the long haul, pulling on bed socks and laying out books, glasses, and packets of sweet-smelling cheese. They'd make me sandwiches, offload their woes and offer advice while I revelled in the cosiness of newfound friendship, the intimacy electric. After blinds were pulled down and lights flipped off, I'd wait for the sound of even breathing before climbing down from my berth and tiptoeing into the corridor where I'd come upon the glow of noctilucent clouds, mists moving through forests like ghosts, and the alchemy of the moon turning water to silver thread.

Outside Europe, night trains remained safe from extinction, at least for the time being. Many passengers simply couldn't afford to pay premium fares for high-speed rail, and tourists kept them going, often choosing to make the journey the destination – saving on hotels and turning the ride into a mobile camping trip with friends and family. But I was curious how the resurgence in Europe was going to play out. There was little rolling stock available, and unless someone took it upon themselves to build a brand-new batch specifically for sleeper trains, fitted with berths, I couldn't see how it could work. It also felt like the right time for me personally to explore the continent's railways. In 2015, when I travelled 45,000 miles around the world for my last book, I'd hotfooted across Europe in a month. An intensive itinerary that centred on major journeys – such as the Trans-Mongolian from Moscow to Beijing, the Canadian from Vancouver to Toronto and the Qinghai–Tibet railway from Xining to Lhasa – meant that Europe had barely got a look-in. At the time there were hardly any sleeper trains left, so I'd skimmed around with a Eurail pass and made my way out pretty sharpish. Now European railways had my full attention and I wanted to know what motivated those passengers drifting back towards night trains. Were they commuters looking to save time and money? Old romantics in search of nostalgia? Or was climate change at the forefront of Europeans rethinking how they travelled?

My own motivation was a combination of all three, but ultimately my love for night trains stemmed from the way in which they allowed me to slow down. Once on board I could relax, knowing I had the whole night ahead of me to read, gossip in a warm dining car, or simply lie in my berth, listening to the beat of the train through the darkness. At times I'd sit in solitude making notes or mulling over troubling thoughts – most of which would fade by the time we drew into a new city, and I nudged up the blind, intrigued to see what lay outside. There were plenty of railway routes to discover but since my last adventure around the world I now had two young daughters, so taking off for a stretch of several months was not an option. Travelling took place in sporadic bursts and around school holidays, sometimes with my elder daughter, Ariel, in tow. Perhaps it was genetic, but she was already showing a strong predilection for railways and had recently ridden along with me on the *Night Riviera* from Paddington to Penzance and the sleeper from Nice to Paris, a perky little Passepartout in striped pyjamas.

Now, to my relief, I saw that the TGV was slowing into Strasbourg, and I peered out to find the Nightjet waiting on the next platform. It was Sunday night. I had a week of travel ahead. If all went to plan, I'd have four more trains to catch before pulling into Istanbul in the early hours of Friday morning.

A harassed-looking woman greeted me on board the Nightjet and handed me a keycard to my compartment, along with a small, warm bottle of Sekt, the last thing I wanted to drink at midnight.

'Wait, don't go to sleep yet, I need to bring you something,' she said, disappearing up the corridor.

Austrian Federal Railways (ÖBB) was playing a major role in resuscitating Europe's night trains. Austria's central location meant that it was ideally placed as a continental crossroads and towards the end of 2016 ÖBB had invested €40 million into acquiring almost sixty sleeping and couchette cars from Deutsche Bahn after Germany officially terminated its own sleeper trains. These cars had been used to launch ÖBB's Nightjet network on twenty routes around Europe. The sleeping cars contained pre-made beds; the couchette cars made up from padded berths that fold down into seats during the day.

I slid the keycard in, and the door swung open to reveal a tatty carpet, scuffed walls and chipped paint. It reminded me of my university halls of residence, minus the stench of fags and WKD Blue. I sat down on the bed and looked around the dimly lit compartment. The offer of sparkling wine made sense now. Still, we were on the move towards the German border. I immediately set to work rattle-proofing the room, laying bottles between clothes, removing coat hangers from the wall and turning down the volume for announcements, the knob coming off in my hand. Although drained and desperate to turn in, I had to wait for the train manager to return. Twice I stepped out to look for her, but she was nowhere to be seen. As I closed the door, a chunk of paint fell off. The compartment was in need of a damn good overhaul. I went online to torture myself with images of Nightjet's brand new fleet of carriages, which was due to launch in the autumn – not a moment too soon. Someone sniffed. I heard it again, followed by a zip being undone, and I realised the walls were thinner than my patience. At that moment a knock at the door announced the manager, Elisabeth, looking far less harassed. Everyone was now checked off her list. She handed me a breakfast menu.

'You tick six items and leave it outside the door,' she said, bidding me goodnight.

After doing as instructed, I rummaged around my washbag for my earplugs and eye mask. Warming the silicone between my palms, I pressed in the plugs, slid beneath the musty covers and switched off the main light. Still, a neon-blue bulb glowed overhead. Although I knew the tiny light would fracture my sleep, I couldn't bring myself to put on my eye mask. I had a strange relationship with darkness: at once unnerving and intriguing; a place I wanted both to flee and explore. Sleeping in pitch-black was too creepy. Travelling by myself meant being suspended in a state of hypervigilance. I needed my faculties to not feel vulnerable, while still relaxing enough to fall asleep.

My choice of reading material did little to help, and I was now lying with my eyes wide open thinking about Edward Ratchett being stabbed to death in his compartment.

Shuffling over towards the window, I took solace from the lights of passing farmhouses, but they soon vanished as we neared the edge of the Black Forest whose folklore was rooted in darkness and the supernatural. I had spent my life trying to reshape how darkness had appeared to me as a child, nervously watching shadows from my bed, and I wondered now if that was why I was drawn to travelling by night train. Perhaps I was trying to reconcile my relationship with darkness or attempting to discover what cast those shadows. I checked my phone: 2 a.m. and the train was approaching the old Baden capital of Karlsruhe. With a final glance, I pulled down the blind and crawled back up to my pillow, tossing my mask to one side.

That night I slept like an actual baby – waking every hour or so, cold then hot then thirsty and occasionally on the verge of tears. The train was bumpy, slinging me around, braking and creaking throughout the night. I stared at the ceiling wondering if it had been so long since I'd regularly ridden trains that I was simply out of practice. Through sheer exhaustion I dozed off, only to wake to footsteps thudding up the corridor close behind my head. Moving to the foot of the berth, I raised the blind in time to see that we were crossing the Saalach river, over the border into Austria. My phone buzzed with a welcome message. Drifting through Salzburg Mülln-Altstadt station, we crossed over a second river, snow piled up its banks, the softness of pastel shades colouring the pre-dawn light. The Northern Limestone Alps glowed in the distance, their scalps turning neon pink in the rising sun. Farms and field scenes flitted past. A family of four deer eating hay. Forests packed with pencil-thin larch.

Elisabeth arrived with my breakfast, and over coffee and a salami roll, I watched curtains opening and lights coming on, catching the eye of commuters clearing snow from their cars. It was this moment that made the journey: when most passengers were still asleep and the outside world yawned and stretched awake, the skies breaking open to let in the first light. My tiredness vanished, replaced by the unmistakable feeling of coming home.

The morning took shape with the Türnitz Alps rising into view. Passengers threw open doors, going back and forth to use the loos. As we passed through the wine region of Traisental, its vineyards covered with protection from the cold, the train slowed. At the Austrian city of St Pölten, a number of people disembarked, and I got talking to Elisabeth. Presumptuous, I'd expected everyone on board to be travelling from one capital to the next, but she shook her head furiously.

'No, there are *many* passengers who take the train because it is so much easier for them to get home. If you fly to Vienna you have to figure out how to get back to your home town, some-times at bad hours.'

'Are there more people using the train now since the pandemic?'

'For sure. I've been working on this train for seven years and people are really bothered about climate change. They could fly for cheaper, but they don't want to.'

I asked Elisabeth if she had regulars on board and she explained that it was a popular route owing to the European Court of Human Rights in Strasbourg, the same few lawyers frequently coming through. I mentioned how stressed I thought she'd looked the night before and she started to laugh. 'People travel-ling for work are often angry, especially when there are delays, but families and others, they are relaxed,' she said. 'The arson did not help.'

We pressed ourselves against the wall as a passenger squeezed by and Elisabeth raised a finger as she remembered something she wanted to say.

'I have one woman: she is a cellist. She plays with the orchestra in Paris a lot and she can't take her cello on the aeroplane with-out buying another seat, so she takes the train. And there is also a dad from Romania whose ex-wife lives outside Versailles with the child. He takes the night train from Bucharest to Vienna and then to Paris to see him.'

'I'm taking the train to Bucharest tonight,' I said.

'The *Dacia*? That's a terrible train – it's so long. And it's a Romanian train. Watch out for your things, yes?'

Beckoned by a colleague, Elisabeth disappeared. I went back to my compartment to pack my bag, caught off guard by the casual racism, but suddenly nervous about the next leg of my journey.

Just after 10 a.m. we drew into Vienna, where powdery snow danced in the cold. This was the brilliance of sleeper trains: the entire day stretched out ahead of me. I had the urge to seek out every highlight of the city, but I took stock. Vienna was only a couple of train rides from London, and I could always return. Instead, I looked up the location of the Belvedere Museum and within twenty minutes of stepping off the night train I was standing in front of Gustav Klimt's *The Kiss* for the first time, welling up at the sight of my favourite painting in all its gold-leafed glory. Paintings were usually smaller than I'd imagined but *The Kiss* was a grand affair, filling a wall, the figures life-sized as they embraced beneath their shimmering shawls. As visitors posed in front of the painting, taking selfies and blocking everyone's view, I found a seat in the centre of the room, and waited for a lull when I could steal a few precious minutes to take in the richness and tenderness of the work, for ever in awe of the power of art to bring peace.

By the time I walked down the Belvedere's baroque gardens towards the heart of the city, the snow turned to sleet, and then rain. As much as I wanted to explore, poor weather presented the perfect opportunity to seek out a café, cut into a slice of Sachertorte and pick up from where I'd left Monsieur Poirot on the train. In a corner of the Demel café, enjoying the din of groups of friends chattering over hot chocolate while the rain hammered down, I foraged around in my bag. The book was nowhere to be found. With a sigh, I realised that I had indeed left Monsieur Poirot on the train.

Opening up my diary, and pulling up a map of Europe on my laptop, I started to compile a bucket list of sleeper trains. After arriving in Istanbul I was booked onto the *Ankara Express* to the capital and then another, the *Doğu Express*, from Ankara to Kars in the north-east of Türkiye. That made a total of five sleepers by the end of the week. I zoomed in and out of the map, realising I'd never travelled around the Nordic region even though it was home to a number of fabulous night trains: the Dovre railway from Oslo to Trondheim; the Nordland line from Trondheim to Bodø; the Norrland Night Train from Stockholm to Narvik; and last but certainly not least, the *Santa Claus Express* in Finland. Italy had also fallen off my radar and there was an infamous journey from Rome to Palermo that involved transporting the train onto a ferry. A few years ago, I'd taken the *Caledonian Sleeper* from Glasgow to London in its former guise, but it had since had a revamp, and I wrote it in beneath the quartet of Nordic routes. If European Sleeper – a Belgian–Dutch cooperative – succeeded with its plans to cobble together enough carriages, there would soon be a new service from Brussels to Berlin called *The Good Night Train*, so I added that in in brackets.

Five months earlier, a EuroNight sleeper train had started running between Hamburg and Stockholm, but there were rumours that it might extend to Berlin. If that happened, I was going to try and ride it back with *The Good Night Train*. More than anything I couldn't wait for Nightjet's new-generation fleet which was slated to go into service on the Vienna–Hamburg route, but this plan was getting hairy. Some of these trains didn't exist yet. They were nothing more than proposals, and I could only hope they would come to fruition.

In the past my rail adventures had involved tight itineraries, allowing for little more than a meal and a cursory glance around the cities of boarding and arrival. This time I wanted to slow down, explore the surroundings for a few days and learn more about the people as well as the places. Scraping up the last crumbs of torte, I looked down the list, wondering what was left to add – perhaps beyond Europe. In 2010 I'd spent four months travelling the length and breadth of India for my first book, and I hadn't been on an Indian sleeper train since then.

Indian Railways had thrived in that time, and I was keen to go back and see how things had progressed, maybe squeezing in a rickety sleeper for old times' sake. There was also the *Silver Meteor*, an Amtrak service that ran from Miami up to New York City. I'd been unable to take it when I had last travelled around the US, and it had recently received an upgrade and returned to the tracks after a hiatus.

The list was taking shape nicely. But one train was missing. I went to write it in, then paused. Not in a million years could I make that happen. Asking for the bill, I closed my diary, gathering my things before flipping it open again and adding my ultimate sleeper train with a flourish. After all, a girl could dream.

2

THE DACIA

Out of breath and bent double at the top of the escalator, I was relieved – and a little concerned – that the train to Bucharest was yet to arrive. I'd remembered at the last minute that it was wise to keep cash on board in case the card machines were down and had got stuck in a queue to withdraw notes. With only ten minutes to departure, the evening crowd at Vienna Hauptbahnhof was thin. Small groups paced around, propping up rucksacks and glancing up the tracks, but this didn't look like it would be a busy train. As I sized up my fellow passengers, a trio of headlamps appeared, and a blue engine hummed into view. Written across the front were the words 'Planet Budapest 21' – a reference to the four-day summit that had taken place at the end of 2021 for Visegrád countries (Czech Republic, Hungary, Poland and Slovakia) to address issues of the pandemic, climate change, water security and sustainable transport. I looked at my e-ticket which informed me that I was saving 224.4 kilograms of carbon dioxide emissions travelling by train instead of driving, which was satisfying to say the least. I could have flown to Bucharest in ninety minutes, but as I scanned the brightly lit compartments sailing past, I looked forward to my home for the next nineteen hours.

After lockdown lifted, many holiday-makers came to the conclusion that it was more ethical to get pissed-up on a cider trail in Herefordshire than on a Tui tour to Faliraki, and I attributed some of this shift in attitudes to Greta Thunberg, who had popularised the Swedish concept of *flygskam*, or 'flight shame'. There was no way I'd do it myself, but I was still inspired by the courage of a then sixteen-year-old with two plaits sailing on a zero-carbon yacht from the UK to a climate summit in New York, as part of a drive towards climate-friendly travel. In turn, *flygskam* had sparked another trend known as *tågskryt*, or 'train bragging', whereby those who gave up flying took to social media to post train-filled content that I watched in bed like porn.

Flying didn't fill me with dread as much as airports. Over time I'd grown ever more irritated at having to arrive hours before departure only to remove shoes, unbuckle belts, collapse buggies, forget laptops, crawl in queues, pay extra for bags, pay extra for seats, pay extra for boarding – and cram my make-up into sandwich bags. I didn't take kindly to being touched by strangers, least of all by security staff running hands along my inner leg and underwire before foraging through stacks of knickers and shaking out tampons, in the hunt for what usually turned out to be an inhaler.

Having children, too, had turned the experience into a circus. On a return flight from Malta, my toddler had charged through the dividing curtain and knocked a passenger's mini bottle of champagne across her table where it fizzed over her passport then dripped into her handbag. Any parent who says they don't judge other parents is a liar: we all do it and I could feel the stares from parents who couldn't fathom how we were travelling without an iPad. Before having kids, I was one of those self-righteous berks, the ones who imagine *their* children will play with wooden blocks and xylophones. Then I became a parent and by the age of three both girls had their own Netflix accounts. As a family it was far less stressful to travel by train. We could turn up five minutes before departure, pack unlimited bags and bottles, run up and down the corridors, wave from the windows, climb around in pants, and make as much noise as we liked – the children too. Now, as I watched a young family boarding, a vision of Disney backpacks, wellies and animal mittens, I felt a pang of yearning for my own little people. It lasted about three seconds, the reality of alone-time too rare and delicious for me to wallow in their absence.

'Can I get a ticket through to Bucharest?' asked a voice with a deep Southern American accent. Halfway up the steps, I turned to see a man push to the front of the line behind me, much to the annoyance of the inspector who steered him to one side. He was wearing a red jacket and an absurd bobble hat that made him look like a Christmas-tree decoration.

'Is there availability?' the man asked again.

The inspector nodded. 'First, allow me to deal with the passengers who have tickets.'

'I want to get on *this* train, you understand?'

'Yes, I understand,' the inspector replied. 'Do you?'

A woman in front of me caught my eye and smirked as we made our way on board. She looked fun and I hoped we'd be sharing a compartment.

We weren't sharing a compartment. She was two up from me, bunking with a young family. The *Dacia* (dats-ya) was a long-distance service that offered a variety of accommodation ranging from private sleeper compartments to couchettes and then regular seating, the last of which was not advisable for a nineteen-hour ride, especially when a couchette cost just £10 more. The private compartments could sleep one, two or three passengers and came with pre-made beds, a sink, coat hangers and – if you got lucky – an ensuite shower and toilet. Keen to have company and conversation, I'd chosen to travel in a couchette compartment which offered six-person berths, women and men grouped separately. Since our morning chat, Elisabeth's warning about the 'terrible' train had stayed in a tiny corner of my mind, but at the sight of newly fitted carpets and velvety couchettes I soon stopped worrying. It was far superior to the battered old Austrian Nightjet.

Two women were already in the compartment unpacking their bags. Through a mix of English and German I established that they were both Romanian. Elena worked as a carer for an elderly woman in Vienna and was taking the train home for a couple of weeks to spend time with her teenage children. She had messy black hair and a goofy smile and as she squeezed by, I could smell the fabric conditioner on her jumper. Maria had curly hair, secretarial glasses and pearl earrings as big as Maltesers. She was at least seventy and reminded me of Sophia from *The Golden Girls*. Maria had been assigned the lower berth where she was deftly tucking in her sheets, before laying out strips of tablets and Tupperware. Elena had the top berth while I was sandwiched in between, and it was here that I went into hiding, trying to keep out of the way as they made up their berths.

At 19.45 the train set off and I soon regretted my decision to climb up, swiftly discovering that I could neither sit up nor kneel in the space where I was crouching like a cat. At one point I glanced over the side to see if Maria had finished and found her scalp and white roots barely three inches from my nose. We were picking up pace when Elena propped up the ladder against the berths and I was soon face to face with the buttons of her jeans, realising that she was unaware of my presence. With pins and needles in one leg, and the other completely dead, the only way to salvage any dignity was to pretend I had been looking for something and I slid down the side nearest the door, brandishing my pen with a loud: 'Ah, here it is!'

I hobbled into the corridor waiting for my leg to wake up and found my smirking friend eating instant noodles and trying to charge her phone. For reasons unclear, there was only one socket in each compartment and the one in the corridor was installed three-quarters of the way up the wall, which meant passengers had to hold onto their phones as they charged or leave them swinging. She gave me a quick wave, tilting her head in the direction of the animated conversation that had begun between my co-travellers since I stepped out of the compartment. Romanian sounded a lot like Italian to me and each woman sounded increasingly outraged on behalf of the other. Suffering a terrible bout of FOMO as they bonded, I was intrigued to know what they were saying, my closet narcissist wondering if it was about me and my game of hide-and-seek. The young woman, conveniently a PhD student in linguistics, translated the conversation for me, which went something like this:

'I started in November, I stayed for five days and then she was taken to the asylum,' said Elena.

'A house with animals, it's hard,' Maria replied. 'As everything has to be maintained and done and you go out and sweep snow and for what?'

'Such dirt in that home I have never seen, so I stayed for half an hour then I called my boss and I said, no offence meant, but I will develop hepatitis. I can't work like this. There were two cats that looked like elephants, they climbed on the table and ate there alongside her. And to let the cats stay in my room?'

'You should have said, "I am sorry, I am allergic to dogs and cats."'

'But I did not know. I was told she had an onset of dementia and I am only to remind her when to take her medication, they didn't tell me about the cats. I stayed four days with the old lady, and she fell during the night in the bathroom and I called an ambulance. She came back from the hospital and on the ninth day I told my boss I could not keep working with her because she would drive me out of the house.'

'It is hard. There are patients with dementia who do not speak and there are those who are restless.'

'Exactly. I could not move through the house, as she was coming after me, she entered the bathroom after me. She would only scream and scream. I was told that I might be thrown out of the house.'

'In Romania I spent two years doing geriatric nursing,' said Maria. 'I worked for ten years at an asylum in Germany until my husband got ill and after my husband died, I thought to myself, I won't go to Germany again, it's a hard road, you know.'

At once I felt dreadful. Elena went on to describe how difficult it was to see her children as she couldn't leave dependent clients for extended periods. Carers were some of the most underpaid and undervalued workers, and I couldn't imagine being away for such long stretches, leaving my own children and travel-ling to another country to look after another family. Our home secretary was about to announce a cruel ban on care workers bringing relatives to the UK in an attempt to curb immigration. Maria took a tablet and lifted her swollen legs onto the berth. I imagined her working while her own husband was ill. It felt so deeply inhuman to split families, separating young children from parents who had few other options for survival but to travel across the world to wipe and wash someone else.

The conversation died down and I glanced in to see both women were eating, and reading their phones in comfortable silence as we rocked through the outskirts of Vienna. Passengers were milling around in towelling slippers, mopping up stew and pouring soup from flasks, the corridor smelling a lot like a school dinner hall. All over the world, from Delhi to Denver, Beijing to Bodø, the dining car is the beating heart of a night train. A hub with an innate sense of harmony, it's where strang-ers become friends, food tells a story, and the air is filled with aromas and laughter. So I was deeply disappointed that there wasn't a dining car attached. Everyone I knew who had taken the *Dacia* had spoken fondly of the bar-bistro carriage, lighting up at the memory of the infamous mixed grill. During one of my *tågskryt* sessions, I'd found a picture of it and enlarged every element of the platter, poring over the crinkle chips strung with melted cheese, the grilled pork escalope, the fatty pork chop, and the sausage which was the same shade as a Saint-Tropez granny. However, the dining car had been discontinued at the end of 2022, with no hint as to whether or not it would return, so passengers had come prepared.

I was nicely full. On my way towards Vienna Hauptbahnhof, I'd passed what I'd thought was a deli named Edelgreisslerei Opocensky. But when I nosed inside the door, the steam from slow-cooked broth drew me in along with the sight of diners in heavy coats being served by a single waitress. She'd waved me over, translating a daily-changing German menu which featured a variety of dishes from lamb cutlets and dolcelatte risotto, to sea bream and crisp schnitzel. I'd taken her advice and gone for the roast pork shoulder with dumplings. Now, on the train, I was thinking fondly about the meal and watching the suburbs roll by.

Slinging the corridor curtain around my shoulders, I pressed up against the window, scanning apartment blocks where children's bunk beds were strung with lights, their ledges lined with plush toys. Residents stood at sinks, looking up as we passed, tea towels over shoulders and dishes in hand. Dog walkers lurked by lampposts and... then it went black. I dropped the curtain, returning to the compartment where Elena and Maria had settled in for the night. Elena leaned over the side to tell me that the berth beside her was free and that I should swap to have more space. Grateful for the tip, I placed my backpack into the storage area behind our heads and watched as Maria immediately got up to shove my empty berth back up and into place. From my new spot, I looked down to where Maria was pulling on bed socks before she made a clucking sound and dropped a pair of false teeth onto the side table, the compartment resembling a residential home.

Far from a party train, this was a journey for reading, sudoku and knitting. The one noisy group of men had gone quiet and were leaning against one another watching films on their phones. It was barely 10 p.m. but most curtains were drawn, the lights off. Elena crossed her ankles, opened a bag of Brot Chips and offered them across the berths, urging me to take 'more, more' as she showed me photos of her children. We lay side by side on top of our duvets, eating giant croutons and chatting – a level of intimacy that I'd only reached after four dates with my husband. And yet to remain relevant in modern times, sleeper trains relied on passengers to embrace this closeness and lack of inhibition.

We pulled into the grand Budapest-Keleti station, and a fourth woman joined us, arriving at the door in a rippling fur coat. Lips red, eyes lined, she glanced at each one of us in turn, the chill from outside on her clothes. It was as though she'd entered from the 1950s. I couldn't stop staring at the way she held herself: *Too good for this compartment. Hell, too good for the rest of the world…* I was desperate to uncover her story, more so when she exhaled and kicked her bag under the seat with such force that I wondered for a moment if it contained the severed head of an ex-lover. Without consultation she flipped off the light and called it a night for us all.

Both Austria and Hungary are part of the Schengen area, so we were free to travel across their borders without any checks. I had my passport in my pocket, however, for the dreaded 2 a.m. halt at the village of Lőkösháza, just inside the Hungarian border with Romania. Unlike the bumpy ride of the previous night's train, this one was travelling at an even pace. Quiet, without announcing itself, it thrummed through the darkness, seducing me to sleep. Alas, at two a bang on the door jolted me awake and I handed down my passport to Hungarian guards, the stench of cigarettes coming through the vent. Burying my nose into the pillow, I kept one eye shut until my passport was handed back, then slept again for an hour before the second check just over the Romanian border at the town of Curtici. I lay completely still, as a mirror was swung into the compartment, under the seats and above my head, then listened to footsteps and muffled voices. The sourness of the cigarette smoke was intensifying, and I began to question the flammability of the bedding. Eventually the doors slammed, the train creaked, and we continued eastwards.

———

'GOOD MORNING!' Elena shouted, sitting up with a big smile. No adult ever greeted me like that. Should my children ever abandon me, she was precisely the kind of carer I hoped to find in later life.

Elena appeared to have slept as well as I had and climbed down the ladder, searching for her shoes before disappearing to the loo. Maria had already gone; only a ring of coffee remained on the side table. To my dismay the mysterious woman had also gone, taking her severed head with her.

It was 8.40 and we had recently departed from Blaj, in Alba County, the heart of Transylvania. I sat by the window observing the Târnava Mare river flow alongside. It was as thin as a burst water main, and I hadn't spotted it until I stood on the seats and saw it submerged between two banks of snow. The greyness of the morning matched my mood as I watched Elena pull on her jacket, picking sleep from one eye. She was preparing to get off at Mediaș, one of the oldest cities in the region, and I was going to miss her presence. A dining car had been attached a couple of hours earlier at the town of Simeria and a pair of catering staff were now wandering the corridors carrying a single tray advertising their wares, which consisted of one type of sandwich, plus paper cups of coffee, for which they only took cash. Elena raised two fingers and I dug out my notes. It was a ham and cheese sandwich, not my first choice by any means, but sleeper trains are not the place to get fussy. I'd once spent five days on the Trans-Mongolian eating only instant mash and noodles, so the sandwich was positively gourmet.

Together Elena and I watched the snowscapes, the Carpathian foothills rolling in the background, ramshackle housing rolling in the foreground. Rusted cars sat in dirt tracks and material flapped across broken windows. Horrifyingly impoverished, the area on the outskirts of Blaj looked abandoned.

'Do people live here?' I asked Elena.

'Yes,' she replied, with a small smile.

Elena disembarked at Mediaș and as I looked back at the shrinking city, I could see the spire of St Margaret's church. A Late Gothic structure dating from the fifteenth century, it appeared to have a herringbone design. I searched online for an image to inspect it closer, zooming in to find that it was covered in what looked like green and blue ludo counters arranged like fish scales. A fortified town surrounded by vineyards, Mediaș was a place I would have liked to explore, and as the train clattered on, I noted it as one to return to. This was a happy hazard of train travel, with every village, town and city presenting itself like a teaser trailer, reminding me how much lay between each end of the journey.

A blizzard picked up and powder billowed past the windows, white skies merging with white fields, nothing but the blurred tops of mountains separating the two. No sooner had it swept up than it died down and I stepped into the corridor as another citadel rose into view surrounded by a cluster of chimneys, turrets and rooftops dusted with snow. Beneath the softness, I could make out coloured walls painted in shades of lemon, lime, strawberry pink and plum. Sighişoara was one of several fortified medieval towns that Saxon-German colonists had built in the region, and as we moved off, I imagined how extraordinary it would look at the peak of spring. On we trundled, past backyards where mean-looking geese pecked at the dirt and chained dogs barked at the carriages. Despite sub-zero temperatures, washing hung outside, collars frozen into points, sleeves fringed with ice. From time to time I'd spot someone sweeping a doorway, but the scene was otherwise devoid of human life.

A couple of hours after my sandwich, I decided to investigate the dining car, and passed through the regular-seating carriage, which was full of human life. It smelled of warm bodies and kicked-off shoes. Under the illusion that this was a quiet train, I realised that the majority of passengers had spent the night crowded into this class of carriage and most were still stretched across the seats asleep, jackets on their chests, sports socks leaving outlines on the windows. Barely a handful of passengers were in the dining car, and the few who were, were sitting in isolation, staring into the depths of forests. I spotted the American from the night before. His bobble hat on his lap, he was lying face down on a table, his jacket for a pillow.

Normally the place where I would while away my day, the dining car was much like the scenery now – uninspiring and cold. I browsed the menu for something to take back to my seat and found twelve variations on the ham and cheese sandwich – none of which was available – and twenty-seven types of alcohol, ranging from Campari to Jägermeister, and Budweiser to Chivas Regal – all of which were available. Not up for getting smashed at ten in the morning, I made my way back with coffee and closed the compartment door, enjoying the solitude. Over the next couple of hours, the train followed the bends of the river Olt, through tunnels hidden by forests, branches heaped with snow. If the Transylvanian winter was a mood, it was a deeply sombre one.

While on the move, I always carried a paperback, usually fiction related to the region in which I was travelling; non-fiction tainted my perspectives, but I liked to read stories that centred on places I could picture. In Vienna I'd sought out a replacement for my lost Agatha Christie and I now took out my copy of Bram Stoker's *Dracula*, which opens with English lawyer Jonathan Harker documenting his train journey to Transylvania to meet the infamous Count. Like Harker, I had found my smattering of German useful and could relate to the scenes of little towns and castles on the tops of steep hills. He'd dined on robber steak and had a couple of glasses of golden Mediasch wine, which produced a 'queer sting on the tongue' – a wine which would have originated from the vineyards of what I would for ever think of as Elena's home town. Granted, Harker's experience with the Count was far from positive, but I was amused by his early judgement of the men in this region as 'barbarian' and 'strange', and the women as 'clumsy about the waist'. Whether in fiction or non-fiction, it was dismaying how travellers moving from west to east often perceived threats and ugliness from the outset, recoiling from the very people in whose land they were to be guests. Casual racism was a common trope, although there was nothing casual about it. The colonial hangover of superiority was so cemented into the Western psyche that it filtered into everyday travel and observations, refusing to die out.

At the end of chapter ten I put down the book, having had my fill of Victorian anxiety and gore. I could hear nothing but the door rattling and looked around the corridor to see if any passengers remained. Peering into one empty compartment after another, I almost gave up, when I saw a pair of legs stretched out with a laptop. They belonged to an attractive young man with sharp features and a neat beard. He smiled and I noticed he was wearing a T-shirt with the slogan 'Green Against the Machine'. Bingo. Inviting myself into his compartment, I got chatting to Charles, a researcher at the Technical University of Civil Engineering of Bucharest. Originally from Normandy, he'd been living in Bucharest for the previous six years, where he had founded an NGO called Climato Sfera to help companies reduce their carbon footprint and environmental impact. A few minutes into our chat we realised that we'd taken the same trains from Paris to Vienna, but Charles had slept in the six-person couchette carriage from Strasbourg.

'I was sharing with a lot of Erasmus students who were travelling there for the first time, so they had a lot of luggage,' he said. 'They told me it was too expensive for the flight plus all their bags.'

'Why are you taking this journey?' I asked.

'My job is to raise awareness about climate change and I wanted to prove that the journey is not only possible but that it's cheaper than a flight if you book in advance. We go into companies and we show people the possibilities along with the calculations of how much this type of travel is saving in emissions.' Charles stretched. 'I slept a lot better in this train,' he said, pointing upwards, 'as it was only a four-person couchette so there was lots of room and also the fluffy pillows and bed comforter are better than on the Nightjet.'

Charles was precisely the kind of passenger I'd been hoping to stumble upon, the poster-boy for night-train travel – and aside from the double stoppage for passport checks, he had little to complain about: 'I love the night train, I can work and am very productive when there is darkness outside the window. And people don't disturb. They see you with the laptop and they don't bother.'

He looked directly at me as he said this and I winced, unsure if it was a genuine observation or a beautifully French way of asking me to bugger off. The staff passed by, and Charles ordered two coffees, so I concluded that he didn't mind me hanging around.

Over the next half-hour he talked more about his work then recounted his only real 'disaster' on the train while en route to a party weekend in the Transylvanian mountains with his friends: 'We had a four-hour stop in the middle of nowhere without heating systems during winter, but it was not so bad, I was with friends and we had beers with us. We were on our way to Sinaia for skiing, we will pass through it between Brasov and Bucharest, I'll show you.'

I took the opportunity to ask Charles for restaurant recommendations in Bucharest, and while we talked the sun broke through, rousing the landscape from its slumber. We were passing through Brasov, a cheerier scene, filled with parks and playgrounds and children enjoying the snow. At the window of one block of flats stood a little girl in pink, a pair of fairy wings on her back. Someone was holding her steady as she waved her wand, and I waved back in a shared moment of magic.

Not long after, Charles gestured for me to join him in the corridor, pointing to the right-hand side where spruce trees packed into the valleys and icicles hung off ledges like a row of wizards' beards. We were passing by the mountain resort of Sinaia. Here, the Prahova river swung alongside, rapids forming over boulders. Now and again chunks of snow fell silently into the flow, dragged off at once. On the outskirts of Bucharest the clouds dispersed, revealing a sky scrubbed clean. It was as though the train sensed the promise of arrival, belting towards the finish. Lakes shimmered into view, fields flashed by, and the *Dacia* entered the city, bringing us to the end of the line.

3

BUCHAREST TO SOFIA

The Romanian capital was a city of wildly clashing architecture that evoked feelings of both misery and awe at every turn. Most buildings were in a state of dereliction so severe that it was hard to fathom their former use. It was as though they were suffering from some terrible disease, facades shedding paint like dead skin, chunks of concrete flesh falling onto the pavement. And yet, as I scanned fractured panes and tiles like broken teeth, a door would open and a resident would step out, securing a bolt behind them. Walk too close and the smell of rot was overwhelming; then a few metres along Doric columns swept skywards, causing me to step back into the street to admire balustrades, domes and ornamental carvings wrapped in vines.

In March 1977 a powerful earthquake hit Romania, killing around 1,570 people. It had originated in the Vrancea mountains, but the majority of the destruction was centred on the capital's residences, churches and multistorey buildings. Taking advantage of the devastation to erase any sign of centuries-old, cosmopolitan traditions and realise his communist vision, President Ceaușescu set about bulldozing Bucharest's beauty to rubble, demolishing entire neighbourhoods, schools and synagogues, replacing them with Soviet bleakness. To my amazement, however, I discovered that a number of monasteries and churches had been preserved at the time by engineers who'd dug beneath them and laid railway-style tracks that allowed the buildings to be rolled away to safety.

Once known as the 'Little Paris of the East', Bucharest was changed for ever by the earthquake, and owing to the universal problem of money and corruption, little had been done since Ceauşescu's time to remodel it. However, there was still charm to discover on foot, and I was glad to have one night to roam before my onward journey to Ruse. As darkness fell, I walked towards the Old Town, the chime of bells drawing me towards a couple of remaining Orthodox churches. Cobbled and dusted with sleet, the passages were cosily lit, awnings hung with bare lightbulbs above bubble tents keeping diners toasty. Specks of snow began to dart around when I found myself outside Cărtureşti Carusel, a bookshop curtained by strings of fairy lights. Gingerbread men sat in the windows holding books alongside toy soldiers with twirly moustaches; behind them a pair of spiral staircases lead up to the three floors. Built in 1903 as a bank, it was now home to a tea shop, an art gallery and a bookshop containing a number of English-language books – at the entrance was a cluster of readers thumbing pages of *Rezerva*, the Romanian edition of Prince Harry's *Spare*. Unable to pass a bookshop without entering, I went in. After browsing the travel books, I remembered what I needed and stepped back out into the snow with a replacement copy of *Murder on the Orient Express*.

Less than a five-minute walk away, I came upon Caru' cu bere, one of the restaurants that Charles had suggested I visit. A vision from a fairy tale, it was housed inside an uplit neo-Gothic building with a spire, stained-glass windows and mosaic floors. Inside it had all the noise and heat of what I was hoping to find in a traditional beer house. I took a seat upstairs, overlooking the atrium, and realised that I hadn't eaten anything since the morning's sandwich, giving silent thanks to Charles for sending me to what felt like a homely church, one that smelled of family cooking. I then remembered we were following each other on Instagram and sent him literal thanks to which he replied with a smiley emoji.

Enjoying the clangs and shouts that came through the swinging kitchen door, I scoured the menu which featured every cut of meat from glazed pork ribs in beer sauce to slow-roasted pork knuckle, pan-fried lamb pastrami to minced meat rolled in cabbage. But it had to be the confit pork *like in the old days*, with smoked sausage, cabbage and polenta, cooked in a cast-iron pan. I ate with the pleasure that comes after long travels, trying hard not to stare at a young couple in the corner, who had begun kissing when I arrived and were still going by the time I'd finished my meal. In between bouts, the young man would pull away to take sips of his beer and I couldn't help but admire his dedication to both causes.

After dinner I was tempted to walk further around the Old Town, so inviting was the glow of bars and thrum of drinkers wrapped in scarves and flirting, but tiredness took over and I made my way back to my hotel room, knowing that the following day of travel would be a long one.

At breakfast I checked my train timings repeatedly, opening the ticket envelope every five minutes to make sure the hour of departure hadn't somehow changed since the previous time I'd looked. Impossible to book online, the tickets had been delivered to my hotel by a local agent and were handed to me when I checked in the previous evening. Although I could have bought them at Bucharest station, I wasn't willing to take that sort of risk when attempting a journey like this one. From my calculations I had barely half an hour – assuming there were no delays – between my arrival into the Bulgarian city of Ruse and the departure to Sofia, the only train of the day. I had no Romanian currency and no way of knowing if there was a dining car on board or even a café at Ruse station, so I asked the hotel staff for a takeaway box and worked my way round the breakfast buffet, packing anything that wouldn't drip, stink or rot by the evening. Sliding a handful of teabags into my pocket, I set off by taxi to Bucharest Gara de Nord, buoyed by the intensity of the winter sun, which usually fired life into any landscape, no matter how worn and weathered. But as the sky blazed a cobalt blue, the city's exhaustion was more exposed than before.

As we drew up to the station, I checked the map on my phone to see how far it was to Giurgiu – the final stop in Romania before the crossing into Ruse. The route, opened between Bucharest and Giurgiu in the summer of 1869, was Romania's first, making it only the third country in Eastern Europe to have a railway line. It was a fifty-mile stretch that shouldn't have taken long to cover, however in 2005 floods had caused a bridge to collapse at Grădişte, about halfway down the line, and it had never been repaired. The reason was straightforward: like the rest of the country, Romania's railways were the victim of poor infrastructure and maintenance, confounded by nonsensical politics, and the train was forced to take an enormous bypass via the town of Videle. Still, three hours sitting at the window on a glorious winter morning was exactly what I needed, after having spent much of the week riding along in darkness, and I was looking forward to this relatively short hop to the Bulgarian border.

On my way through the concourse, I noticed the majority of passengers dressed in the same quilted jackets, the women's belted at the waist, their hoods trimmed with fur. There was not a wheelie suitcase in sight: most people were carrying sports bags or reusable shopping bags, jammed with everything from rolled-up blankets to plastic flowers and bottles of cooking oil.

The train was parked at the furthest platform, where snow piled up between the tracks. A guard – her cheeks as round as apples, and just as red – was guiding passengers on board. It was always a pleasure to watch someone who genuinely enjoyed their job, and more often than not I'd see this on the railways, where colleagues were akin to family.

With a whistle and a wave at the driver, she joked with a couple of regular passengers then checked my ticket, rubbing my hands between her plump palms and directing me up the train to where the heating was on high. No more than two carriages long, it looked more like a school bus than a train, albeit a bus with four smashed windows – including the driver's. The rest, while intact, were sprayed with green and purple graffiti. To optimise the view, I climbed into a pair of seats raised on a platform, opposite a window shattered like a jigsaw puzzle, beneath which I could just make out the small but unmistakable scrawl of a phallus. As the train juddered to life, I felt a kinship with the artist who had correctly judged the pleasure its presence would bring.

Within twenty minutes we were travelling west of Bucharest, past an apiary with multi-coloured beehives, rolling in a straight line between open fields rippled with snow so bright it appeared blue in the light. Untrodden, the hardness of its surface sparkled as we passed through Giurgiu County – at least untrodden by humans: my forehead to the glass, I looked down to where the pronged toes of little birds had left concentric circles, the haphazard movement of a larger animal criss-crossing the tracks. So slow was the train that I could stare between twigs holding teardrops of melting ice to where black pools emerged in the marshland. For more than an hour I stared into the starkness of snow and light, my mind emptying, nothing more than the vibration of the train in my thoughts. There was peace where nature lay clean and untouched.

Once we sailed by the village of Ghizdaru, the land was green and flat, ploughed and deserted. This part of the country evoked the same sadness I'd felt through Transylvania. The homes were broken, with tarpaulins for roofs; the only cars to be seen were stacked up on bricks. A single sheep stood in a road, and I suspected the rest of the herd had fled long ago. Far from a meditation, the journey was now throwing up the parts that other travellers rarely see: heaps of landfill containing plastic water bottles, clothes, shoes, and broken glass. One after the other they went by, the foreground a mountain range of trash.

'So depressing,' said a voice.

I looked over to where a young woman was watching the scene. She wore a beautiful red head wrap and, as she shifted towards the glass, I noticed a Greenpeace badge on her bag.

'Are you travelling through to Sofia?' I asked.

'Yeah,' she said, not looking up. 'It's really insane that this is still happening,' she added, with the kind of American accent that Europeans pick up from watching *Friends*.

'Do Romanians not recycle?'

'This is probably not Romanian waste. Look.' She pointed to a carrier bag from a popular German supermarket. 'We don't have that here. This is imported shit.'

Joanna told me she worked for an NGO in Sofia and was travelling back after a week at home in Bucharest. As we rolled towards the checkpoint at Giurgiu, she explained that since 2017, after China announced a ban on importing foreign waste, Romania had turned into an illegal dumping ground for toxic shipments. A number of investigations had revealed that countries within the EU – including the UK – had been sending everything from broken microwaves to mouldy fridges, as it was cheaper to ship it all off than process it at home. Declared at the Romanian border as recyclable waste, these illegal shipments were being handled by criminal organisations, according to the Romanian environmental minister who had tried to strengthen legislation to make it an imprisonable offence. Before I could ask Joanna more about her work, Romanian guards boarded to collect our passports and she rang a friend to kill time. Wind whistled through the doors, and I pulled on gloves against the January cold. I turned to take in Giurgiu station. Built in 1955 it represented the grand communist style of that era; however I was itching to see the town's central terminus, which dated back to 1869. It was there that passengers from the Orient Express would have suspended their railway journey, disembarking to take the ferry across the Danube to Ruse.

I checked my phone, convinced I would miss my connection from Ruse and remembered how nothing rendered me more impotent than being without my passport. I was at the behest of officials who got to decide my fate. Handing it over always turned me into a wreck, fingers poised to grab it back – particularly at New York's JFK airport, where one eye-roll could spell deportation. The longest I'd ever been without my passport was in

North Korea, when the authorities collected it on arrival and held onto it for the duration of my ten-day trip, returning it as I hovered around on the platform in Pyongyang watching everyone else board the train back to Beijing. Throughout the entire period I was convinced that the North Koreans were scrutinising every stamp, matching my movements to articles I'd written online. Once they'd discovered I was a journalist, visiting the country under 'false pretences', they would burst into my hotel room and drag me off to a gulag. In reality, my passport had probably been chucked into a carrier bag in the corner of someone's office, but I'd been on the verge of tears as it was handed back.

Twenty minutes dragged by as the Romanian authorities did their checks, and meanwhile I got chatting to Murat, a construction site manager from Istanbul who worked in Bucharest. He normally flew home every six months but had decided this time that it was easier to take the train, with his two oversized suitcases packed with food and drink, and spend a couple of days exploring the architecture in Sofia. Curious about my overland jaunt from London, he broke into a smile of bemusement, nodding hard with a series of *wows* as I described each train.

'Can I ask you something?'

'Sure,' I replied.

'Why do you need to do this?'

Put on the spot, I considered his question. My grand travels seemed suddenly small and insignificant. Frivolous, in fact. Here was a man who travelled for work, to earn money – which I suppose I did too. But mine was a luxurious choice and his was not. The train roared to life and before I could answer, Murat began describing places he dreamed of visiting: Singapore, Japan, Hong Kong and Malaysia, all of which I'd travelled to, some on multiple occasions. A younger, more naïve version of myself would have gushed about each place, telling him he absolutely should go. I stayed quiet.

'I applied two times for a work visa in the UK for training in architecture and interior construction but they don't give me one. Two times they say no,' he said.

I watched him closely, studying his rough palms and smooth face and felt a pang of anger, knowing that Murat and scores of others like him, with a simple desire for further education, were forced to spend thousands on applications and jump through humiliating hoops, only to be denied the opportunities that most British people could access around the world with ease.

The guards reboarded with the passports and I spied my burgundy one among the pile being dealt out like playing cards. Our lives were nothing more than a lottery of birth and the luck – or lack thereof – that came with it. Despite Brexit triggering horrendous border queues, roaming charges and the requirement for visas and travel permits, I was still acutely aware of the enduring power of a UK passport and the privilege it granted.

The train set off and I stared at the time. There was nothing I could do if I missed the connection and the majority of my companions seemed to be heading in the same direction, so at least I'd have company.

'What age are you?' Murat asked.

Over the previous fifteen years of travelling by train, I'd been asked to divulge everything from my blood type and bra size to mortgage repayments and, latterly, which of my two children I preferred; so asking my age didn't faze me in the slightest.

'Forty,' I replied.

'Forty?' He raised both eyebrows and turned to survey the river. 'I am thinking you look young. But you are not young.'

Ouch. I was hardly old. Sure, I'd reached the age where I sustained injuries in my sleep, remembered when a Twix cost 23p, and saved Gü ramekins 'just in case'. But old? Never.

Amused at Murat's response, I shrugged as the train approached the bridge, its windows rattling as we accelerated across the steel truss construction. Designed by two Soviet engineers and opened in 1954, the Friendship Bridge had taken two and a half years to build and was one of only two bridges connecting Romania with Bulgaria (the other, between the cities of Calafat and Vidin, opened as recently as 2013). After the end of the Cold War the bridge had been renamed the Danube Bridge, after the spectacular body of water that now drifted beneath us. When I was little, my mum had gone through a period of listening to Strauss while driving, and as the 'Blue Danube' played in my head, I noted that the Danube wasn't, in fact, blue – but a khaki green.

At almost 1.4 miles long, the bridge was the highlight for the rail enthusiasts on board, who were desperate to stand up and film the crossing, glancing around to see who would go first. Unbothered, I hopped up and stood directly behind the driver's cabin to film the view. Everyone else immediately slid across seats and ducked along the aisle to do the same. Geographically, this was also the point when the Latin alphabet turned into Cyrillic, and towards the end of the four-minute crossing, a series of pings, chimes and swooshes sounded out around the carriage as the 'Welcome to Bulgaria' text messages arrived. I returned to my seat as we drew into Ruse station. A stained clock tower showed that we had arrived on time with exactly half an hour to spare and I stretched with relief, just as Bulgarian guards turned up to take away our passports, leaving me once again in a jittery mess.

Ordered off the train, the English speakers gravitated towards one another, hands in pockets, shoulders raised as the wind picked up and billowed down the platform, carrying along with it a couple of empty crisp packets and a pile of leaves that began to waltz. It turned out that everyone on board the train from Ruse, around twelve people, was travelling on to Sofia, including a young Irish woman with safety pins through her earlobes, a French musician, and the American Southerner, who had worked his way on at the last minute in Vienna. He was chatting with a young, fair-haired woman wearing a Barbie backpack and I wondered if they were travelling together. Ten minutes later our passports were handed back, the station's resident drunk taking it upon himself to guide us to our connection. His face a flush of beetroot – and reeking of beer – he shuffled around, a patchwork duvet around his shoulders, giving him a wonderfully regal air as he ushered us towards the underpass. More efficient than the average guard, he checked that each passenger was indeed travelling to Sofia before presenting us with our train – a string of old carriages – and bowing deeply when the Irish woman offered as thanks a half-smoked packet of Mayfair Gold.

Although there were three carriages available, our newly formed clique squeezed into two adjoining compartments in the first one – with the exception of Murat, who heaved his suitcases into a third compartment, put his feet up on them and promptly fell asleep.

At exactly 14.20 we departed, and my stomach groaned so loudly that the others looked up. It was then that I remembered the packed lunch and pulled out my ham and cheese baguette, which was sweating marginally less than I was in the dry, over-heated compartment. I immediately regretted my base layers, eyeing the musician opposite me wearing jeans and a T-shirt. His long hair tied into a loose ponytail, Julien was twirling buttons on a Roland drum machine that lay across his lap. Thankfully, it was plugged into a pair of headphones, saving all of us from what could have been an interesting six hours. Julien was on his way to Sofia to try living there for a little while. Five years earlier he had left his home town of Perpignan and had been a self-confessed 'nomad' since. As an entrepreneur building a tech start-up, he was able to work remotely, and he had been hopping around the world every two months trying stints in different cities.

To me the concept of home has always been a fluid one. Until my early twenties I'd never spent more than three years in any city, moving for my parents' jobs and then my studies, but I was always ready to embrace the new. As I considered the thrill of drifting between the warmth of a Mediterranean coastal town to the wholesome *hygge* of a Scandi city or a snowy Alpine village, my understanding of home thumped in my heart. Home was the sweetness of my children's breath, my dachshund asleep on my lap, the warmth of my husband's neck. Home meant safety and unconditional love, and home was wherever they were.

It was my first time in Bulgaria. When it came to most new countries I had at least some expectation – prejudiced or otherwise – but this time I had no clue about the topography, language or food. As for the people, I'd never met any Bulgarians and was now gazing out of the window hoping to spot some. However, where we were travelling was an expanse of meadows in what could have been a national park. Flourishing in the sunshine, the fields dipped and rolled up towards limestone rock formations; small woods bunched together like chattering groups of friends, the Yantra river looping in the foreground. Not a soul appeared for hours; there were no farms, no shacks, just eagles rising on the wind. As I watched the afternoon sun softening the valleys, I could only imagine the ripeness and abundance of this region in summer.

The idea that there might have been a dining car on board was now funny to me. This was the kind of train that looked as though each carriage was held together by little more than a few staples. There was no toilet paper and I was glad to have swiped a roll from the hotel, which was now gratefully received by my companions who were passing it along like a baton. The American kept poking his head into our compartment and gesturing to me: 'Come on, we got a thing going on next door. Join us.' But I was enjoying the peace and promised to pop in later, opening up my fresh copy of *Murder on the Orient Express* and pressing back the spine.

Poirot was about to reveal to Hector MacQueen that Ratchett was an alias for Cassetti, when the train lurched, and a backpack fell onto my head. Mortified, the owner leapt up and shoved it between her feet, as Julien's suitcase fell against someone else's knees; it had been parked upright in the middle of the six-person compartment, but no one had minded, each passenger twisting away or stepping around it as needed. From my experience, it was only ever on trains that travellers adjusted to one another with such ease, guarding laptops, swapping books, and drifting into a harmony unique to the railways.

Unable to take the heat, I propped open the sliding door which was immediately closed by a young woman shivering in a black fur coat, the sight of which was making the backs of my knees sweat. I decided then to go next door to see what they'd got 'going on'. The American, Joe, was sitting opposite the young woman I'd seen earlier with the Barbie backpack. She was now asleep, twisted awkwardly across the seats, her pale midriff visible from her T-shirt riding up. Not quite what I was expecting.

'Are you travelling together?' I asked, sitting down by the window.

'No, we met back in Bucharest,' he replied. 'She's from Ukraine. I want to try and get us to Skopje.'

Listening to the beat of the train, I paused and asked again. 'Are you travelling together?'

'Me? I'm bouncing between visas. Got my son's wedding in a month's time in the country outside Sofia, so I'm just moving around. Doing ninety days on each then moving on. But I think I'm maybe going to go to Skopje.'

His eyes drifted to her midriff and my own stomach tightened. The woman was no more than twenty and Joe was no less than seventy. Determined not to leave her alone while she slept, I continued to make small-talk with Joe, who was from Georgia.

'How did you find the train from Vienna?' I asked. 'Did you manage to get a sleeper berth?'

'Yeah, they found me one in that multiple-bed section, but I didn't want that,' he said, his blue eyes widening. 'There were going to be other people in there, and you don't know who might walk into that compartment and sleep above you. You don't know who's going to come in,' he shuddered and swiped a hand. I glanced across at the woman then back at Joe.

'Yes, I can understand that,' I said.

'No one wants to sit up all night in a chair, but I got some shut-eye with, you know…' he threw an elbow across his face, '…my head on the table and then a coffee in the morning, so I was good.' He looked at the young woman, still asleep, then back at me.

'She's so pretty, ain't she?'

For me the joy of night trains was that very feeling of uncertainty, the anticipation of who was going to enter my story, but at this moment I was thrown off balance by the dynamic at play.

A patch of pink light appeared on the wall and I turned around to see the sun beginning to set above the forest. It was around 5 p.m. The window was too filthy for a proper view, so I ducked into the corridor, which smelled strongly of heating oil, and watched as a strip of light ignited the horizon where I could make out the ridges of the Balkan range. Within ten minutes the skies erupted, every window in the carriage turning amber in the light. Alone, I basked in the extraordinary sunset that was now sending pink flares into clouds that deepened to a neon glow. It had the emotional resonance of a Whitney Houston key change, and a prickle ran from my wrists to my shoulders. When the show was over, I glanced into the compartment where the young woman was now awake, wrapping her hair into a bun, pins between her teeth. She seemed at ease, so I retook my seat, finally able to read with no distractions from outside.

In the final hour a young couple boarded, one of whom was carrying nothing more than a plastic bag from which he pulled a meaty wrap that he ate with studied care. The woman watched a soap on her phone with the same intensity, her purple nails matching her fleece and backpack. At one point she asked me to plug her phone in above my head and I leaped at the chance to chat.

'Do you live in Sofia?' I asked.

'Yes.'

'Are you a student?'

'No.'

She turned up the volume on her soap which translated into a clear 'Don't talk to me', which was completely fair; after all, not everyone wanted to be interrogated by a thermals-wearing weirdo with a notepad. At Parvomaytsi, a tiny stop, a man with a single tooth boarded and shouted at everybody, before the purple-nailed woman shoved him out of the door, barely glancing up from her phone; it must have been a particularly good episode.

The train was delayed, and we were now following the bends of the Iskar river as it travelled towards Sofia in blackness. From time to time it flowed beneath street lamps, gleaming like a silver ribbon. Lost in thought, I put my head against the window and listened to the *da-da-da-dah, da-da-da-dah* of the motion, eyeing each member of the compartment in turn as they retied shoes, zipped up hoodies and stacked bags in preparation for arrival. After a night train, this point in the journey usually sent my emotions into a state of flux, as the promise of arrival clashed with the passing of a moment. But this daytime journey had not allowed for the blurring of boundaries. We had adjusted to one another – and kept apart. As we drew into the station, I pulled on my backpack and followed the others off the train, watching as the group fragmented and each went about their way.

4

THE SOFIA–ISTANBUL EXPRESS

Now and again someone enters your life and changes it for ever. They might not know it, forgetting your name and your face, but they stay with you in spirit.

In 2010, I'd met Patrick on board the *Golden Chariot*, a luxury train in South India. It was packed with boisterous families and boomers on college reunions, but we were both travelling solo. Over dinner, I'd asked the seventy-year-old if he minded being alone, to which he'd replied: 'I'm not alone. I'm by myself.' He held my gaze for a second then went back to spearing chunks of watermelon.

Something shifted in my psyche. From then on, whenever I felt exposed – asking for a table for 'just' one or taking out a book to hide in – I'd remember Patrick's words and pull myself together. Solitude was a gift. In the absence of company, I paid more attention to my surroundings, tuning in to other people's conversations and watching their lips to read whispers. Birdsong was more noticeable, as was dirt under nails, untied laces and wonky eyeliner. Flowers came into focus, the threads of cloud across the moon appearing like smoke.

There was power in solitude, and I'd spent the previous few days basking in time that was mine to do with as I pleased. But now, as I stood next to Jamie, our breath on the air, I relished the comfort of companionship.

Jamie and I had met at university on a postgraduate journalism course. Tall and gangly, with messy blond hair, an aversion to vegetables and a fixation with the Libertines, Jamie had worked his way up at the *NME* before a sudden move to China, where he'd pursued stories on everything from Beijing's internet-addiction rehab centres and cosplay gatherings to all-gender toilet campaigns and Shanghai's super-club scene. At the start of the pandemic he'd cut his losses and moved back west, but his pursuit of offbeat stories hadn't stopped. He'd made a podcast about the suspicious death of the owner of a bear he'd once wrestled in Ohio, and had recently reported on a heavy-metal festival in Botswana and a group of boxing grannies in Johannesburg.

I'd wondered if staring out of train windows was a bit tame for Jamie's tastes, but nevertheless he'd ventured across from covering a pagan festival in North Macedonia to meet me in Sofia and travel along to Istanbul, Ankara and Kars. So used to arriving at stations then making my own way into the city, I was delighted to spot his familiar face on the concourse, scanning our group of misfits. It certainly took thought to cross town to meet someone off a train. Side by side, we were now standing in the middle of the road and staring up at the golden dome of the Alexander Nevsky cathedral. Its bell tower contained twelve bells that in 1911 were shipped from Russia via Odessa and Varna, then transported by train to Sofia; the largest of them could apparently be heard up to eighteen miles away. Wordless, we took in its uplit magnificence, which seemed to expand with every beat of silence. Neither of us needed to pass comment; I could feel the awe. Sharing the moment cemented it. It was now stamped, saved and tucked away for safe keeping.

For a spot so central, it was eerily quiet, our footsteps the only sound during the walk to what appeared to be an ancient house with a door handle fashioned from antlers. Staria Chinar – meaning 'old sycamore' – was a cosy restaurant housed in a building from the 1920s, with much of the interior looking just as dated. A warren of low-lit rooms was covered in worn floral wallpaper, the diners packed in. It ought to have smelled of old lace and soap, but the aroma of cooking warmed my bones. Only one other Bulgarian couple was seated in our nook as we spooned up sticky wedges of slow-cooked lamb baked in the outdoor clay oven, along with beef cheeks in black pepper sauce. As I licked the saltiness of fried cheese off my fingers, Jamie made a chef's kiss with one hand at what was the epitome of comfort food. It was a good omen for the beginning of our journey together, and we sped through the cold towards our hotel, looking forward to tea, pyjamas and – with any luck – a badly dubbed film to ridicule before bed.

The following morning we were sitting in a café pretending to enjoy a pair of tepid spinach pastries. Behind us the bookshelves were stacked with old copies of *National Geographic* and someone had tossed a couple of board games into the mix, but the pieces were missing and the boards were split. Whoever had chosen the vibe had probably envisioned a hippy hangout with travellers turning up to read dog-eared copies of *The Beach*, play a bit of Scrabble and drink iced coffees by the dozen, forgetting that it took balmy weather, planning, and probably quite a lot of weed to make it work. Neither of us willing to admit we'd picked a dud, we dusted off the flakes and thanked the waitress, who was in the middle of a Facetime session as we left. Fortunately, we didn't have to go far for stimulation.

Tsar Shishman street was filled with art and splashed with colour. Much had been commissioned by the city's authorities to encourage young artists to explore their talents, resulting in decorated electricity boxes and murals on the sides of houses. Every other door opened into a coffee shop, but already trembling from a double espresso, I beelined towards the Elephant Bookstore, which had bookshelves painted onto the walls flanking the awning. Inside was a range of travel books (not mine), scratch-off maps, whisky tumblers, Barabar playing cards and fancy shaving kits – a potential one-stop shop for Father's Day. Singing along to the eighties power ballads playing on a loop, I looked around to see Jamie was now outside on the curb. He was staring intently at his phone, which meant he was either bored or organising a date – or both – so I did one last circuit, catching sight of the cover of *Lolita*, which gave me flashbacks to Joe and the young Ukrainian woman. They'd left the station together and I hoped she had managed to break away and carry on her travels in safety. It was then that I noticed a quote on the jacket from Martin Amis: 'Comedy, subversive yet divine', and I realised that even though I'd read *Lolita* twenty years ago, I couldn't remember the plot so took a copy to the counter, looking forward to feeling disgusted all over again.

'All right?' Jamie smiled, his face flushed as he slipped his phone into his pocket, which meant he'd secured a date. Together we crossed the road and made our way towards the leafy square, where I could hear children playing football in the shadows of the Seven Saints church. I loved the sight of Orthodox churches with their multiple domes. They always looked so plump, jolly and welcoming, unlike their dour Anglican counterparts, which made me feel cold and nervous. Built in 1528 by Suleiman the Magnificent, the Seven Saints was originally an Ottoman mosque known as the Black Mosque, a nod to the black granite in its now-missing minaret. After an earthquake destroyed the minaret, the mosque was abandoned, then used as a military warehouse and prison before finally being converted into an Orthodox church in 1903. I stood at the edge of the grass and tried to picture the church with the minaret and the force of the earthquake that had brought it crashing down: the thought was too terrifying to entertain. The sun emerged from behind a cloud and the gold crosses atop each dome lit up like candles on a birthday cake.

'Come on, let's check it out,' said Jamie, walking off. I followed, kicking the ball back to a little boy and wondering why none of the children were at school on a Thursday morning.

A group of visitors formed a semicircle inside the entrance, and they turned to look as we entered. I nodded, pulling off my hat, my eyes adjusting to the darkness. I craned my neck up, taking in the glorious blue and gold interiors, which depicted various saints, haloes like bronze discs behind their heads. Every time I came upon expressions of human creativity that defied belief, I wondered what we were building that would cause ripples of emotion in a hundred years' time. The Shard? Tracey Emin's *My Bed*? No doubt AI would have taken over by that point, reducing all our wonders of the world to nothing more exciting than a trip to Sainsbury's.

As I dwelled on that miserable thought, Jamie wandered over, muttering about the 'amazing' paintwork. I noticed the group was still watching us. One of my snow boots was making the most awful squeak on the wooden floors and I tried to step quietly around the group who'd all turned back to face the same altar. A lady handed me a flyer and I looked down to see the kindly face of an elderly man. Only it wasn't a flyer, but an order of service. Then I saw the coffin.

'God, it's a funeral,' said Jamie, grabbing my arm. 'Let's go.'

———

The sleeper train was due to depart at 18.40, so Jamie disappeared to a café to file an article before the journey. My appetite for embarrassment unfulfilled, I was now in a pharmacy looking for haemorrhoid cream. Somehow I only ever needed medication when travelling in places that had no hospital or no way of communicating with anyone who could help. I'd once spent an hour going between four different pharmacies in a town in Madhya Pradesh trying to explain cystitis, a savvy flower vendor figuring it out and helping me to buy the correct tablet from a man who sold peanut brittle. On another occasion, while working at a tourist office in Brittany, I'd woken up unable to open my mouth, only to have the doctor exclaim: '*Champignons!*' at what was a biblical case of oral thrush, then inject me in the bum for want of a better idea.

I was now pacing the aisles picking up nondescript items such as chewing gum and paracetamol in the sad hope that they would distract from my main purchase. Feverishly googling the word, I reached the front of the queue where a woman was typing behind the glass. Mindful of the queue behind, I held up my phone for her and she peered at the screen, screwing up her nose and shaking her head. She picked up her specs from where they hung around her neck, reached under the glass and took my phone out of my hand. With a silver nail she tapped the mic on the translation app which announced: 'HYYEMMOROID', with all the vigour of an Oscar win. The tips of my ears turned hot as she nodded and handed back my phone. She then placed two fingers together and made an upwards gesture: suppository or cream?

'Both... anything,' I replied.

No amount of chewing gum could douse the flames of humiliation that were now more painful than the reason for my visit. Very pleased to have helped, the assistant brought everything back to the counter and put it through the till, waving the cream at her colleague to check the price as a small part of me died. Still, I knew no one in this pharmacy or in the city and took my bag of supplies, just as a message came in from Jamie who had finished his work and was now ready to meet up.

'What you get?' Jamie asked, gesturing towards my bag.

'Haemorrhoid cream,' I replied.

'Nice.'

'It will be.'

We entered a warm lounge and Jamie ordered a fruit tea as I fished out our train tickets and approached the bar, curious about the smoke billowing from a highball glass on the counter. The tickets for the final leg of the journey had also been delivered to our hotel and I'd not yet had a chance to double- and triple-check the departure time. One More Bar – a former kindergarten, revamped into a cocktail den with a speakeasy vibe – was the ideal place to while away time before the journey, which would take around eleven hours, passing through Plovdiv, Dimitrovgrad and Svilengrad, before terminating at Istanbul's Halkali station at 5.30 a.m. The timing wasn't great, but dawn arrivals were different. The metamorphosis of the night and the stirring of a city were visible all at once, as passengers watched from the carriage windows, a rare indulgence.

The barman dispatched the smoky jungle along with five green shots to a table of young women and I set my tickets down, scanning the menu for food.

'No dining car,' said a fellow customer, as though reading my mind. A paralegal from Plovdiv, Vasil was eyeing the tickets over my shoulder. 'I have taken this train many times. It's a nice train, you will find chocolate in the fridge,' he smiled. 'But no dining car.'

'Why not?'

'I don't know,' he replied, vaping through a cloud that smelled of strawberries. 'Maybe it's the cost. Also, the train arrives to Halkali very early I think, so there is no need to serve breakfast. But you will be delayed.'

I was starting to feel despondent. Since I'd left London I'd not had a single dinner on a train and the hope of indulging in mixed grills while rattling through the night was fading fast.

'Can you suggest anywhere nearby?'

'You want traditional or something else?' Vasil asked, a vicious-looking tattoo creeping out from his collar, its fangs at odds with the pink e-cig in his hand.

I had nothing against fusion food, fast food or other tourists, but my greatest fear was ending up at the equivalent of an Aberdeen Angus Steakhouse or some Insta-monstrosity with fake flowers cascading down the walls.

'Traditional,' I replied, before adding. 'Where would you eat?'

'Go outside and turn right, then right again, and walk up to Izbata: it's real Bulgarian food,' he added.

'What kind?'

'Meat.'

In seconds we were caught in a downpour, the rush of showers in our ears as we raced towards Tsanko Tserkovski street, the air filled with the smell of rain hitting soil. There, I spotted a side entrance leading to a tavern with stone walls, wooden tables and reassuringly Bulgarian conversation. From experience I'd learned that asking for a 'traditional' restaurant could often result in the opposite. Aged nine, I'd gone on holiday to Cyprus. My dad had booked a traditional restaurant for dinner that had us on a coach, sitting next to Brenda and Mike from Scarborough. The coach had made a number of stops at resorts en route to the taverna, picking up people with various shades of sunburn, in various stages of drunkenness. We were then seated at one long table next to a plastic Union flag and entertained by a dancer with a black waistcoat and billowing sleeves who turned out to be a physics teacher by day. Since then, when abroad, I'd made sure to ask local residents where they ate with their friends.

Izbata was a fabulous find, the scent of freshly baked purlenka drifting by as I watched rain worming down the window overhead. The menu was everything I'd hoped for, all dishes slow-baked in earthenware, homemade or stuffed with cheese, garlic and bacon. With a long night of travel ahead, we went for the sudjuk – fat curves of spicy Balkan sausage – served with raw onion and potatoes pooling in butter, along with granny's chicken and a clay pot of kapama sealed with dough. Popping the crisp top, I watched the steam seeping out, then foraged around the gravy-filled layers of pork and veal. A bed of chicken and rice lay at the bottom, and in blissful silence we dipped triangles of deep-fried bread in the gravy, agreeing that we would be hard pushed to find such a meal on board a train.

Half an hour before departure we arrived at the station. Passengers milled about with restless children, handing out chunks of dried sausage to keep them quiet, when the *Sofia–Istanbul Express* groaned into the station. As the carriages went by, I noticed a white crescent and star on each window – the symbol of the Ottoman Empire. The sight caused a wave of emotion as I realised how close I was to reaching Istanbul, a city that had left me breathless as a teenager and desperate to explore. Around me friends and families hugged their loved-ones goodbye, the expressions of affection more visible the further east I travelled. Elderly men embraced one another, wiping tears on sleeves, and grandchildren were smothered with love, their noses, foreheads and hands kissed and squeezed.

Lost in the sweetness of it all, I realised it was time to board, and followed Jamie up the steps to find a traffic jam in the corridor. A passenger was blocking the aisles with two enormous suitcases: it took a moment before I recognised Murat, the construction worker I'd met at the Romanian border, as the culprit. The rest of us stood sideways on, shoulder to shoulder, with varying degrees of patience. The twang of Turkish house music started up and I peered round the door expecting to find students but instead discovered a family of four stacking their fridge with energy drinks. Eventually Murat heaved his suitcases out of the way and the line filtered off into compartments.

'Well, this is all right?' said Jamie, undoing his scarf and looking around the space. 'Bit hot, mind.' He reached up to where the thermostat offered a choice of temperatures ranging from hot to roasting. Our twin compartment had a pair of berths with checked blankets, full-sized pillows and two sealed bags of ironed linen. In the corner was a sink with high-pressure hot water and pink soap that pumped out like liquid bubble gum, and on the wall was a series of hooks for bags and coats. Curious if Vasil was right, I opened the fridge to find water, apple juice, pretzels and a couple of hazelnut Hobby chocolate bars. All in all, a decent haul.

As the train moved off, I noticed that it had started to snow. I stared at the romantic scene, where flakes spun around, settling against the glass, when a hissing sound cut the reverie short, and I turned to find Jamie spraying deodorant on his socks. Travelling companions could make or break a journey but as long as they observed basic hygiene, enjoyed good food and didn't snore, I was usually content to share a compartment. Now, with a mouthful of something called Dark Temptation, I let go of the curtain and sat back, banging my head against the bottom edge of my berth, which we'd left in place while we watched *He's Just Not That Into You*. Jamie had set up my laptop on his suitcase and was now positioning carrier bags in front of the wheels to stop it from rolling towards us whenever the train braked. He sat back, banging his head this time which we proceeded to do in tandem for the next two hours.

The train was now in its stride, and I cupped my hands to the glass, unable to look away from the snow. Cold air was streaming up from the vent as the outskirts of the Bulgarian capital twinkled through the darkness. Apartments loomed by the track; I could see families at kitchen tables. Grand bookcases and beautiful lamps. Televisions flashed. Bikes and buggies on balconies. Within twenty minutes, the city now behind us, the train broke into a canter, passing fields, farms, tethered horses. Grasping desperately to the last of the night before sleeping, I breathed it all in, catching a final metallic flash from the bend in a river until there was nothing but blackness and the thump of trance music from the compartment next door.

At around ten o'clock I decided to turn in. The first of two passport checks was due at 23.45 at the Bulgarian border town of Svilengrad, the second at 1 a.m. at the Turkish border town of Kapikule. The latter was the one I was dreading, as passengers had to disembark and have their luggage scanned. On my way to the loo, I found a young couple in the vestibule in the middle of a furious row. They stopped when they saw me. As I inched by, I could smell the aftermath of a drinking session. Locking the toilet door, I turned round to find the bowl covered in vomit. Not sure who was to blame, I sighed inwardly. After four months on Indian Railways, little could horrify me. I stepped out, closing the door behind me only to find the couple still there. They introduced themselves as Grace and Alex. Alex was sipping from a bottle of water – most likely the guilty party, judging by Grace's face. Their obliviousness to shame was fascinating, so I started asking questions.

'Are you staying in Istanbul or carrying on?' I asked Alex.

'Bit of both,' Grace replied, with a Scottish accent. 'Istanbul first for a week and then we're going on to Ankara then Kars and then Georgia.'

'Are you taking the train?'

'To Ankara and Kars, yes, and then the bus to Tbilisi.'

The train lurched and Alex fell sideways, dropping his water bottle and casting a mournful look in Grace's direction. I stifled a giggle, too enraptured to leave.

'Where have you travelled from?' I asked.

'Munich,' said Grace. 'I'm from Lanark but work in Munich as a lecturer in psychology. Alex works remotely – and I'm actually on sabbatical – so we're travelling around Europe by train. We love it.'

'You love it,' Alex blurted out. 'I hate trains.'

'I like trains,' I offered.

Grace's expression was one of fury. She placed a hand on the back of Alex's neck, steering him towards the corridor.

'Ah well, I might see you during passport checks,' I said, before darting back to my compartment to recount the interaction to Jamie, but he was asleep, earphones in place.

For a moment I stood watching him, hoping he wasn't secretly awake and wondering what I was doing. At six foot two, Jamie wasn't built for sleeper trains and was almost bent at a right angle, his feet sticking out from his blanket. The trance music had stopped, and I pushed the curtain aside for one last peek outside. The snow had also stopped and the stars were out, scattered like glitter as we travelled east. It was these moments that I savoured: when everyone else was asleep and I felt like the keeper of secrets. Only I could see the twists of river beneath the moonlight, the silhouettes of branches reaching out like arms to embrace. Something released inside me as I stared into the darkness, realising that this intimacy now felt sacred. Satisfied that there was nothing else of note, I dropped the curtain and climbed up to bed, knowing I'd barely sleep with the passport checks an hour or so away.

A thud brought us to a standstill, and I checked my phone. We'd arrived in Svilengrad a few minutes before midnight. I'd slept deeply but sat up straight away, curious to see what it looked like. I slid down the ladder, standing on one of Jamie's ankles as

I jumped to the floor. The corridor was quiet and I stepped out to see we were parked next to a low-lit wall topped with great loops of barbed wire. I often wondered who was likely to break free and risk shredding their internal organs climbing over one of these fences but as the thump of footsteps approached, I held that thought and waited for the border police. In less than twenty minutes our passports were stamped and handed back and the train began to move into Türkiye.

Friends who had taken this train before had advised me to stand by the door to be the first off at Kapikule – which theoretically meant being the first back on. But the next hour was torture. A little before 1 a.m. the train stopped and we leaped down with *Hunger Games* determination, charging towards the first building that looked like an office. No one knew where to go. There were few staff on the platform, and we ended up standing around in confusion as the station cats lapped puddles at our feet.

Jamie noticed a queue forming in a small stone room and we raced to join in, realising after a minute or two that we were moving further and further back as others turned up, sliding in at the front. As each new passenger edged in, I could feel the rage growing around me like a balloon about to burst: the flaring nostrils, the side glances, the heavy sighs. For more than half an hour we waited, watching the cats figure out who was allergic and who hated them, before arching their backs against their legs. A blind shot up from a little window and the families pushed forwards. I held back, willing other passengers to do the same. My neck and shoulders hurt from standing around carrying bags; I was desperate to get back on the train and sleep, but my plight was no comparison to that of parents with exhausted children. Travelling with young children is a mission at the best of times, but the thought of waking them up in the middle of the night to get dressed and dragged off the train into the cold filled me with dread. There was no way I'd bring young children on this journey for fun. After a while I noticed adults tagging themselves onto random children, claiming to be uncles and aunts to get to the front faster, at which point a scuffle broke out and I seized the opportunity to duck around them all and slide my passport under the glass. The first step over, we took our bags to the scanning shed where a bored guard paid little to no attention to what was on the belt.

'Could stick the cat through,' said Jamie, pointing at the skinny ginger moggy that had taken a liking to us. 'He'd never notice.'

Tempted to crawl in myself, I slung my bags in just as the train gave a comical pair of toots and we stumbled back on and into our berths.

———

My entire life I've been a light sleeper. You could whisper my name from over the road and I'd hear. Perhaps it was an evolutionary trait in women to ensure we responded to infants' cries, but even though my children had stopped calling from their room and had instead taken to standing in silence, inches from my face in the dark – I still slept fitfully. Now in Türkiye, the time had moved forwards an hour and it was 2.30 a.m. when I wriggled back under the blankets, a miserable three hours of sleep left to cherish. As predicted, I stirred twenty minutes before we were due to arrive in Istanbul, and checked Google maps. We were passing through the town of Velimeşe and I stretched out the screen to estimate the remaining distance. Vasil had correctly predicted that we'd be delayed and there were still two hours to go. At that moment a message arrived from Deniz, my contact in Istanbul.

'*Goodmorning Monisha.*'

'*Morning, I was about to send you a message to say we are delayed. I'm so sorry,*' I typed back.

'☺))))) *I am still home. Because first metro starts at 6 a.m. Be relax. Can you send me a location?*'

I dropped a pin and replied that I was going to snooze.

After almost two hours of deep sleep I woke at 7.30, and pushed back the curtain. It was not quite dawn. A ruby necklace of brake lights shone along the highway parallel to our tracks. Worried that I was missing something better, I darted into the corridor in time to see the sky splitting open above Lake Küçükçekmece. As though tidying themselves away, bundles of indigo clouds were pulling apart to reveal the blue of the coming day, apricot light crawling up the horizon. Rimmed with silver, the lake reflected the imminent sunrise like a lagoon of lava as we thumped towards Halkali station. Istanbul's hills rose into view, houses jutting off the slopes in a wonderful mess. The city was coming alive, lights flicking on in apartments, roads slicked with last night's rain, yet a fingernail of moon sat in the corner of the sky. A pair of minarets appeared above the rooftops, poking up like sharpened pencils, the mosque's dome soft around the edges. On board I could hear the thud of berths being locked into place, passengers brushing teeth and zipping up bags.

Jamie was now up, rubbing dry shampoo through his hair and looking around for his shoes. Pulling back the sheets and checking for stray books, hats and socks that might have got lost, we gathered bags as the train creaked to a halt. The carriage door swung open with a bang and the morning air rushed in, its freshness in tune with the feeling of newness and arrival. I'd made it. Over five nights and 2,450 miles, I'd journeyed from London to Istanbul in homage to the Orient Express. Jubilant, I hopped down onto the platform as the deep sound of the sunrise call to prayer floated above the rooftops.

5

THE ANKARA EXPRESS

Four months earlier I'd received a message on Instagram. It had been sent by a nuclear physicist named Deniz, whose mother had worked for Turkish State Railways. The message was accompanied by a photograph of Deniz reclining in a sleeper berth on the *Maitree Express* in India, his T-shirt riding up his belly, like a hairy Winnie-the-Pooh. An extreme train enthusiast from Istanbul, Deniz told me that with access to water, naan, and cigarettes he could spend a year travelling on Indian trains. Sensing a kindred spirit, and also a mine of information, I had begun to pick his brains about Turkish trains.

Now, as we reached the top of the escalator, I saw a figure with a shaved head, wearing a black puffer jacket. Deniz had crossed the city at dawn to meet us, and I was astounded by the generosity; I wouldn't wake at 5 a.m. to fetch my own family, let alone a stranger, yet here he was waiting on the other side of the turnstile to take us onto the Marmaray suburban train, and guide us around Istanbul.

Passengers were scattered about the carriage, a crossover of those who were beginning their day and those who were ending it. Of little conversation before I'd had coffee, I sat quietly – acutely aware of my unwashed face – counting the thirteen stops to Sirkeci. Each time the doors opened and commuters crowded in, I could smell the base notes of recently sprayed aftershave, the florals of freshly washed hair. The closer we got to the city, the more I stared up at clean shaves, fat watches peering out of cuffs and the slinkiness of quality silk. Online we'd had much to chat about, most of which had centred on trains, but Deniz was also quiet, and I wondered if I'd failed to meet his expectations. It wasn't hard to deduce character from an online persona, which usually mirrored reality. Several of my closest friends had emerged through Twitter owing to shared politics and a love of books or travel. The community that had found one another was as funny and feisty in the flesh but I wondered if Deniz was more of a wallflower. As though reading my mind, he turned to chat, a slurp escaping his lips, and I noticed then that he was missing his front teeth.

'I'm having dental work done,' he explained with a shyness that suddenly made sense. 'Veneers.'

'There's nothing left,' I said, examining the stubs that remained.

'I must go back for the fitting,' he said. 'Any cosmetic work you want, you should come to Türkiye, it's very cheap. In the UK this would cost thousands,' he added, no longer self-conscious.

'Do Turkish people get a lot of cosmetic work done? Or is it just the English who fly over for fatal surgery?'

'Both.'

There was a troubling trend of tourists travelling to Türkiye for sun, sea and stomach surgery owing to doctors charging less than a third of the cost for similar procedures in the UK. Since 2019, the Foreign Office was aware of at least twenty-eight Brits who had died as a result of medical tourism, and every few months a story would emerge about another botched Brazilian butt lift. Like most women who grew up through the heroin-chic era of the 1990s I'd yearned to be slim and couldn't fathom wanting to pump my bum full of fat from my hips. But who was I to judge? Perhaps looking like the back end of a pantomime horse was worth the risk of dying from an embolism.

Intrigued, I surveyed the carriage through a new prism. Social media and celebrities had given rise to the phenomenon dubbed 'Turkey Teeth', whereby natural teeth are filed down to stubs and bad crowns fitted over the top, making the wearer appear to have a mouthful of piano keys. They were commonly seen on *Love Island* contestants, blinding white against a spray tan the colour of builder's tea. According to the British Dental Association, 88 per cent of dentists surveyed had treated cases where complications had developed after dental tourism, and I hoped that Deniz's new gnashers would give him no grief. Keen to distract from his teeth – or lack thereof – Deniz sat up and pointed a finger at Jamie.

'You are Jem, yes?'

'No, I'm not Jem. That's Monisha's husband,' said Jamie. 'I'm Jamie.'

'Ah, from Beijing!' said Deniz, remembering Jamie's cameo in my last book.

'That's the one,' said Jamie, drawing in his legs as a woman tripped over his shoe. The crowd had swollen to the walls, and I was relieved when Deniz announced that we'd arrived at Sirkeci station.

Once the original terminus for the Orient Express, Sirkeci was now a disused building, few giving its grandeur a glance as they rushed towards the tram across the street. Although much had been made of the celebrations around its inauguration in 1890, it had taken almost two decades for it to progress from a temporary hub to a permanent terminus. The truth was that the building of the station and the introduction of the railway into Constantinople had caused a seismic shift in both the physical and social foundations of the city and its standing on the global stage. It had marked a turning point for the Ottoman Empire, as it finally forged a permanent link with Europe. Until Sirkeci's arrival, railway tracks had remained outside the city's walls, unlike in Paris and Brussels, whose stations lay at the heart of each city. However, the plans for the new hub required tracks to run through the imperial gardens of the Topkapı Palace and a number of densely populated neighbourhoods which had to be demolished, including sections of the sea wall and the Elvan and Daye Hatun mosques. This had posed no issues to the ruling sultan, Abdülaziz, a champion of the railway, who had already shifted his family from Topkapı to Dolmabahçe Palace; but wealthy property owners had demanded hefty compensation for the takeover, hindering what was paradoxically seen as a destructive construction.

'Come, I want to show you,' Deniz lisped, ferrying us over to the station to look through the windows. 'Here, you can see the first-class waiting areas… and on this side, this was the other classes. Can you see the ceilings?' he gestured, presenting the old building with the fondness of a doting father.

Railways the world over are a source of national pride. They were invariably built under physically demanding circumstances, revealing the ingenuity of teamwork and engineering. For some there was gratitude, even reverence, for the way in which the railways' emergence had provided much-needed employment to successive generations. To others the architectural beauty reflected their people's skills and craftsmanship, while many were simply in awe at how their railways had revolutionised the way in which humans formed connections through movement and trade.

Aware that Jamie and I wanted to offload bags, shower and find breakfast, Deniz steered us towards the tram, which dropped us off in Karaköy at the northern shore of the Golden Horn. It was here that we entered the Tünel, a fabulous funicular railway running up to the district of Beyoğlu. After the London Underground, the Tünel is the oldest subway in the world. In 1867, French engineer Eugène-Henri Gavand was visiting Constantinople and observed residents struggling up the hill between Galata and Pera, the former a centre of trade and banking, the latter a lively neighbourhood home to an emerging group of hotels. With approval from Sultan Abdülaziz, Gavand began constructing a railway that worked like a lift and in January 1875 the first train set off, taking just two and a half minutes to reach the top, a life-changing journey for the 40,000 Turks who would clamber up every day.

Never one to shy away from standing behind the driver – a cool young woman with a messy topknot – I steadied myself at the glass as we rumbled up at an angle, exhausted at the thought of climbing such an incline. At the top I discovered a little sign about the Tünel celebrating its '142th' anniversary, a section of which read: 'Even in a short distance, the people started to meet and chat. Over time Tünel regulars emerged. Some passengers routinised to take the first voyage. A warm and special dialogue was established among such first-voyage passengers.'

Translated directly from Turkish, it was as succinct a summary of the community that flourished from train travel as I'd read in a long time.

Beyoğlu was alive and kicking as we followed Deniz to our hotel, and I could sense that Turks here cared passionately about their food. Shoppers inspected pomegranates and punnets of strawberries, takeaways displayed trays of stuffed mussels topped with halves of fresh lemon, and spits were already turning, giving off the scent of slow-grilled lamb. Chefs shovelled pide into woodfired ovens and all along the pavement tables were laid and chairs unstacked, customers sipping slim glasses of dark red tea. Shopfronts displayed fresh baklava, glossed with honey, pressed with walnuts or scattered with luminous green pistachios, each parcel nipped, sealed, scored and tucked into tins.

Much to Jamie's delight, most dogs were dressed for the cold – one bull terrier wearing a sweatshirt with a leather collar and the sleeves rolled up – but it was the cats that stole the show. Sleeping in doorways, stepping across bins, dropping down from balconies and sitting in shop windows, the little felines seemed to emerge from cracks in the walls. Lithe and delicate, they were surrounded by baskets, saucers of water and paper-wrapped pieces of meat – a much-loved and looked-after part of the city's landscape.

As I caught the sweet smell of roasting chestnuts, Deniz stopped and pushed back a pair of heavy curtains. 'We have arrived,' he said.

The train's founder, Georges Nagelmackers, knew that passengers disembarking the Orient Express would expect parallel levels of luxury once they arrived in Istanbul, so in 1895 he opened the Pera Palace Hotel, which still maintains a particular grandness, although a dated one. Marble-floored and lit by candelabra, the hotel smelled of vintage velvet, and wealthy guests from the UAE leaving clouds of oud in the lift. Over time the Pera Palace had seen a string of well-known guests pass through its revolving doors, including Greta Garbo, Franz Joseph, Alfred Hitchcock, and Agatha Christie – who had allegedly shown a particular preference for room 411 – to which I now held the key. Lovingly assigned to the crime writer, the Agatha Christie Suite appeared to me like a shrine of memorabilia. Her collected works were locked in a glass cabinet – for which I did not have the key – and beneath it sat an Underwood typewriter, on which she was said to have written *Murder on the Orient Express*. The space was laid out much like the study in Sigmund Freud's house in London, her wooden bed in the middle, which creaked as I sat down to unzip my boots. Jamie knocked at the door and stepped in to inspect the suite for himself. He was staying on the floor below in a modern room with a much cosier-looking bed – and I had a bit of room envy, as intriguing as mine was. A few newspaper cuttings were framed above a bureau, detailing Christie's stays at the hotel. An image of her deep in thought hung above the Nespresso machine, one hand on her chin, as though asking: 'Now, what'll it be this morning? Ristretto or Livanto?

'Quite a clever little bit of PR, isn't it?' said Jamie, peering into the bathroom at the deep tub. 'Must be loads of fans who book this up. Weirdos wanting to sit in the bath where she did.'

Whether or not Christie had written *Murder on the Orient Express* in that particular room, it was certainly a great spot for super fans, and I was definitely going to use that bath. But it would have to wait. Deniz was sitting downstairs, excited to give us a tour of his favourite spots around the city, beginning with a rail-related treat.

Not even tarpaulin could hide the elegance of Haydarpaşa train station in Kadıköy as it rose into view. From aboard the ferry, I watched the mid-morning winter sun bounce across the Asian side of the Bosphorus Strait and light up the sheets that were wrapped round its body like towels preserving its modesty. Built between 1906 and 1908, the railroad terminal at Kadıköy was the starting point for all major eastbound services in Asia under the Ottomans, and served as the Istanbul connection for the Berlin to Baghdad line. For many years, until 2010, it was the origin for trains running to Anatolia until a fire suspected to be arson ripped through the roof. Now still under reconstruction, it remained a place of pilgrimage for railway fans.

The ferry docked and the salty smoke from grilled mackerel floated by as workers on their lunchbreaks milled around, biting into balık ekmek – fish sandwiches – and waving off Roma women in leopard-print leggings who were thrusting flowers into their hands.

'All the fish is from Norway,' said Deniz, declining a drooping posy from one angry woman wearing Crocs.

'Norway? Wow. I'd assumed it was fresh out of these waters,' I said, noting the numerous fishing boats in the harbour.

'How do you say… there has been overfishing in the Black Sea,' said Deniz. 'It became very costly. Now all the mackerel is shipped in.'

Whenever possible I deferred to street food for the freshness and the fun of discovering local flavours, but I was now coming round to the understanding that 'local produce' wasn't always the most climate-friendly or viable option.

Haydarpaşa was closed for renovations but Deniz had wangled a tour for us to see the work in progress. As we neared, he pointed to a nursery school, the sound of little voices and bubbles of laughter carrying across from the yard.

'That was my school as a child. It is where all the railway workers' children go. Even me, forty years ago.'

'What did your mother do for the railways?'

'She was a tailor. She sewed the uniforms of railway workers.'

With an air of superiority, we squeezed around other tourists held back by the barrier and walked past the workmen towards the entrance. After a couple of phone calls a young woman with red hair arrived to take us inside.

Fatma was the lead architect overseeing the renovations, the sound of drilling drowning out her unusually high-pitched voice, which made her sound as though she was trying not to cry. Following Fatma, we trooped up a wide staircase and around hallways lined with red carpets and lit by low-hanging pendant lamps. While Deniz and Fatma chatted, I ran my fingers along the dust-covered wood, the whine of sanders coming from different directions. Stained-glass windows let in muted pools of light as I walked around conjuring up an image of Haydarpaşa in its heyday – the roar of engines, the slam of doors and hoots of trains chugging in and out.

'They are doing everything to keep it original,' said Deniz, pointing out the details in a cornice. 'But not all of it is from the beginning. There was an accident: two ships collided, and one was a petrol ship, so it exploded and blew out the windows, so the glass has been replaced before.'

On the opposite wall was a golden face, like a Bafta award stuck to a marble slab.

'Who is this?' Jamie asked.

'That is Mustafa Kemal Atatürk,' said Deniz, smiling as though introducing a family member, rather than the founder and first president of the Republic of Turkey. Jamie looked blank.

'Are they going to start trains from here again?' I asked, desperate for the answer to be yes.

'They are not sure. Maybe they will start again the *Doğu Express*.'

'From here?!'

'It's a plan but not certain. We hope that it will again be the station, but we are not sure.'

Deniz and Fatma spoke quickly again. Fatma shrugged and pursed her lips, then each gave the other a look that I recognised as one of resignation.

'There is fear that it will be a boutique hotel, perhaps. We hope not. We hope that it will be the station. The workers want it to be again the station. They are looking at masterplans and blueprints, and they are watching old movies so that they can get it back exactly as it used to be.'

Downstairs the grand hall looked close to completion. Tiled floors echoed with our footsteps as we passed beneath arches framed by gold inlay. On close inspection the freshly painted strips featured green, intertwined phoenixes, their tongues unfurling, a symbol of the station rising from the flames. Gold foliage sprung from their backs, twisting its way up and over the arches, through flowers and aquamarine fountains giving life. That this might one day be a hotel lobby was a horrifying prospect. During the restorations, archaeologists had uncovered among its treasures a Byzantine-era fountain and a skeleton wearing a scented necklace, along with gold coins and jewellery believed to date as far back as the sixth century. The station was a working piece of history and it deserved to be preserved as such.

It was late afternoon by the time we wandered back round the harbour and I was now considering the balık ekmek, but Deniz urged us to hold on a few minutes longer, until he'd shown us a few more spots. Around us stray dogs were in abundance, great Anatolian shepherds with golden coats and dark faces. Most wore pink ear tags to show they'd been jabbed, spayed or neutered, and were lying around in coffee-shop forecourts hoping for someone to pet them. Hip-height and as rideable as horses, they weren't easy to shake off and sloped after us, lumbering into bookshops and whacking displays with their tails before spotting their pals and wandering off for a sniff.

Entering a passageway, Deniz gestured for us to follow, the space opening up into the most extraordinary two-storey collection of new and used books. Akmar Pasaji was the kind of place I could trawl for a week, one stall after the next stacked with worn paperbacks, neatly aligned classics, textbooks and tables piled like a librarian's nightmare – hundreds of books slipping and sliding across each other, forty copies deep. The mustiness fluttering out of pages, I stepped around the English translations before coming upon a copy of *The Time Regulation Institute* by Ahmet Hamdi Tanpınar. One of the greatest Turkish novels of the twentieth century, it dealt with the clash of tradition with modernity and I'd longed to read it. Paying barely 50p for it, I shoved the book into my pocket as Deniz signalled that it was time for our long overdue lunch.

The crowd thickened as the streets narrowed and we were soon surrounded by Turks shopping with one hand and eating with the other. At close quarters I noticed men with hairlines that looked as though they'd been dotted with red felt-tipped pen, their scabby scalps revealing recent hair transplants. The more I scanned the crowds, the more I saw them all hanging out together, bloodied and smoking shisha. On one side of the street were fishmongers in wellies selling slippery-looking tuna, headless pollack and boxes of anchovies as slim and bright as burning magnesium ribbon; on the other were deli owners rearranging Gemlik olives so fat they looked like dates, glistening in their brine. Some were stuffed with chillis, bobbing about like Halloween eyeballs, while others blushed pink, their flesh as tangy as lemon. Fridges hummed with slabs of bresaola, marbled beef and mortadella, and vendors hawked vats of midye dolma – mussels stuffed with rice. Stopping at Gözde Şarküteri, Deniz bought a couple and passed them to us, each one opening up to reveal a plump mussel on a bed of warm, herb-flecked rice. Scooping up the load with the loose shell, I could taste the sweetness of cinnamon.

Enjoying the smoke and noise, I was happy to forage around for lunch, but Deniz steered us away, determined to take us to Yanyalı, a restaurant that had been around since 1919. Serving broths, casseroles and various meats grilled, stewed or wrapped and fried in aubergine, it was in here, over tea and baklava, that I felt a renewed rush of love for Istanbul. As a teenager I'd sensed its magic but had come to realise that no matter how much we roamed a city's streets, trawling its bazaars or pacing barefoot around its mosques, it was impossible to truly open up a place without its people at our side.

We got up to leave and I patted my pocket. On the ferry Deniz had brought out a small badge featuring the symbol of Turkish Railways, along with a silver Serkisof pocket watch connected to a chain. Inside was a Turkish inscription that commemorated the 125th birthday of Atatürk. The badge had belonged to a train driver and the watch to a train chef, and he had given them to me as a gift. 'You are now an official member of Turkish Railways,' Deniz had said when he handed them over. As I gathered my bags and watched him hold open the door for Jamie, I felt a gut punch of debt to the kindness of this stranger who had unlocked his city for us both. Far from being a wallflower, Deniz was the embodiment of the wonderful ways in which trains brought people together.

A little after 10 p.m. Jamie and I arrived at Söğütlüçeşme station, also in Kadıköy, to catch the overnight *Ankara Express* to the capital. From there we would take the *Doğu Express* to Kars. The temperature had plummeted, an icy wind skirting the ground while we hunted for somewhere to sit. During the day, fifteen high-speed trains ran to the capital, taking an average of four and a half hours to make the 330-mile journey, so I was confused as to why the waiting area was full of passengers who had opted for a service that took twice as long – at three times the cost. It made little sense. I looked at the time: the train would have just departed Halkalı station on the European side of the city and would soon be passing through the Marmaray Tunnel, beneath the Bosphorus, before emerging on the Asian side of Istanbul, where it would pick us up before continuing south-east. A number of elderly passengers were in the waiting area along with young children asleep across laps, parents hushing the smallest. From my own experience it was much easier to manage little people at night, when they were more likely to conk out and sleep through the journey, rather than demanding entertainment, snacks and hourly trips to inspect the toilet on a day train; so the families on board made sense.

The queue to scan bags was growing by the second and I realised that this was the first time since leaving London that I'd come across tight security measures. Then I remembered the twin suicide bombings outside Ankara station which had killed 109 people in 2015. No group ever claimed responsibility but the prime minister at the time suggested that Islamic State was behind the country's deadliest terrorist attack, which had appeared to target a pro-Kurdish peace rally. Like most people in the West, I didn't spend my days fretting about potential terrorism, but as I dumped my bag onto the belt I thought about some of the railways that had recently been targeted: India in 2014, Germany in 2016 and our own London Underground at Parsons Green in 2017. I surveyed the crowded waiting area. Most people were glued to their phones. Some were finishing kebabs; others dozed on loved ones' shoulders. They looked so exposed. I could understand why the worst of humanity would see fit to exploit the vulnerability of travellers. Before spiralling into a vortex of paranoia, I saw the gates open to the platform and signalled to Jamie, who was lightly oscillating on the spot. We'd spent the afternoon in the Grand Bazaar looking at tea leaves, Turkish delight and jewellery before visiting the Hagia Sophia, and although neither of us had said it, we were flagging. Taking comfort in the knowledge that we were moments from bedding down in a toasty compartment, we followed the line upstairs as the train drew into the station.

'Hey, there's a dining car!' I shouted, as the carriages sailed past.

'Ah, nice one,' said Jamie. 'Looks like our carriage is right next to it. Want to get in there quick and grab a table?'

'It seems fairly empty at the moment, let's stash bags first.'

Our compartment was laid out exactly like the sleeper from Sofia, with twin berths, two checked blankets and the heating set to volcanic. If only to escape the feeling of my pores steaming open by the second, I was keen to get to the dining car.

'There's no lock on the door,' said Jamie, fidgeting with the latch.

'Then chain your suitcase and bring the laptops.'

As an afterthought I went back to draw the curtain and turn off the lights to dissuade anyone who fancied a snoop, then manoeuvred up the train, which was already twisting out of the station.

The dining car had fairy lights draped from one window to the next and a dated stereo system was playing what could have been a soundtrack to *Game of Thrones*: big drums and a saz, until a man began to sing with the pain of a spurned lover. Through the Shazam app on my phone, I identified the owner of the mournful voice as Serkan Kaya, a Turkish folk-classical singer, and brought up the video of 'Dağların Dumanı' on YouTube, which featured Kaya sitting on the floor of his living room with one hand pressed against his heart.

'What you watching?' Jamie asked, leaning over.

'Not sure, he's either been dumped or is suffering from acute angina.'

'He's sad 'cos his TV's not working,' said Jamie, pointing out the white screen jumping in the background. 'And now his water carafe's spontaneously exploded. I'd be sad, too. Want anything?'

While Jamie queued to buy me a chocolate bar, I sent the song via WhatsApp to a Turkish-Cypriot friend, curious about the lyrics, and she replied immediately:

'Me and my friend call it "My-Wife-Left-Me Music". They sit there drinking Red Label to it, smoking fifty Rothmans and wailing about their ex-wife after they drove her to insanity by shagging the twenty-third woman they met that year. And yes, he's singing: the mountains have no smoke, tomorrow has no faith, my emotions hit the shore. It's so unbelievably Turkish. Where are you?!'

I looked round at the restaurant-car manager, a gentle man named Harun with a small, feline face. The only heartbreak he appeared to be dealing with was deciphering Jamie's attempt to buy a can of Coke Zero – his fourth of the day. Five or six solo travellers were seated by the windows, one young woman in the middle of an argument, her phone wedged into her hijab. I then noticed her friend gesturing wildly from another table before putting her head down and laughing at the scene, for which I was desperate for subtitles. An elderly couple were spooning up lentil chorba that smelled so good I asked Jamie to order me a bowl – the only hot dish available, despite the extensive list of panini, köfte and kebabs.

Rain slashed the windows, the wind tearing at palm fronds as I sat watching neon hotel signs reflecting off the wet ground, mosques and minarets rising in the background. Running along-side a residential boulevard, the route allowed me to stare into the apartments in a wealthy neighbourhood where owners had set up extensive bars in their chandeliered living rooms featur-ing grandfather clocks and cacti arranged in ascending order. Portraits of Atatürk hung from the walls alongside guitars. At one window a mother stood holding her baby, pointing at the train. It was almost midnight, and I felt a surge of empathy as we locked eyes, remembering my many sleepless nights.

With a pudding in hand, Jamie slid into the opposite seat as Harun placed down my chorba and a bread roll.

'Really nice this, isn't it?' Jamie said, peeling back the lid.

'What, the train?'

'This,' he said, waving an arm behind him. 'Everyone just here in one place. Doing their own thing. But together.'

This was what I'd been longing for since I'd left London. Like a common room, the dining car provided ambient company. Even those who chose to sit apart, earphones in, and without ordering anything, had drifted in here for a reason, towards the innate sense of belonging. A place where you could be alone together. Two ticket inspectors sat down at the next table and smiled like a pair of old uncles, one giving Jamie's pudding a thumbs up. I liked that the staff were hanging out with passen-gers instead of hiding away in their own compartments.

'Might get another one, actually,' Jamie said, waving at Harun as I squeezed out my Dido bar, which might have looked like a dark KitKat Chunky had it not melted in the heat.

I took out my diary and worked a finger down my list of trains, crossing off the journey from Sofia to Istanbul and the one we were currently on. It was midnight. Cupping my hands against the glass, I looked out to where workers were unloading lorries behind a supermarket. Night trains are ideal for the nosy. From my seat I was privy to cleaners vacuuming offices, waiters stacking chairs, and the homeless gathering together in doorways, their faces briefly lit by cigarettes. The after-darkness of their move-ments went unseen by most, but I had a front-row ticket. Did they know they were being watched? Or did the train clatter by as background noise, there for a moment then gone?

My empty bowl began to shudder and I felt the train break free of the city, speeding along the outskirts, fewer lights and more rain striking the glass. Most passengers had drifted back to their carriages and, not wanting to keep Harun up for longer than necessary, we gathered our things and went back to our compartment. Jamie hauled himself up and into his berth and within a few minutes I could hear the faintest of snores. Quietly, I eased open the door for one last trip to the loo as the train slowed into Gebze station, where a family was waiting on the platform. A woman boarded with a little girl – no more than three years old – and a baby in a onesie so padded she looked like a starfish. Depositing the bags inside the door, their father just had time to jump down and wave off his family before the train jerked and moved on. He took sidesteps for a few seconds, peering in to check on the mother as she hauled up both children, kicked the bags along the corridor, then disappeared into the compartment at the end of the carriage. So many questions ran through my mind: which berth would the toddler sleep in without safety nets to stop her rolling out? How would the poor woman use the loo without taking in both children? What if the little girl needed the loo in the night while the baby slept? Would she have to leave her and duck out? On my way back to bed, I thought back to my time in Japan where toilet doors had harnesses fixed on the back to stick babies in. I stopped outside the woman's compartment. I wanted to knock and offer assistance, then changed my mind in case she saw me as an interfering busybody. Perhaps the family did this journey all the time and I was just riddled with maternal anxiety.

Grateful that I'd finally reached the point in life where I could use the loo without a baby watching from a bouncer or sitting on my lap, I spread out my blanket and scrolled through photos that Jem had recently sent me of the girls dressed as butterflies at a birthday party. I loved the freedom of being back on the rails, but I was missing their small faces. Shuffling up to the window,

I looked out to where the Sea of Marmara poured into what was essentially a bay reaching up to the city of İzmit. On the opposite shore lay Gölcük, where the lights of restaurants, resorts and bars shone like a string of sapphires and diamonds. My blanket wrapped around my shoulders, I sat in the glow of the nightlight, the drum of wheels the only sound. Savouring one last look, I nudged down the blind, patted my pillow and turned in for the night.

6

THE DOĞU EXPRESS

It looked like it had snowed inside the train overnight – shoeprints pressed into the powder which had blown in through the gaps. It was piled up on the steps and sprayed across the doors, and as the connection between the carriages flexed like an accordion, I wobbled across the coupling, feeling the freeze from outside.

The time was 7 a.m. and we were passing the town of Polatli, the *Ankara Express* running at least an hour behind schedule. Warmed by the aroma of coffee and toast, the dining car was soundtracked by upbeat pop this time, as I found a window seat and stared out to where darkness still clung to the landscape. The scene looked like a Turner painting, thick impasto snow almost violet, the moon a yolk-yellow haze. For a moment I pictured myself out there, trudging through the drifts in terrifying terri-tory, where sound would go unheard by anyone but the birds roosting in bare branches. A battle between light and dark ensued, each pushing against the other as cloud swept across the moon and the might of morning brought the first rays of sun above the horizon. And with it the energy now radiating from atop the hills turned the wilderness into an expanse of calm and safety.

The two hijabis were asleep face down on the table and a third passenger was playing solitaire on his laptop. His jacket was rolled into a ball and I wondered if he, too, had slept in the dining car. Yawning, then readjusting his jumper, he got up to ask Harun for more coffee. I leaned across.

'Are you travelling to Ankara?' I asked.

'Sincan,' he replied, 'and then Ankara.'

'Why are you not taking the high-speed train?'

He laughed. 'It is not stopping at Sincan. This one,' he pointed downwards, 'this is the only train that will make that stop.' I asked why he was travelling there.

'I live in Ankara and I go sometimes to work in Istanbul, but my mother she is in Sincan, so I try to stop sometimes and visit with her.'

A tech engineer, Mehmet was a regular user of both the sleeper and the high-speed train, but much preferred the latter for the comfort, cost and efficiency.

'And you?' He wiped what looked like tomato paste from the edge of his mouth.

'I like sleeper trains. But this one's expensive compared to the high-speed train, no?'

Mehmet shook his head. 'Only if you are in the sleeping carriage. Before the high-speed train there were twelve sleeping carriages. Now there is only one sleeping carriage. The other six are Pullmans, with seats, and they are the same price as the high-speed. Usually it is with all the people who could not get tickets for the high-speed.' He pointed at my diary. 'You, you like to look out of the window? It is very nice. Many people are like you, they like the nature, the drinking tea. Older people they are having the time also. In summer it is beautiful.'

Mehmet got off at the next stop. Owing to the bad weather, we were almost two hours delayed, but I could sense from the movement around me that we were approaching Ankara.

Jamie was once again rubbing dry shampoo into his hair when I returned to the compartment. Shoving up the blind, I saw that it was a clear day in Ankara, ideal for exploring on foot. As the train came to a standstill we jumped down to the platform and were about to follow the crowd when I remembered the mother with the two children.

'Wait,' I said to Jamie, 'I need to find that mum.'

Hanging back, I scanned the carriage windows to see if I could spot her, but the train had emptied. Then I saw her, squatting on the platform with the baby against her chest. She stood up, holding one bag strap while her toddler held the other, and together they attempted to walk, the bag tilting downwards and banging against the child's side. Unable to help myself, I relieved them of the bag, the woman taking her daughter's hand and chatting away to me in Turkish while I showed her my screensaver picture of the girls. Her eyes brightened as she patted each of her daughters on the head and rolled her eyes, gesturing at all their things. No matter where in the world we were, the Motherload translated across every culture into a universal language that each one of us understood.

A plate of hot börek was the perfect way to start the day. Stuffed with minced lamb then baked, the fatty filo pastries went well with cups of clear, unsweetened tea. We were sitting in a pastry shop between tables of elderly men wearing sweater vests and sandals, who were chatting with theatrical gruffness. They were either annoyed with one another or expressing the deepest love and admiration, and their indifference to us was cheering.

Certain capital cities have a way of making visitors feel that their presence is neither welcome nor unwelcome and I liked being left to navigate at my own pace without questions or judgement. Along from the pastry place was a shop selling Turkish coffee. It had cezve – traditional copper pots – hanging from the ceiling and hessian sacks full of beans. The assistant was in the middle of a Facetime conversation with a busty woman in a vest top and showed an understandable indifference to my potential custom as I walked about scooping up handfuls of beans, the bitterness staying on my fingers. Wherever I travelled, I got caught up with local customs and invariably found myself coming home with oversized bags of masala chai and boxes of silvery barfi. They would then lie in a cupboard while I sat on the sofa drinking PG Tips with a packet of Custard Creams. Much as I loved the tweeness of the Turkish coffee pot,

I knew it would end up unused. Instead, I picked up two tins of hot chocolate for my kids, which would last a week at most.

Standing on a mound of snow swept up on the pavement, Jamie was taking photos of an elderly vendor selling simit – burnished twists of sesame-coated bread – when my phone buzzed. Around the same time Deniz had written to me, I'd received a message on Twitter from Vedat, a Turkish train driver who worked between Ankara and the city of Kayseri. '*I wish you health and well-being,*' he wrote. '*The doors of my country and the doors of our trains are wide open to you. You have a brother in Türkiye.*'

Struck by the heartfelt message – and thrilled to hear from a real-life train driver – I had written back and forth with Vedat and he was now waiting for us at Ankara station, along with his friend Ferhat, a high-speed-train driver who would interpret.

A Turkish version of Peter Kay was waiting in the foyer of the old Art Deco station, which I'd been too sleepy to notice when we'd arrived. Vedat had taken the day off work to meet us, and we now stood beaming at one another, chatting in broken phrases and willing Ferhat to arrive. Rummaging through his rucksack Vedat pulled out a paper bag patchy with grease. I could smell the honey in the pastries as he handed the bundle to me, then felt it on my palms.

'For *Doğu Ekspresi,*' he said, before going back into his bag and bringing out a brass train whistle, gesturing that it was mine to keep. I turned it over, the growing collection of train gifts making the child in me dance a thousand jigs. Placing it between my lips, I waited for Vedat's approval, then allowed a shrill blast to echo into the rafters as Jamie made a video. Quiet, unassuming, and more content to observe other people in their element than put himself at the centre of activity, Jamie slipped his phone into his pocket and listened to Vedat.

'A whistle is a life,' Vedat said. 'Sometimes a whistle saves a life. Earthquakes and trains speak this phrase better.' He pointed up the platform. 'Ferhat is come.'

A tanned, good-looking man with a natural set of teeth strode over wearing jeans and a pair of aviator sunglasses. The two drivers clapped one another on the back before steering us upstairs and across to the modern side, where the high-speed trains arrived and departed. A glass expanse, much the same as a shopping centre, the new station had been described by train buffs as an eyesore and a 'monstrosity'. The gatekeeping so particular to train afficionados always struck me as odd. Any contemporary railway building was bound to represent the sophistication of modern design, vaults and gargoyles a thing of the past. The station was bright, spacious, filled with plants and practical, much like the ones I'd seen in central China, and it matched the slick new trains parked underground.

Amused by my obsession with sleeper trains, Ferhat was keen to show off the high-speed trains, leading us down to where they were all lined up as though about to start a race. He opened the doors of one which usually journeyed to Ankara, and we climbed up. Carpeted, well-lit and wide, it smelled of new leather and featured a dining car with curved glass dividers between tables, giving it the air of a Soho diner striving for vintage charm. Sliding doors hissed open to reveal private compartments containing business-class seats with TV monitors tucked down the sides. I felt a mixture of envy and irritation: envy of Turks who got to use these trains that were clean, high-spec and affordable, and irritation at the stinking, expensive excuses for trains in the UK. After a quick play around in the driver's cabin, I sat down at a café to quiz the experts on the *Doğu Express*.

A sleeper service running from Ankara to Kars near the Armenian border, the *Doğu Express* – meaning Eastern Express – had existed in various guises since 1939 and was wildly popular with local tourists, who mostly travelled the 800-mile route in winter, decorating the compartments with coloured fairy lights and spreading out picnic blankets covered with baklava, börek and cold cuts. Tickets were snapped up as soon as booking opened, so in 2019 Turkish Railways launched a parallel service called the *Turistik Doğu Ekspresi*, which developed a cult following. Whereas the classic train had standard carriages with both seats and couchettes, the new one was fitted with twelve carriages containing couchettes only and made long stops along the route, allowing passengers to get off for up to three hours at a time to explore historic sites in İliç and Erzurum, when travelling eastbound, and then at Erzincan, Divriği and Sivas when travelling westbound. Jamie wanted to ride the tourist train but I got palpitations at the mere thought of spending thirty-four hours with a bunch of wannabe influencers waving selfie-sticks, blocking up the aisles with tripods, and decided instead to book tickets on the original service.

Only it was impossible. Tickets went on sale twenty-nine days before departure and with just one sleeper carriage – with a capacity of forty passengers – the spots were taken in seconds, usually as a result of group bookings made through tour companies, which had a monopoly. Men and women weren't permitted to travel in the same compartments unless they were in the same group, which lessened our chances further still, and our agent had failed to secure couchettes. But like a fairy godfather with shaved-down teeth, Deniz had come to our rescue. Pulling a few strings within Turkish Railways, he had secured a compartment then sent me a link to buy the tickets. If he ever tired of nuclear physics, then Deniz had a promising career ahead as a tour guide and fixer.

'You are lucky,' said Ferhat, laying down his aviators and massaging his stubbly jaw. 'It is not easy to get tickets.'

'When did the train become so popular?' I asked.

'*Doğu Express?*' he said, pronouncing it *doh-ooh* without the 'g'. 'It was always a popular train and then a young Swedish man, he put a video on YouTube. He rode this train and then young Turkish people they saw this video of a train in their own country and then they wanted to ride it.'

'Have you ever driven it?' I asked.

'Ah no,' Ferhat replied. 'Let me show you,' he said, taking my pencil and drawing a line across a page. 'Here, you have Ankara, and here you have Kars. In between there is Kayseri, Sivas and then Erzurum. There is one driver for here, one driver for here and another driver for here and here,' he explained, shading in the stretches between each of the five cities. 'One driver cannot do this whole journey, only eight hours. Usually it takes twenty hours' – at this he and Vedat started to laugh – 'but with delays it is about twenty-five. And each shift is two drivers. So, you have many drivers for one train.'

Vedat was watching our exchange and I asked if he had ever travelled on the *Doğu Express*.

'Yes, I was on the train last year. Passengers decorate the compartments with lights. It's a romantic and fun journey, people are smiling and cheerful. But it's a long journey and an opportunity to meet new people.' He turned to Ferhat and spoke quickly.

'There is the Erciyes mountain, you should see it when the train passes through Kayseri. And also…' Vedat picked up his phone and showed me a photograph of Selim station, a wasteland but for two parallel lines of bright red trees flanking the slim tracks. He began to explain then stopped and typed into his phone, holding the note up to me, which read:

'*Thanks to an eco-friendly railroader working here, they grew all these trees. There are very few in this area but he grew them all. Also, in the past, whenever railroaders ate an apple, they buried it instead of throwing it away. So there are now very many apple trees in interesting places on the railway route.*'

'Do you drive night trains?' I asked Ferhat, who was looking for videos of the *Doğu Express* on his phone.

'High-speed only. But all 4,000 drivers in Türkiye, we have to do it for training.'

'Which do you prefer? Night trains or day trains?'

'For us night is much better than day. Nobody is outside. Nobody is rushing, it's better for safety.'

'Would you say that Turkish trains have a special place in people's hearts?' I asked.

Vedat wrote into his phone again:

'*The trains are very much a part of Turkish life. In the past doctors travelled from station to station, treating people and educating the public against epidemics. And you know, some train drivers have distinctive horn rhythms.'*

'Why?'

He typed and held up his phone, smiling:

'*So that the children understood in that rhythm that their father is coming home.*'

Vedat spoke rapidly to Ferhat again, before writing another note.

'*Once, I picked pears from the trees at a small station and offered them to all the railroad workers at a large station. An old railroad worker asked me where I got this pear. I told him the station and the location of the trees. He said he started working on that train station and planted those trees forty years ago, he was very happy. I told him I brought you the fruit you planted forty years ago. Train stations should be seen as cultural facilities. Stations are structures that promote art and landscape and agricultural production.*'

'Yes, it's true,' he said, putting his phone back into his pocket.

To my horror, Ferhat announced he was late for a funeral, so we disbanded immediately, thanking him for his time as Vedat led us out onto the main road. Before I realised it, we were walking in single file along the edge of a dual carriageway, stepping around puddles and piles of dirty snow.

'Where's he taking us?' Jamie asked.

'I have no idea,' I replied, trying to open up Google maps and avoid being killed at the same time. Cars sped past, spinning sludge in our direction as Vedat marched on, too far ahead to hear our shouts.

'At least the weather's picked up,' said Jamie, with the quintessentially English take on what was beginning to feel like a suicide mission. No other pedestrians were on the road. Ten minutes later we darted across a slip road and Vedat stopped to ask if we fancied anything from a roadside café. In need of something a lot stronger than caffeine, I politely declined then followed Vedat across the road, down a side street and into a courtyard.

'Is this his house? Or like a friend's house or something? Jamie asked.

Shrugging, I started to giggle, thoroughly enjoying the impromptu tour of the city. Vedat had brought us to a small gallery showcasing traditional Turkish crafts. He then asked if we wanted to experience a hammam, leading us around the corner to a traditional bath house, a welcome relief from the cold. As the wind stung my ears, I watched Vedat disappear into the men's side of the hammam to organise Jamie's treatment.

'Such a nice guy,' said Jamie. 'How'd you meet him?'

'Twitter.'

Unlike the old men at the coffee house, Vedat was not someone indifferent to our presence. He wanted nothing more than to show us the best of his home and he was doing what he'd promised months ago when we chatted – throwing wide open the doors of his country.

Steamed and scrubbed raw with olive soap, we taxied through streets which reeked of coal. I felt at least an inch smaller all over after watching with a mixture of glee and disgust as shreds of dead skin were rolled off my arms, legs and stomach by a matronly woman with highly processed blonde hair, and parsley on her breath. An infantilising experience, but one that mentally and physically prepared me for our onward journey to Kars. I looked out of the window. Ankara was not a city I'd sought out, but stumbled upon out of necessity, and it didn't fill me with joy.

'Weird place,' said Jamie, staring at soulless apartment blocks. 'Feels a bit dry.'

'Yeah… quite like it though.'

'In what way?'

'Dunno, just has a bit of an edge.'

Colourless and lacking in character, Ankara wasn't walkable, a mass of ring roads and boulevards, which made it hard to fathom. Built for administration and functionality, this was a grey, government city: the equivalent of Washington DC to Istanbul's New York. As we drew up at a restaurant, I suppressed my instinct to see only ugliness in a place that had suffered much violence and poverty. What it lacked in aesthetic it made up for in spirit. Inside the hammam I'd found a delightful mix of women – cotton muslin wrapped around their curvy, wet bodies. Seasoned bathers, they weren't afraid of eye contact and had observed my nervous nudity with amusement. They'd chatted about trains, scolded me for not travelling down to Antalya, and asked about my kids with the sweetness of Muslim sisterhood. Now, as we pushed open the door to a restaurant Vedat had recommended to me, I realised that it wasn't the city that needed to warm up, but me.

Ciğerci Aydın was one of those rare spots that made me reconsider returning to a city for the food alone. Staff sped around bringing loaded skewers hot off the coals, grabbing empty ones from holders, as though carrying a bunch of tiny swords. Over chilli-flecked chicken thighs and Adana kebab, satisfying Jamie's vegetable aversion, we discussed our plans for the following day of departure, leaving just enough room for a slice of künefe.

'What is that?' Jamie asked, inspecting the laminated menu.

'Cheese,' said a passing waiter. 'Sweet cheese.'

'Mmm, not sure about that,' Jamie replied.

Looking round the room, I spotted the crisp triangles on other people's plates and, despite suffering from ever-worsening lactose intolerance, figured it was worth the misery.

'Go on, I'll share one with you,' I said. Soaked in syrup, the cheese was baked between crisp layers of shredded filo pastry and devoured with urgency – hot, stringy threads stretching into the air as we failed to cut it apart and ordered a second.

'God, that was amazing,' said Jamie. 'I'd totally come back here tomorrow before the train.'

Night had closed in by the time we returned to the hotel – a high-rise Radisson Blu located in the Old City. Having travelled on a budget for the previous few days, we'd now got separate rooms, Jamie declaring: 'You'll have some privacy now,' as he disappeared to bed.

If anyone needed privacy it was Jamie. The truth was, I hated being on my own at night. Since the age of six I've suffered from night terrors, waking every couple of months to the sight of a faceless figure standing at the foot of the bed. At times it would lean over me, inching the duvet off my chest as I struggled to scream myself awake. During these moments I'd be immobilised, unable to sit up, as though weights were pinning down my limbs. Somehow, I'd yell myself awake. I didn't suffer from terrors as long as someone else was in the room. Sleeping next to my husband Jem, or my children, I'd not experienced a terror for at least a year, the safety of another human presence enough to ease my subconscious.

Being in hotel rooms made me uncomfortable, and I was secretly wishing Jamie and I had booked a twin. Stepping out onto the balcony, I expected the roar of traffic, but heard nothing but the flap of wind along the parapet. From here, eleven storeys up, Ankara looked like a different city: brake lights flashed like jewels; the Melike Hatun mosque lit up like a Las Vegas hotel. As though licked by flames, museum facades were warmed to shades of gold – and I saw now, through the treetops, how many parks and lakes lay in between, their bodies brightened by the reflection of neon lights. Ankara looked like a big fairground. The wind whipped harder, and I stepped back inside, sliding the door closed. Double-bolting the main door, I got into bed and tapped the nightlight app that I used for the children, swiping to find their favourite scene of dancing unicorns. With my final thought of my girls at home, I flipped off the main light and hoped for the best.

I sat up. Unsure why I was awake, I listened, hearing nothing but the blow heater. Touching the back of my neck, I found my hair damp with sweat. A night terror? No, not this time…

The unicorns were still glowing and I reached across, swiping them away to check the time. It was 4.17 a.m. Confused,

I decided to use the loo and felt my way around the corner to the bathroom, wincing as the light came on. I sat down, closing one eye, then both. I lurched forwards. Despite the fog of tiredness, I felt it again, stronger this time. Then again. On the shower rail two hand-towels were beginning to move like windscreen wipers; then my toothbrush clattered into the sink. Was the wind making the building sway? The wall behind me creaked as the bathroom shifted back and forth. Earthquake!

Bolting from the bathroom, I jumped onto my bed. Before going to sleep I'd slung a bra over the back of a chair and I watched it now, swinging, my stomach turning over as the teaspoons trembled on the table. Grabbing my phone, I searched 'earthquake', the top news alert reading: 'Major magnitude 7.8 earthquake – 29 km north-west of Gaziantep... 4 minutes ago.'

I'd forgotten that Türkiye lies across one of the most seismically active regions in the world. As the wall groaned again, I called Jamie, who didn't answer. The curtains were swinging; was it getting stronger? Would the ceiling fall in? Was the whole hotel about to come down like the Twin Towers? Should I ring the children, send a voice note to say I loved them?

A cup fell off the table and I leaped off the bed and threw open the door to go to Jamie's room. Other guests were in the corridor, or peering around their doors.

'My room is moving!' a woman shouted from across the hall.

'There's been an earthquake,' I replied, banging on Jamie's door. He still didn't answer. I tried again.

'Who is it?' came a muffled voice.

'It's me!' I said. 'There's been an earthquake.'

Jamie opened the door. 'Shit, you okay?' he asked as I stood trembling in my pyjamas. 'Come in, come in,' he said, throwing an arm around me. 'I'll make tea.'

Wrapping himself in a gown, Jamie foraged around for tea bags, as the roar of a cheap kettle filled the room. Baffled by his nonchalance, I watched him place the bags in a cup, laying the strings carefully over the rim.

'Can you not feel that?' I asked, glancing around as the after-shocks continued.

'Nope,' he replied, pouring out a cup and bringing it over to where I sat cross-legged on the sofa, suddenly aware of how nice his suite was. His indifference went some way to calming my frenzy. We sat in silence, checking Twitter for live updates from residents in Gaziantep, a city of more than two million people in the south-eastern Anatolia region. Snowflakes spun outside the window. The temperature was below zero and footage showed people screaming into rubble and digging by torchlight. If anyone buried had even the slightest chance of survival, it would be severely hampered by the freezing weather.

Aching with pain for parents searching for their children, I asked Jamie if I could sleep in his room, dragging my duvet round from next door and curling up into a miserable ball at the edge of his king-sized bed, both of us scrolling in the darkness, tapping on videos of collapsing buildings, bloody survivors and men lifting slabs of concrete. There was nothing to be gained from live-streaming the horror, so I sent a message to my family to let them know I was okay. The trains would be cancelled, I was sure of that. Such was the nature of travel: no matter how much we try to control our journeys, researching, planning and checking, there is nothing any of us can do if the earth chooses to buckle beneath our feet.

———

At breakfast guests ate in silence. Most were on their phones, trying to call loved ones. We sat in a corner, picking at cereal and dried fruit, unsure what to do with ourselves. I contacted Vedat, who replied that his friends were fine, adding '*but every pain my people go through is my grief*'.

Vedat reassured me that the trains operated outside the earthquake zone but warned that there might be delays owing to humanitarian aid trains heading to the area and that the journey might not be a very pleasant one. By that point I had stopped caring about the onward journey. It was the first time that I'd been in the proximity of a natural disaster: watching the fallout and feeling the intensity of Turks' pain hit me in a way I didn't expect.

The *Doğu Express* was set to depart just before 6 p.m. and with half a day to explore the city, Jamie was keen to visit the mausoleum of Atatürk, whose name he'd learned of only in Istanbul.

'Apparently he's this great leader.'

'You could say that,' I replied.

'Never heard of him, but I read about his mausoleum, which is apparently in some massive complex.'

'You've never heard of Mustafa Kemal Atatürk?'

'No. Who is he?'

'He's the founder of the modern-day Republic of Turkey?'

Jamie shrugged as the taxi drew up to Anıtkabir in the Çankaya district. Stamping ice off my boots, I passed through the security gates and thought back to my history lessons at school in India when I'd first learned about Atatürk. Aged nine, I'd studied world history that encompassed everyone from Atatürk and Christopher Columbus to Giuseppe Garibaldi and Lakshmi Bai, Rani of Jhansi. After returning to the UK, I became acutely aware of how the curriculum was so narrow and focused on British history – albeit a deeply distorted version – that it wasn't unusual for people to assume that Garibaldi meant biscuits. I'd spent two years at A level memorising useless tales of George, Duke of Clarence drowning in a butt of Malmsey wine, instead of learning how Winston Churchill had starved 3 million Indians during the Bengal Famine, or how Carl Hagenbeck had showcased Somalis in London zoos, truths that would explain much of the modern-day geopolitics affecting Britain and the world at large.

The mausoleum complex was indeed massive, with regimental guards housed in boxes, like life-size Action Men. Snow was falling in giant flakes, visitors slipping around the wet grounds with hoods up, waiting for the changing of the guard. Housed in one corner of the square was a black 1935 Lincoln, encased and

84

gleaming with polish. A seven-seater with bulletproof windows, the vehicle was ordered after assassination attempts against Atatürk.

Two shouts cracked like gunshots and I went outside in time to catch the guards performing the ceremony, handsome in long, belted coats, rifles over their shoulders as they marched in single file. Following them at a distance, we climbed the steps and entered the main building, which housed the late leader. I could hear the sound of careful footsteps behind me and was reminded of the two embalmed bodies of Kim Jong Il and Kim Il Sung which I'd visited in North Korea, their waxy faces a mixture of grotesque and enthralling to behold. We'd been forced to bow three times around them both. Fortunately, there was nothing nearly so tasteless here, only a beautiful marble cenotaph.

Unable to help myself, I'd been scouring social media for updates on the quake, watching the death toll climb every hour from just after four in the morning – by noon it had reached almost 1,200. I thought back to my time in Japan when a hotel owner had explained the country's many preventative measures in place for earthquakes, its high-rise buildings sitting on special blocks of rubber to absorb the motions. It seemed short-sighted, if not downright reckless, that Turkish engineers hadn't incorporated similar motion-dampers given the country's location across multiple fault-lines.

The sky was a sombre grey, the air heavy with a dampness that was now sitting on my eyelashes. From our elevated position I couldn't see any details across the capital, low cloud and drizzle blurring the skyline. Walking and scrolling in silence, Jamie and I emerged on the opposite side of the grounds from which we had entered and found ourselves barely five minutes' drive from Ciğerci Aydın. In need of food and a warm place to wallow, we traipsed back into the restaurant, the staff amused to see us again, the same waiter showing us to a table by the radiator where I dried my gloves and hat. After several skewers and another slice of künefe, the hollow in my stomach filled a little, but I couldn't shake off the images of suffering just 400 miles away.

Back at the hotel, Jamie went to his room to work, and I settled onto my bed to read reviews of the *Doğu Express*. Unable to focus on more than a line at a time, I started researching 'What to do during an earthquake', realising I had no idea of the protocols. 'Protect your head and neck with a large pillow or seek shelter under a table or desk. Drop, cover and hold on.' Just then a cracking sound travelled up the wall to my right and my armpits prickled. My eyes shot to the curtains where I could see the inner layer beginning to swing. It was 13.26. The uplighter lamp was now swaying in the opposite direction. Instinct told me the epicentre was elsewhere. I sat still, watching. Almost two minutes passed with no sign of it abating. This was no aftershock but a second, violent quake. As each moment passed, I pictured the devastation unfolding somewhere nearby: roofs falling in; bridges collapsing; roads splitting; people being crushed.

People were dying, right now, as I sat here. The phone rang on my side table.

'Did you feel that?' Jamie asked.

'Course I bloody did, I'll come over.'

Running round in my socks, I found Jamie at his laptop. He'd noticed the desk moving but hadn't realised what was happening. So attuned to terra firma, our bodies had gone into fight or flight mode at the sensation of the ground refusing to do its job; our brains unable to process the broken pact that it will hold us up and keep us safe. For the next hour I stood by the bed detecting tremors, glued to the new scenes of carnage unfolding in Kahramanmaraş province. Houses were sliced open, half a living room falling out, armchairs upside down. Floral duvets were piled with snow, surrounded by wires, cladding and windows hanging from their frames. Mothers cradled the bodies of dusty, dead children. A flurry of WhatsApp messages came in and I swiped them away until my friend Ramin called.

'You okay, Mon?'

'No,' I said, crying into my hands and sliding to the floor.

Powerful and shallow, the quakes proved to be two of the most destructive in modern history. The region was already home to refugees from north-west Syria, many of whom were living in makeshift accommodation, and the brutal cold was exacerbating the punishing conditions in which rescue teams were attempting to pull out survivors. I couldn't understand the depth of my grief. I had no family or friends in the region, but hearing the primal screams of parents, their faces contorted with pain, was making me unravel. My own children were at home, safe and warm. I would soon be able to reunite with them and kiss their cheeks. Unlike the thousands of Turkish and Syrian families on my screen, the sound of their agony in my ears, I had a home. Survivor's guilt maybe? I had an urge to abandon the whole journey and head south to offer assistance, but that threw up its own ethical challenges: who was I to arrive and take up space, food and water from those on the ground who needed it? No. I would be more useful observing, telling their story and doing what I could to encourage aid to the displaced.

On board the *Doğu Express*, Jamie opened the door and sat down. 'Just been talking to those girls next door. They're really sweet: two mates on their way to Kars. Think they're in their twenties or something? They've put up lights around their compartment,' he shrugged off his jacket, looking highly entertained, 'and they've got a candle lit, for "atmosphere",' he said, doing air quotes and stifling a laugh.

'Awesome, that's just what we need, a nice atmospheric fire breaking out on board,' I replied, watching the platform move away. A pair of young men jogged alongside, filming as we rolled out of the station.

'Oh cool, we're moving.' Jamie peered through the window, unwinding his scarf. 'Only fifteen minutes behind schedule.' He sat down and took off his hat, scrabbling his hair back into place and scrutinising the compartment. 'Big journey ahead... shall I just take this berth that I'm on?'

We were sharing a four-person compartment with no other passengers, owing to the rule that women couldn't travel with strangers. I stared at the two empty berths: a dreadful waste given how desperate people were to book tickets. Wracked with guilt that Deniz's contact might have booted out other passengers to accommodate us, I stepped into the corridor to scout out who we had as neighbours for the next twenty-four hours. The two young women were sitting cross-legged on one berth engaged in what looked like a séance and the rest of the carriage was taken up by a large group of Turkish friends in their mid-fifties. They reminded me of my parents and their university pals who got together annually from all over the world, each wearing fleeces and walking shoes borrowed from their kids.

The *Doğu Express* was once a migration train carrying seasonal agricultural workers and members of the military who trained at Erzurum. Transporting telegrams, letters and parcels from one side of the country to the other, the train had been a Turkish lifeline and probably still was – just not to the people in our sleeper car. This was for the fun-time folk: the ones who boarded to party or ponder life while staring into the scenery expanding outside. But I had strong suspicions that the seating carriage would be full of commuting Turks and regular travellers, who I was eager to seek out.

In less than twenty minutes, the twilight turned the snow blue, streetlights lighting up the foreground like a winter wonderland as we entered a long bend around a series of apartment buildings where cars were buried in snow up to the windows. Between the blocks, Ankara's eastern exit gate shone brightly, a clear indication that we were leaving the capital behind. Unable to see much more, I made my way to the dining car, only to find Harun, our restaurant-car manager from the *Ankara Express*. He waved, confirming that he'd be on board all the way to Kars, and ushered me towards a table where a young man in a turquoise hoodie was working on a Samsung tablet, making notes. I'd recently learned that *turquoise* came from the French word for Turkish, to describe the colour of the mineral that was transported west, and the more I looked, the more I saw it in clothes, tiles and jewellery. Worried that I was invading his space, I asked the young man if he minded me sitting down. He shook his head, waving me into the seat. The car was filling up, trance playing from a nearby phone, so the young man took a break to chat to me.

Ender was a twenty-year-old medical student from Ankara, studying in Erzurum. He was a regular commuter who never flew, not least because he couldn't afford the cost, but also because he enjoyed the laidback set-up of this train journey, and received a substantial student discount which reduced his ticket to around £4. A steal, considering the length of the ride.

'I like train trips because I am meeting a lot of people on the train and it's comfortable for me,' he said.

'Are you travelling in the sleeper car?' I asked.

'It's very hard now, there are a lot of tourists. In the beds it is hard to get tickets. I have a chair. It is normal, you can take it easily. I'm used to it.'

'You don't mind being upright in a chair for twenty-four hours?' I asked, ashamed to reveal my inner princess.

'No, I don't mind,' he said, twisting a large silver ring on his thumb. 'There is a culture here. I make a lot of activity, watching movies and studying, that is the advantage rather than being on the plane. I think I have a lot of time. We listen to music, we make friends, and also Türkiye is a natural beauty.'

'How many times have you done this journey?'

'Maybe seven I think?'

I looked out of the window at the drifts, amused that a student's commute was now one of the most sought-out journeys in the world, by both domestic and international travellers. 'Which do you prefer? The journey in winter or summer?'

'I think it is better in winter because in the summer is too hot in Türkiye. It's very popular now, a lot of Turkish people want to travel to Kars from Ankara.'

I glanced at the tablet lying on the table and saw the writing was in English. 'Are you studying medicine in English?'

Ender pushed his tongue between his teeth. 'I am learning histology in kidneys and learning it all in English. In Türkiye there is two types of medicine: one in English and one in Turkish. The teacher teaches in both. Not everyone learns English at school. It is hard but we must.'

Not for the first time I felt deeply in awe of young people around the world who moved between languages with little choice in the matter. I couldn't imagine British medical students being made to learn anatomy in multiple languages without throwing a fit in protest.

Jamie joined us – 'It's the same guy from Istanbul,' he said, pointing at Harun – and then introduced himself to Ender.

'He's a kind man, I know him well,' said Ender. 'He will order you cağ kebab.'

Unprompted, this was excellent information about the infamous kebab delivery. Rumour had it that it was possible to order hot kebabs to be delivered to the train at Erzurum the following afternoon by making a phone call an hour or so in advance from either Kandilli or İliç. During our chat, I'd been gearing up to ask Ender if he wouldn't mind making the call, but he had beaten me to it.

While Ender and Jamie got acquainted, I decided to check out the seating carriage, what sounded like Led Zeppelin growing louder as I neared the door. Inside was a scene of mayhem with boxes and bags in the aisles, twenty-somethings wearing neck pillows and the metallic sound of multiple films, dramas and soaps playing at once between the music. I clocked one young woman asleep – assuming it was a woman – with her head wrapped entirely in a cotton scarf to block out the light and noise, her plait dangling out from the bottom. Condensation dripped down the windows from the density of humans and someone had drawn 'FUCK YOU' into the fog. Not one seat was empty, so I eased the door shut and went back to our table.

Ender got up to talk to Harun and I nudged Jamie. 'Shall we ask him if he wants one of our berths? Better than sitting up all night?'

'Yeah, sure, I mean we've already paid for them.'

Ender came back with a cup of tea.

'We have a spare bed in our compartment if you would like to sleep there?' I asked, realising as I heard my own voice how creepy the proposition sounded.

'You can join us, then it's more comfortable,' said Jamie, making it worse.

'We don't mind, we have two empty ones, so it's fine,' I added, trying not to come across like a modern-day Fred and Rose West. 'You don't have to if you don't want to.'

'Thank you,' said Ender, looking shy. 'I would like that. You are kind.'

'Have you met many British people before? Jamie asked suddenly.

'God, I hope not, he won't want to share with us.'

'A few,' said Ender, 'but not on this train.'

Aware that other people wanted to eat while we hogged the table, we returned to our compartment, giving Ender the number.

'Are you on Instagram?' he asked.

We swapped details and Ender slid out from the table. 'I will get my bags,' he said brightly, disappearing into the carriage of carnage. By the time I reached our compartment he had already found me and sent a message that read:

'Hi Monisha, I'm Ender. You wanted to order çağ kebab. Harun brother in the canteen will order çağ kebab. You can tell him if you want. 90 Turkish lira. The menu includes dessert, salad and çağ kebab. Let me know.'

After dark, there was never much to do on board sleeper trains but read, chat and watch films. Not that there was anything wrong with this. With so many distractions throughout the day, it was a welcome relief to be presented with a block of time in which to indulge. Long train journeys were perfect for reading books cover to cover, binging box sets and thinking through as many of life's conundrums as possible. There was no pile of laundry staring at me from the corner, no lunch boxes to pack, no uniform to iron, no Lego to pick up, no dog to walk and no library books that needed returning. It was just me and the precious gift of time that I'd always taken for granted until it was no longer mine to enjoy.

I shook my blanket across my legs, the drum of the train settling in for the night – and my mind went straight to the earthquake. I'd stayed offline, unable to cope with the images coming out. While Jamie unhooked the ladder and laid it across the berths as a makeshift table to prop up his iPad, I reluctantly opened Twitter: it was impossible to stop picking the scab. There, on my feed, was a photograph of a man wearing an orange jacket. He was sitting halfway up a pyramid of rubble, his right hand in his pocket; his left hand reaching on top of a mattress with a pink sheet hanging down. Zooming in, I saw that his rough hand was holding a smaller, pale hand – the hand of his daughter who was dead in her bed. My nostrils stung and hot tears poured down my face, the saltiness filling my mouth as I wept as quietly as possible.

'You all right?' Jamie asked, as I wiped my face.

'Ugh, god,' I sighed. 'I can't bear how horrific this is.'

Jamie shrugged. 'There's always something bad going on somewhere. What you fancy watching?'

I let Jamie put on something called *Beast of Bangalore* that he'd downloaded from Netflix, and tuned out, wondering how he was so unbothered. Perhaps numbness to suffering was an act of self-preservation, a way to stay sane amid life's hardships. Maybe the real question was why I was so deeply affected? Was it the proximity? That we were so close to the disaster? Or was it that I was now feeling intense pain as a parent? Having babies thrust you into a state of hypervigilance, knowing that your only job is to keep them safe and alive. The guilt if anything happened to them felt like a knife to the heart. A stab of failure. I'd once turned towards a cupboard as Ariel, then eight months, had leaned so far out of her high chair that she'd fallen headfirst onto the tiled floor with a sickening thud, my blood turning cold when I saw her lying face down. It had taken me days to forgive myself – other parents blushing with similar stories of knocking babies out of beds at night, or slipping down stairs with them while carrying too many things. Perhaps the horror at the sight of this father holding his dead child's hand came from knowing that until that moment he had probably spent his entire life doing everything to protect her, until a greater force had left him powerless.

Ender arrived at the door wearing his backpack and we both stood up, flipping on the light. Before we could welcome him in, the train manager came up behind and began to question him.

'It's fine,' said Jamie. 'We told him he could have one of our berths.'

'He is saying it is not possible,' said Ender. The train chose that moment to jolt, sending both of them into the wall.

'No, really it's fine,' Jamie continued, going to the door, 'we've paid for both the berths, they're ours already.'

The inspector shook his head.

'He is saying, it is not possible because we cannot travel together,' Ender said, gesturing towards me.

'Oh, I don't mind at all,' I said, holding up my hands. 'I told him he could stay here because they're both spare and we've paid for them already. They're going to waste.'

Ender looked crestfallen. 'I cannot, he says.'

Jamie exhaled with annoyance, his shoulders dropping as he tried again with the inspector.

'But that's really stupid because we've paid for them, it's kind of up to us if he wants to sleep here.'

The inspector took a step to the side to allow Ender to pass, and I realised that he would probably get it in the neck, so I dropped the matter, apologising repeatedly to Ender as he eyed what could have been his bed for the night. Maybe it was for safety reasons, in case of a fire or other emergency that would place him in the wrong seat, or simply that women couldn't travel with men, but I let it go. If I didn't feel dreadful enough already, I now wanted to crawl into my berth and pull the blanket over my head as Ender gave a small wave and walked back down to his carriage, trying his best to look cheerful. In a trough of misery, I left Jamie alone to watch *Beast of Bangalore*, which I'd assumed would be about a man-eating tiger but was in fact about a woman-murdering serial killer. Enough death for one day. I decided to turn in, reaching across to pull down the blind – and watching it slither up in response, broken. Spent, I shuffled down my berth, the blue light of Jamie's iPad flickering in our compartment as I lay still, willing the morning to come.

Harun put down coffee and freshly toasted kumru. It was a little after 7.30 a.m. and the dining car was buzzing with elderly couples, the younger passengers presumably asleep. A monochrome scene lay around us, the river Kızılırmak flowing between banks of snow. Black and topped with sheets of ice like panes of broken glass, it looked both beautiful and deadly. We were nearing the city of Sivas and the river was looping alongside, following the turns of the train. The longest river lying entirely within Türkiye, the Kızılırmak originated in the Kızıl mountains in north-central Anatolia and was now at its fullest, replenished with melted snow and ice that boosted its journey to the Black Sea. I had barely slept, the night filled with jolts, slamming doors and ear-splitting brakes that had sent me thudding into the wall. But as we tunnelled through the mountains, snow rising up to twice the height of the carriage, I felt calmed now by nature at work. Sunlight began to prise open the clouds, warming the hills whose summits were lined with single-storey houses in pastel greens and yellows, each one smaller than the next. With single windows and roofs slicked up into mohawks, they looked like birdhouses propped up on plinths.

Ender had told me that the majority of passengers would disembark at Sivas, and as we drew into the city of sickly yellow buildings, half the carriage vanished. Unsure how long we would stop, I stayed on board, but moved to the window and looked down to where a man in a tracksuit was squatting in the snow. He buried his arms in the powder then lifted handfuls to his face, squeezing his eyes shut as he rubbed snow all over his head and stubbly neck. Gasping, he opened his eyes and saw me watching, signalling for me to join him in what was a guaranteed way to wake up. He laughed then made his way up the steps and back on board. I felt frustrated that, with my lack of Turkish, I couldn't chat to the remaining group who were eating chorba and scrolling news bulletins about the earthquake on their phones. No one used headphones, yet no one seemed to be bothered by the noise of other people's tablets and phones.

Behind me a man sat wearing a beard as long and thin as a stick, which was tied into segments with tiny black bands. His wife was knitting and across from her a table of Indonesian students sat chatting away with excitement as another group of Indonesians entered the carriage and joined them. Diverse in age, ethnicity and faith, there was a mixed group on board. I was relieved that we hadn't taken the tourist version of the train. Here, the passengers weren't interested in showcasing their journey to strangers. Few took photos, choosing instead to stare through the windows, unaware of the serenity that came to rest upon their faces.

A rush of cold came through the vents as a blizzard encircled the train, the woods nothing more than a blur through the haze. Snow thudded in chunks against the glass, threads of water unspooling up and across the windows. And then it stopped. A series of short tunnels brought us to the foot of a mountain range in Kangal, not a jagged edge in sight. Their snowy curves were smooth, as if silk flowed down their sides. As we curled around them, the sun chose that moment to beam upon their heads as though calling down from the heavens. Over millions of years, the earth had pushed and pulled apart, sending up the peaks that stood here now with silent grace; the same movement that had, only yesterday, caused such a magnitude of death and devastation.

For hours I sat at the window, my thoughts lost in the wilderness. I could all too easily forget that only 14 per cent of the earth's surface was modified. It was only by train that we saw the vastness, uncut, unfenced, unmined and untouched by the destruction of human hands. Since I'd woken, not a soul had appeared between the woods, drifts and valleys. A flock of birds took flight from a single bare tree, so small they looked like a swarm of bees, but no humans. Still no humans. On board was a different story. There were too many humans, crammed into booths, flapping open papers in each other's faces and kneeling up to watch as the train snaked around canyons, the Çaltı Suyu stream turning green in the midday light.

Jamie emerged after a long lie-in, wearing sunglasses and reading his phone. I was now eavesdropping on a German conversation between the large group of friends who'd taken up the remainder of our sleeper carriage. I got chatting to Irfan, a Turk in his mid-fifties who switched straight into English and explained that they were a group of forty from Wuppertal near Cologne, Turkish by origin.

'These guys,' said Irfan, pointing to two tables, 'they're all from Kars.' He is actually from the Black Sea and he took this train fifty years ago.'

I asked his friend what he remembered of the *Doğu Express* then, and he mumbled a reply then looked out of the window with a grin. Irfan started laughing.

'He said he took the train from Kars to Istanbul and then all the way to Germany. At the time he said the seats were wooden. It cannot be comfortable. You had to bring all your food yourself. He was a child, he was nine, but he remembers it being really fun.'

The train drew into the town of Divriği and I saw that we were at least five hours behind schedule. As a result of the earthquake, the trains were running at slower speeds. Jamie looked around the empty carriage.

'Interesting isn't it, how everything ebbs and flows with passengers,' he said. 'It's cleared out at this stop.'

I sniffed. 'That's because they've all gone out for fags.'

Struck by the fact that I hadn't tasted fresh air for the best part of twenty hours, I jumped down the steps to where most of the dining car's residents were now strolling about the tracks, laces undone – no time to waste with nicotine in demand. Here the ground was dry, the station scattered with bent-backed ladies waddling along with plastic bags, a handful of men doing very little, and all the young people from the night before jumping around in hoodies, trying to stay warm. The train signalled its departure, and the smokers inhaled with desperation. Anything to see them through for the next couple of hours.

Back on board, there was fresh kinship between the smokers, united in their struggle. As they embraced new friendships we carried on north-east, surrounded by the wonderful aroma of chicken skewers grilling in the galley. This was the part I loved the most: deep into the journey, sitting in comfy sweatpants, sipping tea, ordering one hot snack after another, and making idle chat with anyone who sat down. I looked out to where the Çaltı Suyu stream now joined the Karasu river – meaning 'black'– that was worming its way round boulders, so slim at turns I could have crossed it with a running jump. Over bridges we clattered, the river stretching and growing by the turn until we approached the Bağıştaş dam, where its boundaries fell away and its body appeared to me like an ocean, green with neon marbling.

We soon slowed into the station at İliç. Here, three passengers disembarked: a little girl and her parents, who heaved their cases onto the platform as she waited patiently on the tracks, carrier bags in hand. Departing as quickly as we stopped, the train picked up pace and I sensed something happening in the vestibule. One of the Indonesian students was standing behind a man I'd seen earlier in the seating carriage. They had the main door thrown open. My eyes watered from the wind, and I stepped back in case the train chose that moment to lurch and fling us out. The sound of the wheels thundered in my ears and a wave of nausea rose up as I watched the first young man swing out to take a photo. Wearing little more than trousers and a T-shirt flapping in the wind, his springy hair matting itself into dreadlocks, he leaned out for a second time, yelling into the thump of cold air that caught in his throat: a hit of adrenaline right into his veins, one I was willing to forego in the face of death. Jumping back in, he took off his glasses and then gaped at me, his mouth curling up at the edges. Madness or hedonism, I couldn't decide.

Through his gasps, I deciphered that Metin was a 32-year-old from Antalya, and en route to Kars.

'Do you travel by train much?' I asked, as he wiped his head on his sleeve.

'No. But after this I will do it,' he said. 'I like it.'

'So why are you on this train, then?'

'A friend showed me on Instagram. He called me and he said "You should do this train" and so after that I decided.'

Madness, definitely.

'But what are you planning on doing when you get to Kars?' I asked.

He gave his hair a shake, sending droplets into my face. 'I will go to this Armenian place called Ani, yeah? I will wear my shorts, yeah, and then I will get in the snow, yeah? I will go to Çıldır lake, yeah? Then I will go centre of Kars, I will go some museums and take some photos and then eat pizza. What about you?'

In fairness to Metin, this sounded perfectly reasonable and not that far off my own plans once I arrived in Kars – without falling in snow in my shorts. 'I'm also going to Ani and then I'm heading home.'

'Do you like whisky?' he asked.

'Whisky?'

'Yeah.'

'Not really, no.'

'We've got some here, I give to all my friends.'

'Ah, that's kind. But I like gin,' I replied, eyeing the Indonesian student as we swept into a tunnel, the wind screaming past the still-open door.

'Gin and tonic? With some lemon?'

'Cucumber.'

'I don't know what that is. Oh, cucumber!'

To my relief, a guard walked through the vestibule, slamming the door shut, and I felt my cortisol levels return to normal.

'Do you travel alone a lot?' I asked.

'I do, I can do what I want, I like it.'

'Are you not cold?

'No. Because of the whisky. I also have something here, but I will not show you,' he said, pointing inside his trousers.

'Ah, thermals.'

'Yes. But my god, last night, when it was two or three o'clock, I came out here and I had to take this off, it was very hot.'

Passengers were coming through every few minutes and we were getting in their way, so I invited Metin to join us in the dining car. A theatre actor, he had tried a number of different jobs including minivan driver and bellboy at a luxury hotel in Istanbul. Interested in the pros and cons of the latter job, I probed Metin as the train ran alongside a rockface so closely I could see fissures gleaming with wetness.

'When we had Arab guests, they had a lot of luggage but that is the job. But the worst bit is when people are talking with you, they don't even look at you. They think you are smaller than them,' Metin said, wiping his glasses.

'And what's the best bit?' I asked.

He took a deep breath and looked out of the window with a frown. 'Meeting people. You meet friendly people from other cultures who talk with you in their room. I travelled so much without leaving the city. Also, as a bellboy you should know everything about them, if they say they remember me I must say I remember you. But the best thing is getting tips: I got £200 from a Scottish guy once and $100 from a lady from Kuwait.' He smiled. 'When you work you should work with rich people! But really, you must work hard and remember the laundry and the tickets and the things they like. I am not religious, but they say when you give to people, god will give you back.'

'Where do you live now?'

'I live with my mum in Antalya, maybe it's strange?'

'No, I don't think so at all. In Asian countries it's normal to live with your parents – even after you get married. And actually, more young people still live with their parents in the UK now as no one can afford to buy a house.'

'Oh, okay? Yes, my father died and for her it is company. Look he is polishing shoes,' said Metin, as an elderly man came up the aisle, carrying numerous pairs. 'He is smart.' Metin looked around, 'I like it, on trains. You know Atatürk decided to push railways in Türkiye, to make more lines as it was not so okay. And I'm happy. I was reading the books of the Turkish writer, Sunay Akın: he said trains made our life different; he said when you go somewhere flying you can't see anything you know: you get your ticket and you go to aeroplane and one hour later you are there. But when you go with train you see mountains you see people, you see everything.'

'Is that why you're here now?' I asked.

Metin thought for a while. 'I watched this train on a video and I think I should go there. Also, I'm from Antalya where it's hot, and the snow makes me come here. I like to go where I don't know what it's going to be. I feel curious. I'm very lucky to see this.'

I gestured towards his carriage. 'And how was it last night?'

Metin put his head down on the table in mock horror. 'I get some drinks or I don't sleep. Without cognac I don't sleep. Some people snore, some people are talking, it was also smelly. They take off the shoes, it smells of cheese. It is like that.'

More than six hours behind schedule, we were now around thirty miles from Erzurum and it was time to put in our kebab order with Harun. As we lined up, the train took a turn beneath a cliff face. On its edge stood the Turkish flag, now lowered to half-mast to mark the beginning of the seven-day period of national mourning for all those who had died in the earthquakes.

On the approach to Erzurum we broke down. For more than two hours we sat on the tracks, sighing and looking out of the window in the hope of spotting engineers. By this point we were at the mercy of fate and I had decided that arriving at any time within the next week would be a blessing. Most passengers had convened in the dining car where a rumour was circulating that the engine needed replacing. A chill crept in; I put my hand onto the heater to find that had stopped working too. Splinter groups formed and I saw a number of students running to the doorway. Not wanting to miss out, I got up in time to see Metin return from throwing himself into a pile of snow. 'Yes, I will do that again in Kars,' he announced, shaking his head like a dog and sitting down opposite us. To avoid any language issues, he offered to ring our hotel to let them know we'd be arriving at 4 a.m. at the soonest, just as a replacement engine arrived to take us on to Erzurum.

It was around 11 p.m. when we eventually drew into the city. Ender disembarked, giving me a thumbs-up sign as a mass kebab delivery arrived on board, and Harun handed out more than sixty bags of kebabs and yoghurt drinks to ravenous and restless passengers.

As the wrappers were balled up, the cartons drained and teeth picked clean, I could feel the beginning of the end. Sleet was striking the windows like shards of glass; the dining car had emptied, and the train had only one task – to take us to Kars. Thanking Harun, who had somehow managed to maintain good humour throughout the ordeal, we swayed up the carriage to our compartment which was warm and welcoming, like a nest. Sitting up in our berths, we watched towns flash past, more snow flying at the window. In two or three hours we'd be in Kars, but for now there was nothing for us to do but wait and sleep.

A few days of travel had felt like a lifetime. My body ached, but for what I wasn't sure. Soon we'd be in the north-eastern corner of the country, not far from the Armenian border. It was where I'd wanted to be, where I'd set out to reach, and yet something didn't feel right. The death toll from the earthquake was now an estimated 15,000 and I realised that the ache was for my family. I needed to be with them. I looked around to make sure we'd not left anything behind, running my hand along the two upper berths to find my hat and a stray base layer, unplugging my phone from the charger. From under the blanket I listened to the sound of Jamie's even breathing. In the darkness I scrolled through my messages, and found one that Vedat had sent a few hours earlier:

'*Travelling is living. Hug your husband and children tighter. I hope you always have good memories. Turkish railways have a saying*: "Hayat ulaşınca ve sevdiklerinize kavuşunca başlar." *Life begins after you've arrived and reached your loved ones.*'

7

THE NORRLAND NIGHT TRAIN

One of the great contradictions of train travel is how it forces a traveller to slow down and see the world around them – while at the same time, seeing it at speed. From my seat by a frost-rimmed window, I stared at the gold reflections in a canal, my eyes flicking from side to side as I tried to take in the red glow of a Westfield shopping centre, followed by a Miele showroom, ribbons of motorway, back-to-back hotels, and the edge of a lake. A blur of forest and brown snow. It was just after 6 p.m. and the sky was a midnight blue, the moon waxing in a corner. The lights inside the carriage made it hard to scour what remained of Stockholm before the city vanished from view. This was a belter of a train, one that wasted no time in fleeing the Swedish capital as passengers were still stowing luggage.

A few weeks had passed since my journey from London to Türkiye and I was now on board the night train from Stockholm to the Norwegian town of Narvik. The aftermath of the earthquake had deeply unsettled me. It had taken days for me to sleep soundly, and I experienced recurring dreams about being buried, seeing images of children covered in dust. I realised that the only way to shake it off was to get back on track and keep moving through my bucket list.

A daily service, the Norrland Night Train takes around nineteen hours to draw passengers up the backbone of Sweden then over the border, ending its journey 137 miles inside the Arctic Circle. From there I planned to take the Arctic Train back along the Ofoten line down to the Swedish village of Abisko, a hotspot for the Northern Lights, which I was desperate to see. The ideal time of year for sightings was between October and March and it was now the first week of March, so I booked my tickets, hoping I wasn't too late.

Founded in 1902, the port of Narvik was key in exporting iron ore extracted from the Swedish city of Kiruna and sending it around the world. The warm waters of the Gulf Stream meant that the bay was free from ice year-round, making it the natural choice for the shipping industry. In November of the same year the railway was completed to transport freight, officially opening in 1903.

The last section of this journey ran along the Ofoten line, and I was keen to retrace the segment on the Arctic Train to learn a bit about the route's history. I knew it had been significant in the Second World War and wanted to find out more. Leaning against the window, I watched as the train sank into a bend, a shelf of snow hovering overhead.

'A lot to take in,' said an unusually tall man sitting next to me. Although for Scandinavia, he was probably considered average.

'Yes, but it's a bit too dark now, so I can't see much,' I replied, closing my diary and noticing that the top of my head just reached his shoulder.

'My name's Karl,' he said, extending a large hand.

'Monisha,' I said.

Karl was wearing a Prada wool jumper as thin as skin, the kind that costs four figures until you snag it on a nail and render it worthless. A venture capitalist from Stockholm, he was heading to Jukkasjärvi for a stag-do at the Icehotel; the other stags had taken the ninety-minute flight to nearby Kiruna. To their amusement, Karl would arrive the following morning at eleven and their WhatsApp group was blowing up with brutal gifs mocking his choice of transport.

'I have little vacation and I like to travel slowly,' he said, slipping his phone into his pocket. Karl told me he was worried about a reshuffle at work and that he needed space to 'stare into the snow and think'.

Since lockdown, the concept of 'slow travel' had come back into play. The idea was to move around in a more thoughtful way, stopping to connect with people and places. Slow travel encouraged taking the time to explore our own backyards, with the concept of 'staycations' causing online spats between those who believed it meant holidaying in your own country and those who felt that holidaying in your own country was still by definition a holiday and not a staycation. On the surface the trend of slow travel seemed perfectly harmless, but under scrutiny it had more than a whiff of middle-class whimsy, the kind that appealed to Shoreditch trustafarians and readers of Goop. Rail travel embodies the essence of slow travel – but lord it can be expensive. Growing up in Yorkshire in the 1980s, I had friends whose summer holidays took place year after year in the same caravan at the seaside town of Bridlington, an hour's drive from home. Wasn't that exploring your own backyard? None of them had ever flown and flopped on a beach in Jamaica or Bali, instead making do with buckets and spades and magenta sticks of rock. Others had no choice but to fly: immigrants with far-flung families; travellers with disabilities requiring access or assistance. Not everyone had the time, funds or circumstances to kayak down the river of life and indulge.

A stream of passengers was heading towards the dining car and I looked around for my companion. He was sitting a couple of rows behind, hands clasped, legs crossed at the ankle, his eyes closed. Deep in meditation, Marc jutted his neck ever so slightly forwards as though listening for something and I wondered what thoughts were running through his mind. I'd met Marc while volunteering on the *Lifeline Express*, a hospital train in India. Half Welsh, half Indian – with a strong Scottish accent – Marc was a photographer from Hackney who'd been documenting the surgery that took place on board the train and we'd immediately been drawn to one another, my words and his pictures coming together to form a symbiotic relationship that had carried us through many subsequent rail journeys. At the time Marc had just finished a ten-day silent meditation course in Nashik, inspiring me to do the same, and the practice of Vipassana was now a firm part of his life. He had joined me and Jem for my second book, accompanying us through China, Tibet, Kazakhstan and Russia, lifting our spirits when we needed it most. Marc was always up for adventure and had jumped at the chance to come with me to Narvik.

Hungry and worried that we wouldn't find a table, I squeezed around Karl, who was furiously typing a comeback to his pals. Not wanting to disturb Marc, I hovered in front of him, aware that others were now watching me lurking like a creep. I tapped him on the knee and his eyes flew open. In keeping with his cleaned-up lifestyle, Marc was now teetotal and vegetarian, while I was still a mess, yearning for pale ale and a plate of reindeer stew.

'Fancy dinner?' I asked.

'Let's stash our stuff first,' he said, hanging his headphones around his neck.

I nodded, looking round as Karl raised a palm in farewell, then went back to his phone.

We were sharing a couchette compartment with two couples: one from Norway and the other from the US. An hour earlier the train had pulled out of Stockholm Central Station, and we'd arrived to find the corridor jammed with three rucksacks rotating in the tiny space. A pair of socked feet were balanced across the middle berths, their flustered owner trying in earnest to shake out sheets while the train offered unhelpful jolts and I suppressed the urge to laugh. After my ride with Elena and Maria on the *Dacia* I had realised that there is an unwritten rule of etiquette when it comes to sharing compartments on trains and that involves taking it in turns to make up berths. No one wants to endure the inelegance of stretching across strangers and bumping your bum on their heads while they unpack pillows. There was little to gain from six people trying to negotiate a space that had less room than a downstairs toilet, so we'd let the other four settle in first.

'Who's that guy?' Marc asked as we wandered up the aisle. 'Was he trying it on?'

'God, no, not at all, he's off to a stag-do at the Icehotel and his mates are taking the piss 'cos they all flew and they're already there.'

'Where's the Icehotel?'

'Jukkasjärvi, not far from Kiruna. I actually looked it up to see if I could get us a room but it was fully booked. It's nuts, it's like something out of *Frozen*.'

'Ah, that's a shame. I'd have been well up for that. What the rooms like?'

'They've got normal rooms, but I was looking up the art suites. I think it's about −8°C inside? The whole place is carved in blue ice, including the bed.'

'That's mental,' said Marc, scanning the numbers of each compartment. 'Where'd you sleep?'

'From the pics, they've got reindeer hides on a block of ice. I think they give you thermal sleeping bags. But that one was about £1,000 a night.'

'A grand? To sleep on a fucking ice cube?'

We arrived at the door to find the compartment far less frantic. The Norwegian couple were sharing grapes and giggling in the top berths as we shoved away bags, peeled off jumpers and went back to the dining car where the air was thick with the heat of bodies, the sound of cans cracking open and the smell of sweaty gravlax. I sat down at the last empty table, across the aisle from a young teacher heading to Kiruna for a weekend of cross-country skiing with her colleagues. She was holding a plastic cup that contained what appeared to be a tube of squeezy cheese with a boiled egg at the bottom and proceeded to mash it all onto crispbread.

'It's called Kalles,' Cecilia said, showing me the blue tube. 'It's made from cod's roe. It's very Swedish, like, kids eat it in their lunchbox. Would you like to try some?'

I declined, lifting the lid on my bowl of reindeer stew to find it bubbling over mash, the sweet tang of lingonberry jam cutting through the richness of smoked meat.

The car was abuzz with the jollity of Swedes in snow boots and knits, most of whom seemed to know each other. I couldn't work out if they were incredibly friendly people or drunk – or a healthy mix of the two. The menu had a variety of items that were vegan; gluten-free; lacto-free, and lacto-ovo-vegetarian – which I had to look up – and around me passengers were chatting over steaming boxes of bean chilli and mushroom risotto.

'Are you going to visit Abisko?' asked Cecilia's colleague, Henrik. With his dimples, round blue eyes, and thinning hair, he resembled a middle-aged toddler, only his breath smelled of Riesling, the dregs of which were trembling on their table.

'We are,' I said, 'a quick stopover in Narvik then Abisko on the way back down.'

'Then you must go to the Aurora...' he paused to burp into his fist, 'Sky Station. At night you can take the chairlift up the mountain and, how do you say, chase the auroras at the top.' He made a running-around gesture with two fingers. 'It is quite something.'

'I know, I've seen them before,' Marc added, smiling over a blueberry soda.

'What? Why are you here then?' I asked, crestfallen. In my head we were aurora virgins, looking for the magic together.

'Why would I not be here?' Marc said. 'This is amazing. I've not been on a train since the pandemic. In fact, I don't think I've been on a long train journey since our last big ones together. It's nice, man, such a great atmosphere. And I bet the scenery tomorrow will be epic up by the fjords.'

'Have you seen them before?' I asked, sulkily.

'No, never, I've been to Oslo though.'

'It's not easy to spot the lights,' Henrik said, his scalp now pink from drink. 'You can plan for days but it depends on the clouds and your guides sometimes have to drive far out. Did you see the aurora in Sweden?'

'No, in Reykjavík,' Marc said. 'I was literally sat about in the middle of town, drunk at a bar one night and they just appeared overhead.'

Our American companions arrived and sat down. Colin and Eimear were recently engaged and celebrating with a trip to

Kiruna to chase auroras on snowmobiles. Over a grumble about US politics, race, and extortionate rents in Brooklyn, Colin unwrapped a slab of gravlax and nudged it across.

'I don't want to alarm you or anything, but the other couple are… kinda sketchy,' he mouthed over the din.

'In what way?' I asked, peeling off an orange strip and flicking off the dill.

'So, they've locked the compartment with all of our stuff inside and they're not opening the door.'

Eimear shrugged and sipped her beer.

'Should we go and look?' Marc asked. 'I don't want my camera bag getting nicked.'

'No, don't worry, I'm done, I'll go,' I said, wiping up the last of my stew.

'Come on, I'll show you,' said Colin. I followed, watching him pick his way up the carriage before swinging into someone's lap as the train wailed and braked into a bend. We passed through the standard carriage where passengers would sleep upright all night, their shoes off, hoods pulled up, and phones showing dramas and films. It reeked of socks and stale ale. I asked Colin if he'd checked the numbers on the carriage.

'Yeah, it's definitely ours,' he said.

'Are you sure?' I pressed, as we stepped into the next carriage. 'We're in 15 and I think this is 14.'

'Totally sure.'

There was less confidence in his voice this time. We came to a compartment where the curtains were drawn and the doors locked.

'It won't open,' he said, tugging at the door, his stance wide as the train bumped along.

'Keep walking,' I said, as Colin turned a similar shade to the lingonberry jam.

In the next carriage we found our compartment. The door was open, the curtain tied back and the couple were still in their berths, the woman playing *Minecraft* on an iPad.

'Hey,' said Colin, weakly. Neither one looked down but some-one grunted. He rummaged around his berth for nothing in particular while I bit my lip. Back outside, we staggered around the aisle in hysterics. Colin held up his hands.

'I swear, in the States this is totally what people do. They will take over a compartment, even if your stuff is in there, and they will not let you in.'

'Wait, what? That sounds horrendous.'

'I'm serious,' he said, as we rejoined Marc and Eimear in the dining car. 'You could spend the whole night out there sitting upright without your bags and no bedding and they wouldn't care.'

We started giggling again and in that moment a friendship was formed. The kind you only find on a train.

Using my elbow, I wiped the condensation off the window and took in the lights from a passing town. Most houses were dark, but on those where the curtains remained open I could still see people standing at sinks or watching TV, oblivious to the train rushing by. Daft Punk was now playing in the car, voices louder, inhibitions long abandoned. I wanted to stay up, to bask in the warmth of this rolling community, but it was late. While the others chatted, I slipped out and made my way back to find the Norwegians already asleep. In the darkness I lay awake trying to get comfortable on a pillow as flat as a postage stamp. It was cold, too, wintry air blowing up from the vent. Eventually I bundled up my fleece and shoved it under my head as the others appeared, the stench of beer on their clothes. They rummaged through washbags before they too climbed into bed and fell silent. Certain that everyone was asleep, I lifted the corner of the blind for one last look. Until this journey, Scandinavia had never crossed my radar. There was no particular reason; I'd simply not felt the pull towards this part of the world. Perhaps it was the cold, the aggressively outdoorsy vibe and perceived lack of exciting food that had put me off: I'd once had a conversa-tion with a Norwegian who described a delicacy that was 'cod soaked in bleach' which had done little to tempt a traveller like me who hankered after flavour, my spice cupboards running out of space. So far though, I liked what I saw.

The moon was at eye level, girdled by black cloud. We were on the ascent, curving up the north-east of Sweden, where swords of ice hung from wooden houses. In the beam of the train's headlamps, woods lit up like stills from a Tim Burton film; branches reaching out with grabby, bony hands. I drew my knees up and watched as villages clustered then dispersed. Ski slopes twinkled in the distance and tunnels swallowed us whole. I thought of Karl, yearning for slowness while busy on his phone. Slow travel was a mindset. This was my meditation, my journey to peace when the world flashed by, quietening the noise of my thoughts. One town passed, then another, a forest followed by the next, until nothing remained in my head but the thump of the train.

───────

Marc was in the corridor watching a blizzard. Colin and Eimear were packing, and the Norwegian couple had gone, leaving grape stalks in their sheets. It was 8 a.m. and the sky was a mucky grey. Colin and Eimear got off at Kiruna along with most of the train and we sat in the dining car with coffee and kanelbullar – squidgy cinnamon buns that we'd picked up in Stockholm.

On the ascent, the sun began to burn through the cloud. Skeletal and buried to the waist in drifts, the trees were now white and laced together, branches touching, like a child's paper chain. On the approach to Abisko, the train circled above Lake Torneträsk, one of the largest in Sweden, its surface thick with snow. White peaks rose in the distance, wrapped in shawls of cloud. The train wound even higher, so close to the forest edge that I could make out sweet little loops where birds had hopped around the snow. It was crisp, hard and sparkling, like compacted broken glass.

As the train swept over the Swedish border, we passed the resort of Riksgränsen. Here began the Ofoten line, Europe's northernmost railway and the most spectacular stretch of the journey. I looked down and took a breath as the fjords emerged. Like black silk ribbons they wound around the base of cliffs, a terrifying majesty in their movement. Peach-gold sunbeams now fell upon the scene, softening everything in sight, just a handful of passengers privy to this glorious finale. Curling in and out of twenty tunnels, the train began to slow, hissing as it drew into Narvik.

'Ready for adventure?' Marc said.

I nodded, as we stepped onto the platform.

———

Narvik was a curious town, one that felt like a gateway to anywhere better. It wasn't particularly pretty and smelled of fish, gulls circling the pier as we skidded along black ice to find somewhere to eat. A starter point for travellers wanting to hike, cycle, ski or visit the Lofoten Islands – none of which we were doing – Narvik itself could be seen in a day with a long lunch and a couple of hours at the war museum. After walking a few hills and stocking up on thermal socks, I needed an early night. It came as no great shock, but I was starting to experience mild bouts of MDDS, otherwise known as mal de débarquement syndrome. Literally translating to 'disembarkation sickness', the symptoms left me feeling like I was still moving after exceptionally long journeys. They never lasted for more than half an hour or so, but I was conscious, while reaching for cutlery or reading a paper, that my brain thought I was rocking. The sensation often gave me nausea and this bout was yet to subside. We had booked into the Breidablikk guesthouse which overlooked the fjord. It was a snug pad with underfloor heating and furs on the bed. Marc was meditating on his bed, and I slid under my covers, wondering what animal was sprawled at my feet. As I scrolled the hotel's website looking for info about breakfast, I came across the blurb about their categories of accommodation:

'The family on a trip? We have room!

Love weekend? We have mattresses with resilience!'

My initial confusion turned to admiration for the searing honesty. Nothing was lost in translation; they were simply mindful of their guests and catering accordingly. I shuffled down the resilient mattress, willing the rocking to go by the morning, while wondering how many love weekends had taken place where I lay.

———

After a breakfast of cold cuts and coffee we walked down to the station. The Arctic Train departed at 9.55 a.m. and would take an hour and a half to go back to Abisko. Introduced in 2020 this was a tourist service with speakers, Wi-Fi and an audio guide, yet we were the only two on the platform. Five minutes before departure I started to panic and phoned the cancellation number.

'Hallo!' said a cheerful voice.

'Hi there, I've got tickets for the Arctic Train and I'm on the platform at Narvik, but there's no one here.'

'Ah,' said the voice. 'You did not get the email?'

Marc flashed me an exaggerated frown of query.

'No, I didn't get the email,' I said, kicking at a lump of ice that was a lot harder than I was expecting.

'Oh, there you are, on the platform, *hallloooooo!*'

I looked up to see a man in a mustard polo-neck jumper waving at me from a first-floor window. 'We have had an avalanche on the tracks and we are not running the train this morning. Wait, let me come down,' he said.

I exhaled hard, my breath coming out of my nose like a bull.

'I can't believe this,' I said. 'There's been an avalanche up ahead so the train's not running.'

'An avalanche? Shit man,' Marc said, dropping his bags into the snow.

I crouched down, trying to stay measured. I'd travelled 630 miles only to find the train cancelled.

'To be fair, we're not really missing anything though, are we? We've already done the route, we've seen it, just not with any of the info.'

We had already travelled along the line on the way up, but I had wanted to experience the slower train while listening to the audio guide at each stage along the route. The manager picked his way across the snow, a thin line of mucus shining above his lip as he clasped his hands before me in apology.

'I am so sorry you did not receive the email. It was an oversight and you will be fully refunded. Such a shame, it was only recent, if you'd taken the earlier train you would have been in Abisko by now,' he laughed.

I was only too familiar with the power of Mother Earth. Whether it was earthquakes, storms or avalanches, we were always at the mercy of the natural world, and I knew better than to fight it.

The manager paused and looked up the tracks to where a short version of the train was now slowing into the platform. When the doors opened a group of Gen Zs got out, carrying skis. In their red hats, yellow gloves and green leg warmers they looked like extras from a Wham! video, which wasn't such a bad assessment when I learned they were with a crew, filming promos for the train, travelling back and forth up a small section of the track. After a quick chat with the director, the manager crunched back across the snow towards us. He was feeling bad and keen to make amends.

'Would you like to go on board with them? They are only doing a little of the route, up to where the tracks are closed, but they say you are welcome to go.'

'That's amazing,' said Marc. 'Absolutely, thank you.'

While the pretty young things frolicked around at one end of the train, we set off, snaking through one tunnel after another. With no one else on board, we spread out across the seats. After a couple of minutes the manager came by. Kjetil ('like kettle but with a "j"') explained how to download the app that would allow me to use my location to listen to the train's history, then showed us to the crew's catering carriage.

'This is so much better,' said Marc, sipping a hot chocolate and looking out to where the Ofotfjord was moving diagonally in the wind. During the Second World War, the battles of Narvik took place in the immediate vicinity of the railway. Owing to the town's strategic position, it was one of the first cities the Germans attacked. On 9 April 1940 a fleet of ten destroyers sailed into the fjord with many of the Norwegian forces retreating on foot along the 27-mile Ofoten line during a conflict that raged until early June. At the bottom of these magnificent waters lay a registered twenty-two shipwrecks.

I wandered up to the driver's cabin and peered in. A young man with a shaved head was reclining in the seat, as though playing a video game. Gesturing for me to join him, the driver pushed a pair of black Oakley sunglasses up onto his head and accelerated, one hand resting casually on his thigh. Never had anyone made driving a train look so sexy. Jan was originally from Oslo before relocating to Narvik. One summer he'd worked on a salmon farm – 'like being a janitor for the sea' – and discovered that his cousin earned four times as much being a train driver. He quit his job, began training, and started his career on the airport express train.

Marc had followed me into the cabin and was now photographing the scene from over Jan's shoulder, while he pointed out what looked like ski poles lined up at the track's edge.

'Do you see this, these red poles? It's for an avalanche warning,' he said. 'You know this was built in 1903 and they put them there and they've lasted this whole time and never been serviced.'

'Apart from an avalanche, what's the scariest thing about driving a train?' I asked.

Jan rubbed his hand across his head. 'In Oslo, it was kids on the track. They used to sit on the edge with their legs, you know, dangling. I would have to brake so hard when I saw them.' He smiled out of the side of his mouth and described how they'd not just get hit, but dragged under the train. So each time he would have to stop the train to go back and check. 'Only later, when the adrenaline has gone down, you start to shake. Kids are really stupid. Especially drunk kids.'

'When did you move up to Narvik?' I asked.

'In 2020, right before lockdown, so no one was on this train as they soon couldn't travel.'

'Why Narvik?'

'I was fed up. The murder rate in Oslo... and the fact that the police were more bothered about people driving five kilometres per hour above the speed limit than the fact that kids were getting mugged on the way to school.'

The global murder rate was 5.8 per 100,000 people. Oslo's figure was less than 0.5, making it one of the safest cities in the world. Jan's fear was an insight into the standard of living in Norway and the high expectations of a tiny population.

The train passed into another tunnel, the stones covered in aquamarine waterfalls, frozen mid-flow. Looking down, I could see long animal tracks which Jan explained belonged to moose and reindeer that strayed towards the railway line. He turned a handle and the train slowed into a bend.

'On the Swedish side of the line you can even see bear and wolves. When the reindeers go in front of the trains and the trains hit them, in Norway we take them and collect them. In Sweden they don't do that. They just leave them by the sides of the railroads so if they hit like a big pack of reindeers and there's a lot of dead reindeers there, the bears and wolves come out for the buffet.'

A voice spoke over the radio and Jan paused to chat. He turned to look at us both and started laughing. 'Guys I'm really sorry, but... there's been another avalanche, so we're going to reverse up and head back to Narvik.'

Within half an hour we'd shunted around and the train was sailing back the way we'd come. Jan put his sunglasses back on and leaned back.

'Well, if you're ever back here, you can always knock on the door. Even if I'm not driving, we're quite happy to have people in here.'

More than content with our ride, I closed my diary as Marc gathered his bags and gave me a huge smile. 'That was awesome. I'm sure you can Google the rest of the missing info.'

'Do you climb?' asked Maja, handing me what looked like an upturned skateboard with metal teeth instead of wheels.

'Just stairs,' I said, tapping at the edges.

'Then we will go slow,' she smiled. 'Come.'

It was 6 p.m. and we were setting off on a guided snow-shoe hike through the woods behind our lodge. Lying around 150 miles inside the Arctic Circle, the village of Abisko had no light pollution and was deemed one of the prime locations in the world for solar activity. As Henrik the school teacher had suggested, we'd spent the previous night on the chairlift up to the Abisko Sky Station on Mount Nuolja, a twenty-minute ride looking down on treetops; a soundless journey through the darkness. At the top we'd stumbled around like drunks before giving up on seeing the aurora, sitting quietly in the midnight cold. I've always associated low temperatures with sadness and depression, but it was so extreme up there, needling into my ears and catching in my throat, that it jump-started my body to life.

Now, dressed like the Michelin Man, I twisted around in my snowsuit, trying to keep up with Maja. I was annoyed by the haze of cloud that had moved in from Lake Torneträsk. Other than a single ski trip to Saint-Moritz, my experience of winter activities extended to little more than snowball fights and sled-ding. Marc, of course, was a seasoned skier and snowboarder and had already disappeared into the shadows as I lagged behind, trying not to kick my own ankles.

'Instead of lifting your feet, try to walk like a duck,' Maja called, smiling at me like a nursery assistant. It was −5°C and ice flecked the air, stinging my cheeks as I tried to mirror her move-ment, legs wide as though I'd soiled myself. Tugging off a glove the size of an oven mitt, I switched off my headlamp to pause and take in the surroundings. Powder squeaked underfoot. Then silence. Any noise was absorbed by the snow, which was blue and sparkling in the moonlight. All I could hear was my breathing, a bewitching aura around the trunks of skinny birch.

Hikers had already hardened the ice as we shuffled in single file behind Maja towards Stornabben, a small hill whose outline

I could barely make out through the darkness. Shining my torch around I found tracks in the snow: elongated rabbit paws; cloven hoofs of moose; and the frozen filigree made by tiny birds. Twigs snapped as Maja ducked between stray branches. I'd given up on sightings by the time she stopped.

'Ha! Aurora!' With three claps like gunshots she veered left, plunging knee-deep into the snow and I stumbled behind her. Above us was a twist of aurora. I stopped, holding my breath and gazing into its body. Like steam, it lengthened and performed a pirouette, radiating a Ghostbusters green. As though alive, the neon hovered in the sky, and I felt time stop. Out of darkness had come this natural beauty. It needed complete darkness to be seen, to grow, to thrive. For the first time in my life, I stood surrounded by darkness, fearless and filled with appreciation for its power.

Buoyed by the sighting, we pushed on. Historically this northern region of Sweden was inhabited by the Indigenous Sámi people, reindeer-herders for whom the land is sacred. Before the ascent, Maja paused, her breath in clouds. She pointed to a mountain range, fearsome but peaceful.

'Do you see this semi-circle in the valley?'

I nodded at the curve which appeared as though the Sámi gods had taken a bite out of the range.

'This is Lapporten. Between those mountains are two small lakes and the story is that there is a portal to the other dimension. Halfway to Lapporten is Paddus, the holy mountain of the Sámi people. In the past, Sámi men travelled there once a year to pray to the gods. When you hike there, you feel like you are not alone, that someone is watching. Sometimes you can see shadows running around, but it's not a feeling of fear, just the presence of something.'

As we crunched through the snow, blades scraping, I thought about what Maja had said. I needed to find a way to push away my fear of darkness and accept the existence of shadows for what they were.

In a few minutes we reached the summit where visitors had signed their names on a notepad tucked inside a little bag.

Sweating, yet cold and exhilarated, I unzipped my outfit, panting as I looked down across the town to where a fire burned on the frozen lake. Maja pulled out a flask of hot lingonberry juice and we drank in silence, the liquid furry against my throat. Marc joined me as another aurora beamed into view, its green body like a light shower of rain. For a few moments it shifted like a screensaver, until the clouds moved in, knitting together a blanket so thick that the moon was obscured from view.

'Shall we?' asked Maja.

I nodded.

'Go slow, we have time,' she said, as we threw one last look at the sky before descending into the magic of Abisko's woods.

The following evening we were back on board the sleeper, returning to Stockholm. In a private twin compartment this time, we played cards, occasionally glancing up to watch the midnight blue sky from the window, the moon bobbing alongside. Other passengers had reported occasionally seeing the Northern Lights from the moving train, but the forests were obscuring the view and, besides, I'd had my fill. The dining car was less rowdy this time, the ski groups recovering in their compartments. There was a distinct Sunday-evening feeling on board, returning to work, playtime over. Indulging in a final bowl of reindeer stew, I opened up my diary and scrolled through my list, coming to rest on a pair of trains. I drew a circle around them both. It was time to explore my own backyard.

8

THE CALEDONIAN SLEEPER

On a Friday evening in London, there is nowhere more terrifying than the concourse at Euston Station. It's a place to observe the human nervous system on the brink of mass malfunction. No one arrives at Euston in a good mood: the expectation of delays, cancellations or an overcrowded service causes heart rates to soar on the approach past Pret and Itsu. Inside there's a crowd – always a crowd – staring at overhead screens, like a trading floor from the 1980s. No one blinks in case the platform number appears and a millisecond is lost in bolting to the trains. You can hear the ticking of brains mapping out the quickest route. You can smell the pheromones of fear, white knuckles tightening on bag handles. Then the number appears and the frontline sweeps forwards like a scene from *Squid Game*, commuters sprinting to get on board.

In 1837, Euston was the first mainline station to open in London. A few days before the inauguration of the line that would eventually run up to Birmingham, the company directors took a party of friends on a test-run to Boxmoor and back. On the return leg, the train had reached the back of Euston Square when the brakes failed and the carriages hit the barrier wall, causing a number of passengers to suffer broken noses and sprained wrists, while others lost their front teeth. It was a prophecy for a station that modern-day commuters described as a 'petri-dish of chaos' and 'one of the nine circles of hell'.

Throughout my twenties I'd endured the Euston Dash when travelling up to see my parents in Birmingham, but had given up once I'd had children. One summer evening in June was all it took.

Laden like a pack horse, I'd tried to steer a buggy with one hand as my kindly fellow Londoners shoved past, clipping the front wheels and knocking bags off my shoulder. The electronic seat reservations were down and I'd been left standing for the duration of the journey, newborn in arms. Overnight I abandoned Virgin Trains for the Chiltern line and from then on travelled in relative peace, enjoying the mild-mannered charms of Marylebone.

Now, I barely recognised Euston. It was 10.30 p.m. on a Tuesday night in April and all I could hear was the squeak of my trainers as I crossed the concourse. A fraught woman with bad teeth shook a Burger King cup at me, charging off and muttering obscenities before I had the chance to fish in my pockets for change. Propped up against the wall, a couple swigged from cans of M&S gin and tonic and then I smelled it: the station piss, rivalled only by the stench of NCP stairwells. Oh yes, this was the same old station.

To my relief I saw the teal-green train already parked at platform 1. The blinds were pulled down and the windows tinted. So at odds with the grime of its surroundings, the *Caledonian Sleeper* appeared to have shimmered into being, like a Tardis. One of only three night trains in the UK, the Lowlander service departed Euston a little before midnight and would arrive into Edinburgh Waverley at 7.30 the following morning. The Highlander service split at Edinburgh, continuing to Aberdeen, Fort William and Inverness. My mum was waiting for me in Edinburgh. She was turning seventy and I had organised a surprise birthday treat for her, asking only that she meet me at the station.

For the sake of research, I'd coughed up an eye-watering £345 for a double room. At almost ten times the cost of the hour-long flight, I was intrigued as to who bought up these spots. Most sleeper-train travellers argued that they were saving on the cost of a hotel room, but a flight plus a night at the Travelodge was still cheaper than this fare. For all my grumblings, I was permitted to board an hour before the plebs in seated coaches, where tickets were £50 a pop. In addition, I had access to the station's guest lounge where I could find snacks and shower. No money in the world could persuade me to strip naked at Euston Station and I was eager to hop on board for a long-awaited hot dinner. The conductor scanned my ticket and handed me a keycard. At once I felt the flush of excitement of stepping into a world that would soon be sweeping up the country through the darkness, a moving mini-city of sorts, its residents curled up in bed or nursing a nightcap.

I'd ridden the *Caledonian Sleeper* before, but only in its former guise. In 2019, at seven months pregnant and unable to fly, I'd travelled from Glasgow to London, a month before operator Serco had rolled out an upgraded fleet of carriages a year behind schedule. At the time of booking I'd hoped for fancy compartments with plush bunks and Wi-Fi, but instead I'd arrived to find the same shabby old train, its walls carpeted with what looked like blue duffel, the light just bright enough to make out my disappointed face in the mirror. I'd lain awake for most of the night, grateful for the added centre of gravity holding me in place as the train braked and jerked, tipping me out pale and exhausted into London's thin first light, prepped for premature labour. Soon after, Serco's inaugural train made its journey from London up to Glasgow, with the *Guardian* newspaper reporting that the historic journey had 'struggled to stay on the rails thanks to booking mix-ups, water leaks into cabins and a delayed driver'. Despite being short of berths – a basic requirement of a sleeper service – passengers had rather generously put the chaos down to 'teething problems'.

When taking British trains it's best to expect the worst – and then some. But tonight I was willing with all my fibre to be impressed by this recent incarnation of the Anglo-Scottish sleeper service, which dated back to 1873. I climbed aboard and turned down the corridor, my carry-on wedging between its walls. Barely the width from my elbow to my fingertips, the bag was stuck fast, and I couldn't believe how tiny the space was. A large suitcase would never fit. Nor, for that matter, would a large passenger. With a two-handed tug, I managed to pull out my bag and locate my room, which was mostly taken up by the bed. A leather band ran around the walls, which were carpeted again, but with natty, Sherlock Holmes-style tweed this time. Eye masks lay on the covers, along with an organza bag of Arran toiletries. The ensuite had a loo that folded down to create a shower area and I knew at a glance that I'd not be putting bare soles on a floor that had all the allure of the footbath at my local leisure centre. That aside, it was a comfy bolthole, and I was looking forward to slipping under the duvet later. Cranking up the heat, I stepped back out, but my door refused to lock. I looked across to see my neighbour, an American, also wrenching the handle before he waved his card in the air.

'I can't lock this fucking thing,' he said. 'But I don't have anything to steal,' he added, as he squeezed past me towards the dining car. I shrugged and followed.

The smell of pies and gravy filled the carriage, which resembled a private members' club. To some degree it was, owing to the restrictions that granted only sleeper-car passengers access. These night owls were poring over notes for morning meetings, their suit jackets hung by their sides. Most were on Glen Garioch whisky, its hue like honey under the light of little lamps. Fittingly, a number of passengers were travelling up for a green-energy conference and I realised that the rooms were mostly taken up by corporate use. I slid onto a banquette and ordered a plate of haggis, neeps and tatties, which arrived piping hot from the microwave in a pool of whisky sauce. According to a Scottish writer friend, haggis is primarily eaten around Burns Night, 'or in bon-bons at hipster weddings and tourist restaurants in Edinburgh'. He explained that while it was theoretically a year-round dish, 'only psychopaths eat it in summer'. It was spring, but I tucked into the spicy mound of offal and mash all the same. Over dinner I began to eavesdrop on a young couple who were sitting across the aisle, peering at a plate of toasted sandwiches.

'I'm not sure that's what I ordered,' said the woman with a Lancashire accent, lifting one with a fork.

'That's annoying,' said her partner.

'It's fine, it'll do, I'll have it,' said the woman, who I noticed was around six months pregnant and probably hungry round the clock.

A staff member walked by and asked if everything was all right.

'Yeah, fine, thank you, it's lovely,' said the woman smiling, then shrugging at her partner when he'd gone.

Like the passengers happy to write off their awful journey as a result of teething problems, the couple filled me with puzzlement. Why did the British have such reticence about complaining out loud? Stoicism is so hardwired in our psyche that consumers would rather eat the wrong food and go without a bed than voice outrage and risk offence. There is a lot that is mad about the British, but the feverish determination to keep calm and carry on is something I can't abide. After living in France, watching my colleagues spend more time on strike than at work, I understood how they'd rid themselves of their royals, enjoyed a 35-hour week and indulged in long wine-filled lunches while we poked at sandwiches we hadn't ordered and sat at low-paid jobs in a sulk.

I saw we were on the move and my mood leaped as the station's lights beamed across the carriage. The couple pointed out of the window and I saw the man squeeze his partner's hand, absent-mindedly turning round her engagement ring. She wrinkled her nose at him as I reached for my book. I always had one on the go, mostly to hide behind while listening to other people's private chats. I'd picked up that the woman was named Molly, and as she leaned in, I looked sideways to read her lips.

'Do you reckon people shag on these trains?' she whispered.

'I have,' said the passenger sitting across the aisle from her. Small and slim, with a devilish goatee and sharp ears, he looked like Puck from *A Midsummer Night's Dream*. His black trousers ballooned beneath the table and he was sipping a whisky so large it looked like a beaker of apple juice. Squinting, he licked and rolled a joint, pinching the end with liquid silver nails. The couple laughed nervously as he kept talking in a voice as deep as he was slight.

'It was in 1999. I was in this punk band. We'd been playing the Edinburgh Fringe and it was my first big international gig, seeing as I was from, you know, England.'

Molly glanced at me and giggled. 'God, I didn't think anyone was listening,' she said, fanning herself.

'Everyone's listening,' said Puck. 'All the time. You're on a train, that's what people do. Anyway, I was booked back to London on the minibus but everyone else was so fucked up on drugs and shit and raising the hell out of the flat we'd rented. One of them cut his wrist after putting it through a wall and then numbed it with coke instead of going to the hospital. Anyway, you get the picture.' He tapped his roll-up and put it in his jacket pocket. 'So, me and my girlfriend – my first big love – we wanted to get away from these pricks and so we got the sleeper train. The very last empty coach, seats with old wooden armrests. There's this line in Madonna's "Justify My Love" that talks about making love in a train cross-country and so we just got down to it and kicked up so much dust and shit.'

Molly's mouth was open. Puck was enjoying the effect and carried on.

'This train clearly hadn't been vacuumed since it was built and all this dust was flying up and making us cough and shit. So yeah. That's it. I've fucked on a few trains. I've fucked on buses. I've fucked everywhere to be fair. Give me an orange and drill a hole in it and, well, happy times. Anyway, I'm turning in. Sleep well, kids.'

With that he downed the contents of his glass, giving his neck a crack, and floated out of the carriage like a mischievous sprite. Molly looked as though she needed resuscitation.

Molly and Simon were from Burnley. In the absence of smelling salts, she recovered over a pot of peppermint tea and told me this was their first sleeper train. In return I prepped them for future interactions, explaining that this was average on the grand scale of train confessionals. Over years of gadding about the world's railways I'd heard people admit to crimes, sob over estranged family members and recount abusive relationships. One memorable tale emerged on a train to Beijing, from a woman detailing how her boyfriend had thrown her out of their house in Adelaide for having scabies and sent her to prune vineyards on a farm with illegal Chinese migrants. Fortunately, they had taken pity on her and helped her get rid of the rash. Scoring zero on the scale of one to insanity, Molly and Simon had no such revelations. It was her first pregnancy and she was too nervous to leave the UK or fly, deciding that a sleeper train was the safest option. I'd seen numerous pregnant women on sleeper trains and only when expecting a baby myself had I twigged how reassuring it was to know that help wasn't far away if needed. Wheels on the ground felt infinitely safer than being airborne. Simon had booked a surprise hotel in Edinburgh and Molly gushed like a young child talking about the fancy bunk beds in their sleeper compartment. I didn't dare mention the double bed I had to myself, wondering for a moment if I should offer to swap with them, then deciding I was mad and far too generous.

'There's another one of these trains going down to Cornwall,' said Simon, 'I'd quite like to do that one, but that's dead expensive.'

The *Night Riviera* ran between London Paddington and Penzance. Its name suggested wistful window-gazing, a train that would deliver a romantic ride – not one that would halt at Reading at 1 a.m., picking up pissed-up passengers who fell against my door and rattled at the handles all night. My five-year-old daughter Ariel and I had taken the train the previous autumn. We'd collected complimentary packets of shortbread and chocolate from the kindly staff in the bar car and she'd climbed up to her silky-soft berth, arranging the treats around her pillows then falling asleep before departure. I'd spent half the night worried she'd roll out onto the floor and the other half blocking out the voices jabbering through the walls. Before dawn I'd drawn up the blind to find mists hovering above the moors, the clouds like puffs of pink steam. A knock at the door brought 'Delboy' with hot bacon rolls and we'd watched waves crashing up to the track before arriving into the damp and grey of Cornwall's morning mizzle.

For all the fun of the sleeper, the Paddington–Penzance route was best taken during the day. The nineteen-minute stretch that lay between Exeter St Davids and Newton Abbot was one of the railway community's most guarded secrets. Soon after accelerating past terraced houses and car parks, the vast green marshland narrowed to a point, the trees fell away, and the train curved around the mile-wide River Exe. To the untrained eye, it appeared like an ocean dotted with kayaks and sailboats. The wetlands teemed with birdlife, teals, bar-tailed godwits and avocets picking their way through the sands like ladies holding up skirts. Around

Dawlish Warren the Exe joined the English Channel and a sliver of foam rimmed the water's edge, waves rippling across the shore. Winding down the coast, the train swung inland once more then ran up against the River Teign before pulling into Newton Abbot. It was a tragedy to miss it all at night.

As we passed Watford I took myself off to bed, handing Simon a spare packet of earplugs and promising them both that babies didn't mean the end of travel, just different travel. My neighbour was now apparently in my room, so thin were the walls that his shuffling and sniffing felt like we were sharing a bed. With earplugs in place, I shoved keys, water bottles and shampoos into my boots and dimmed the light. This did little to mitigate what turned out to be one of the worst nights' sleep of my life. From Berkhamsted the train hummed sweetly to itself and I dozed off until another train went past with a *shoop... shoop... shoop*, sending us thumping to one side. For the next few hours we were pulled into sidings or held up, freight screaming past the window, until I realised I was never going to find peace. My eyes drier than dust, I lay on my back counting each of those £345 in my head before possibly crying myself to sleep. Who knows how I got there, but I woke at 6.30 and scrabbled out of bed and into the corridor. Beams of sunlight wheeled through as the train skimmed the edge of the Cobbinshaw Reservoir. It was a bright morning, the Pentland Hills fresh and green, yellow gorse bursting at the edges of the slopes. I imagined its smell, like coconut, the grass likely filled with dew as we rushed past on the way to Carstairs. At once, all was forgiven: the faulty door; the mucky floor; the jammed bag; the two hours' sleep. In my pyjamas, unbothered by others walking to breakfast, I allowed the serenity of the Scottish countryside to take hold and soothe.

Over the full Highland breakfast – a full-English but with two triangles of potato scones – I watched the Clydesdale countryside flit by, trying to ignore the headache at my temples.

Only one other passenger was dining until a plump woman in a badly fitting suit sat down, hoicking up her tights as she did so. I nodded and wished her good morning.

'Well, it might have been I suppose, but I've not slept, and I've just found out we're going to Edinburgh and I need to be in Glasgow.' She checked both her phones then laid them down on the table.

'Hello, lovely to see you again,' said the train manager, stopping by to pour coffee.

'They've booked me onto the wrong train,' she said with a sarcastic smile.

'Ah, well, it's still lovely to see you,' he replied, winking at me from where I was watching the scene with a mixture of amusement and pity. Glasgow was only an hour from Edinburgh by train, and whichever minion had fluffed her booking would no doubt be scrambling to order her a cab. At that moment another member of staff ran through, followed by two others. My American neighbour was now stuck inside his room, the door jammed. Handing a knife to his colleagues, the manager went back to wiping down the tables as the others disappeared, presumably to stab open the door. I glanced down at my own keycard which said in silver writing: *Your key to a good night's sleep.*

'This new tech,' he said. 'It's not always that reliable.'

'So I've gathered,' I replied, spearing the last chunk of sausage and wiping it around my plate.

'It. Never. Works,' he mouthed, drawing a finger across his neck and rolling his eyes to the sky.

Arthur had worked on the train for almost fourteen years and was far from in thrall to the upgraded fleet. 'The cost is putting people off,' he said as the car emptied. He missed his regulars, the ones who bagged cheap berths at the last minute. It was still popular with politicians, civil servants and TV presenters like Kirsty Wark, but Arthur had witnessed a complete overhaul in his customers. Tourists and corporate travellers had replaced his faithful riders. Six months earlier, the Scottish government had announced that Serco would be stripped of the contract seven years early and that the *Caledonian Sleeper* would come back under public ownership. It remained to be seen how the train would evolve.

To my knowledge only one person had ever slept through the entire night. According to the tabloids, Jim Metcalfe, a charity chief executive based in East Renfrewshire had boarded the train in Glasgow and gone to sleep before it departed to London. At 5 a.m. there was a knock at his door and he woke up to a man with a coffee and roll and sausage who kindly informed him that they were still on the platform at Glasgow after a heatwave had caused the tracks to buckle, leading to the train being cancelled.

We arrived into Edinburgh and Arthur warned me that unless I wanted to end up shunted into the shed as the train decoupled, I'd better disembark. I thanked him, handing him a tenner after learning from a fellow passenger that none of the credit card tips went to the staff and jumped onto the platform, ever dismayed by big corps' capacity to swindle. Behind me the train rolled away and I turned to face Auld Reekie. It was 7.30 a.m. and my mum wouldn't be with me for a couple of hours, which was perfect, as I had lined up a wee rendezvous. Oddly nervous, I crossed the station and parked my bag, scanning the crowd for my friend. While I was travelling around India we'd got chatting on Twitter. A fan of Bombay and its roadside dhabas, she and I had swapped tips on kheema pav and pani puri and kept up a friendship online. Then, during lockdown, when a traumatic incident sent me into a spiral, she'd posted a package of tea and a number of vintage train stamps that she'd found in Gdansk. Our friendship shifted to WhatsApp, and now, after more than a decade, we were about to meet. She was taking one of the Lumo trains to London, which gave us barely half an hour for coffee. However, neither of us knew when we might cross paths again and our corresponding timetables felt like kismet.

I saw her before she saw me. Her hair was a shade darker than I'd expected, her voice deeper, her accent less posh. But the warmth was the same. In the middle of the station we embraced, thirteen years of friendship compressed between us as passengers hurried around us and trains came and went.

9

THE ROYAL SCOTSMAN

A few hours later, a crowd was gathering outside the Pasty Shop, drawn to the strapping bagpiper and the skirl of his pipes. Commuters slowed to peer over the stairs as a maroon train slid gracefully out of the shadows and drew to a standstill. I turned to look at my mum as sunshine poured through the station's glass roof, lighting up the livery of *The Royal Scotsman*, a Belmond train. Putting on a handful of luxury journeys around the world, Belmond had cornered the market when it came to decadent slow travel by rail. Four brass stanchions went up, linked by red rope, and a carpet was laid out.

'Oh wow,' she breathed.

'Ready for the ride?' I asked.

Along with around forty other passengers who had flown in from New York, Paris and Coventry, we boarded the train, our designated home for the next two nights on a journey around the Scottish Highlands. To date, I hadn't included my parents in any of my train shenanigans, deciding perhaps unfairly that they wouldn't take kindly to clambering into dusty berths or going for days without a shower. Not all trains suit all travellers and I assigned my companions accordingly. From what I could tell *The Royal Scotsman* was a joyride, one that would involve spotting wildlife, eating Dundee cake, and dozing under tartan blankets, which suited my mum to a tee.

The train resembled an Edwardian country cottage, a long and narrow one that held the musky scent of heather. It rocked lightly beneath the footsteps of its new residents, who were now crowded into the carpeted corridors, pausing to glance into the galley where chefs with meaty forearms nodded in greeting. We were sharing a twin cabin panelled with polished wood and lit with wonky candle bulbs. I peeked into the bathroom where the fittings gleamed, then squeezed out some Bamford moisturiser, savouring the lemony scent of geranium and the feel of thick, expensive cream polishing up my hands. A glass jar of mint rock sat on the bedside table and I popped a piece into my mouth, running my fingers along the softness of the bed covers. Pulling off my jumper, I threw one last look of approval at our digs before locking up with a satisfyingly heavy key: no faulty tech on this train.

On board there was one member of staff for every two passengers, along with a whisky ambassador named Sylwia, whose job it was to size up passengers and handpick the perfect malt from hundreds of bottles. After a quick period of orientation, the train glided away from the platform, the bagpipes wailing until we were out of earshot.

In the lounge car wooden fans turned slowly in the heat of an unusually warm spring afternoon. I looked around: the car was tastefully furnished and decorated. Sage-green sofas were draped with herringbone throws, light cream curtains belted back to reveal the Lowlands. The muted shades matched the earthy tones of the hills, moors and mountains and, with the exception of a few tweed and tartan cushions, it resisted the urge to scream: *Och aye, you're in Scotland!* Passengers clutched short-stemmed glasses of champagne, and I realised then that they were less likely to fall over than traditional flutes. It was fun noting the details tailored to rail travel, like padded coat hangers that wouldn't rattle at night, cans of water that couldn't smash, and heavy silver vases unlikely to slop or topple.

While the others exchanged names and nationalities, I picked my way through the car, at the end of which was an open-air observation deck. Departing Edinburgh at 2 p.m., we'd veered west, clattering over the River Almond, and in ten minutes we were passing through sunlit fields towards the Forth Bridge.

I could see its distinctive rust-red body approaching and I pushed open the door and stepped onto the deck as we began to make the mile-and-a-half crossing above the Firth of Forth. The first major structure in Britain made of steel, the cantilever bridge was completed in 1890 and was now a designated Unesco World Heritage Site. I looked down onto the estuary, where the village of North Queensferry lay along the shore, boats tipped sideways as though tidied away in a hurry. The wind tugged my clothes in every direction, my eyes watering as the train passed within arm's reach of the railings. And then we were off the bridge and pulling east towards the coast. I turned around to find a couple of other passengers standing behind me, hair swept up, noses running, hands clutching the sides – but each one was wearing the singular smile that came from the rush of leaning out of a moving train.

Afternoon tea was served in the two dining cars, named 'Swift' and 'Raven', and we seated ourselves across from the first couple who looked most likely to chat. I often saw people freeze, pupils dilating with the fear of being made to socialise, but these two looked approachable.

'We are what you call a Thalys couple,' said a sparrow of a woman with cropped blonde hair. In matching white jeans, blue suede shoes and blazers, the pair explained that they lived between Paris and the Hague, each one taking a Thalys train to Rotterdam to meet the other. I couldn't help but feel that the Paris commuter was getting the rough end of the deal, but kept my thoughts to myself.

'When I was young, maybe four, I travelled on the Orient Express with my parents,' said the woman, whose name was Valérie. 'I went to Yugoslavia, I went to Switzerland, but my father said to me: "Your mother is priority, you are second priority," and they would have separate holidays once a year without me. It is important that you do that. Do you do that?' she asked me, turning my hand and looking for my wedding ring. 'Do you have children? Do you travel alone with your husband?'

There was something gratifying in how direct and nosy this woman was. A woman after my own heart. I explained that my children were still young and perhaps not quite ready to be left alone overnight. She sat up, her cream silk blouse revealing a décolletage that had suffered decades of sunbathing.

'But this is your mother, yes?' she said, pointing a thick red nail at my mum, who was amused by the exchange. Valérie's hand trembled slightly. 'That is what grandparents are for!'

Valérie's father had worked for SNCF, France's state-owned railway company. Over sticky Dundee cake and tea, she told me about her time on *Le Train Bleu*, departing from Paris and waking in Saint-Tropez.

Launched in 1886, *Le Train Bleu* was one of the world's first night trains, ferrying the rich and famous between the French capital and the riviera.

'We were not rich or famous. My father worked for them so everything was free, but the breakfast, my god, it was so special. And then you would pass by the ocean and get off and then each person went back into their own world after. It's important to go by trains, that's the only way you learn about the culture.'

Budget flights and TGV trains had killed off France's sleeper services, the last Paris–Nice night train making its final journey in 2017. However, four years later it was brought back on track. After a week in Antibes together, Ariel and I had taken it from Nice to Paris. I'd booked us into a six-person, women-only compartment and she'd stood at the window, enthralled as we rushed past homes with bougainvillea pouring down the walls, the Mediterranean flashing in between. It was her first ever sleeper-train experience and we'd been assigned the top two berths, only to have a man take a bottom one at Toulon. 'It's okay it's my husband,' the woman in the other bottom berth had explained with a shrug. Ariel had looked down, panicked at the sight of the strange man, then burst into tears. I protested to the wife but it was nearing midnight, the other two women

Jamie sprays deodorant on his socks on the *Sofia-Istanbul Express*

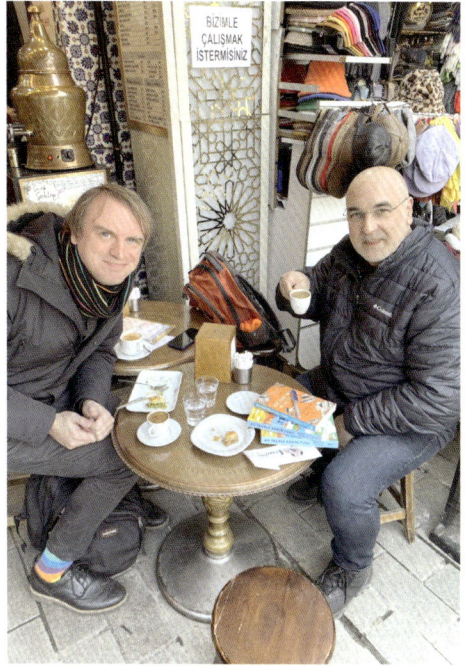

Jamie and Deniz enjoy Turkish coffee and baklava in Kadıköy

Deniz presents Monisha with a railway worker's watch on the Bosphorus ferry to Kadıköy

Vedat gives Monisha a brass whistle on the platform at Ankara station

Marc at breakfast in the dining car on the Nordland line to Bodø

Passengers in the dining car on board the Norrland Night Train from Stockholm to Narvik

The train curls into a tunnel on the Ofoten line

A twin compartment on board *The Royal Scotsman*

Ariel says hello en route to Palermo

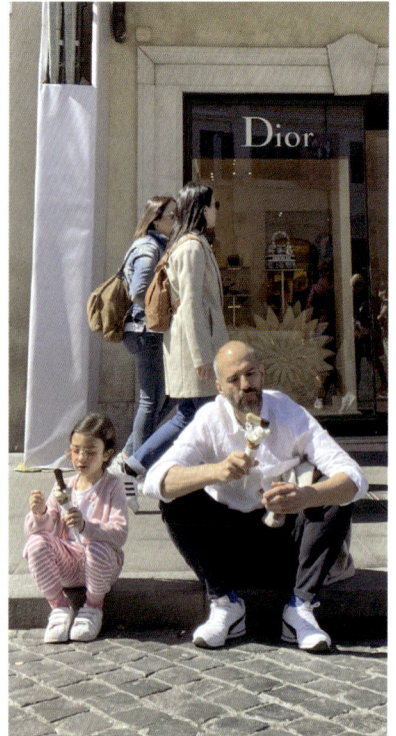

Ramin and Ariel with gelato in Rome

The uncoupled carriages on board the ferry to Sicily

Jem sits in Don Corleone's chair at Castello degli Schiavi

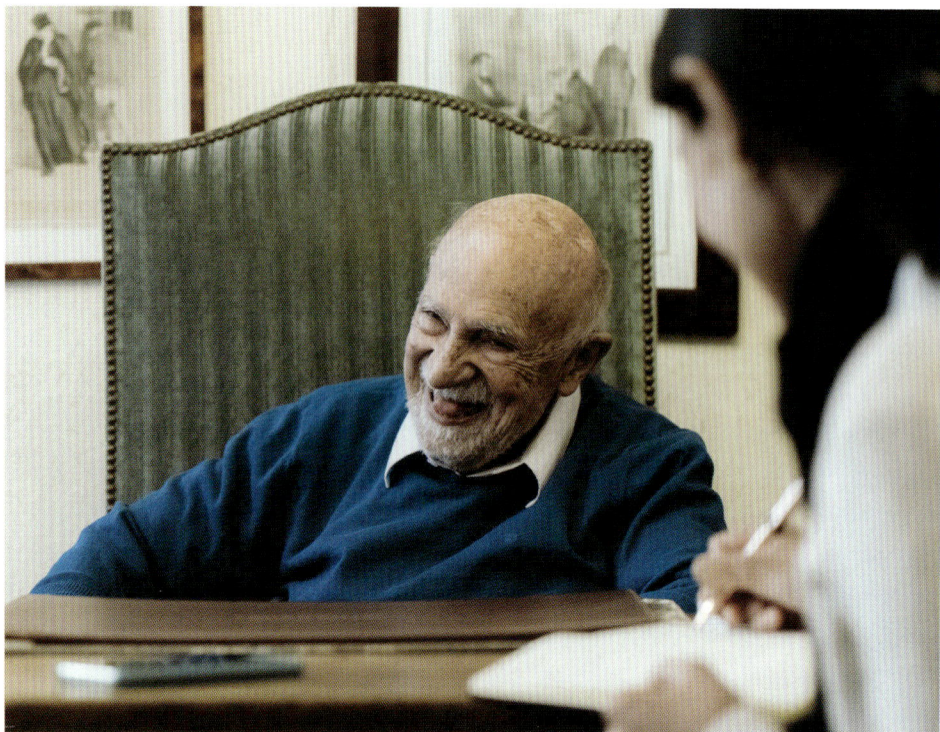

Simon Gronowski laughing along with Monisha at his home in Brussels

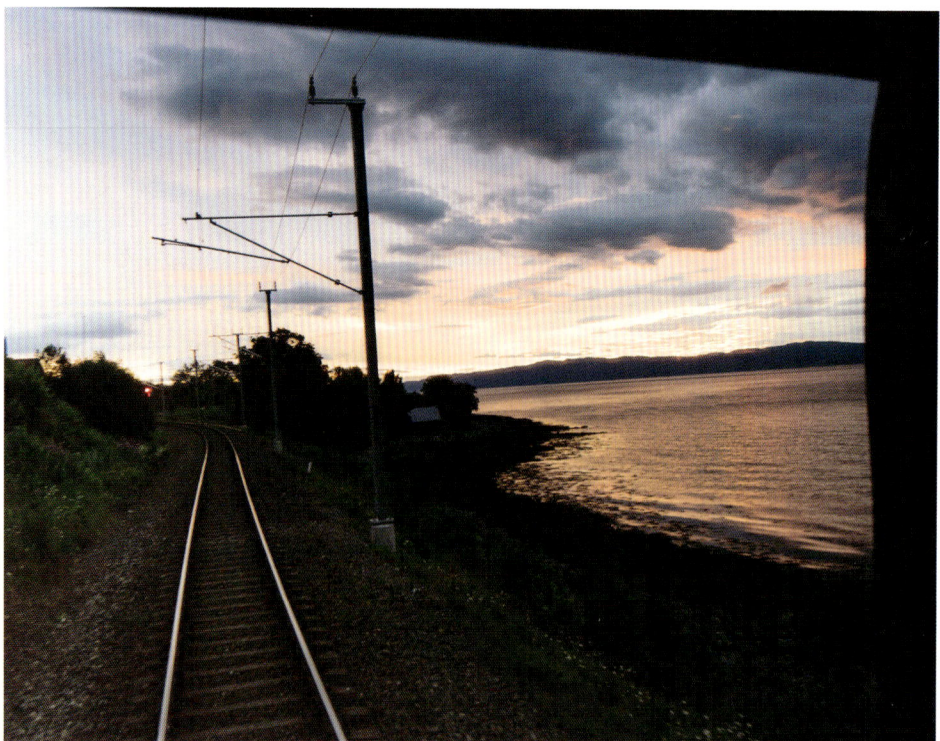

The Trondheim fjord reflecting the golden light

Monisha asleep at 3 a.m. in the Premium Pluss compartment

Denny on board *The Good Night Train*

Mahaveer Singh in Jodhpur's Old Town

Trains parked at Jaisalmer station, the fort looming in the background

Ghanshyam Gawlani: the 'Omelette Man'

Maya looking at a regional train on the platform at Helsinki

Jem and Maya by the *Santa Claus Express* on arrival in Rovaniemi

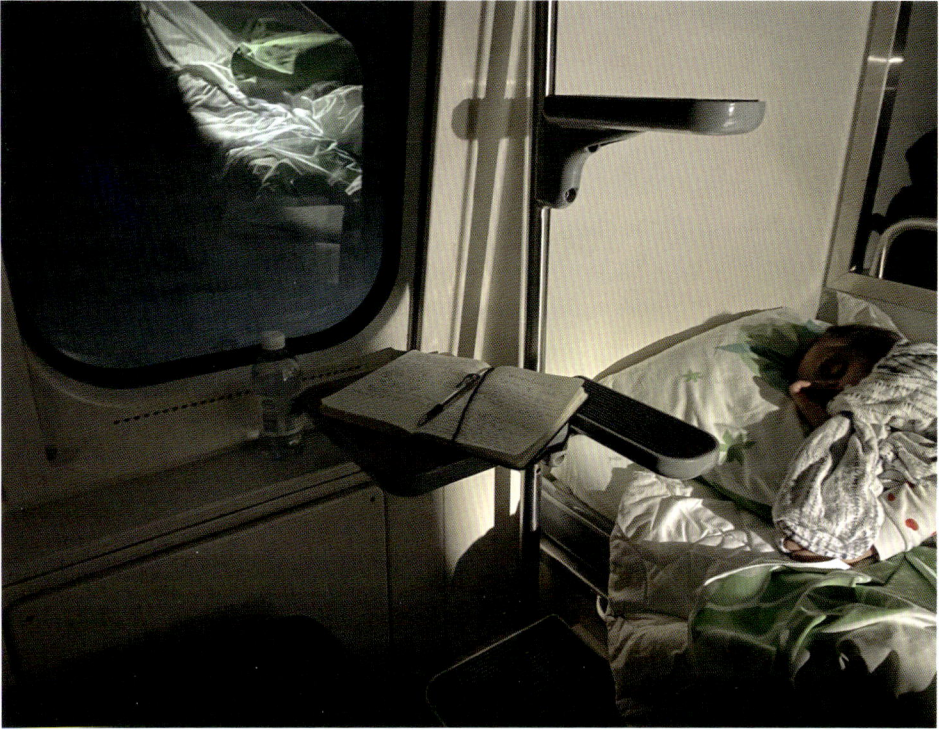

Maya sleeps soundly as the train travels towards Rovaniemi

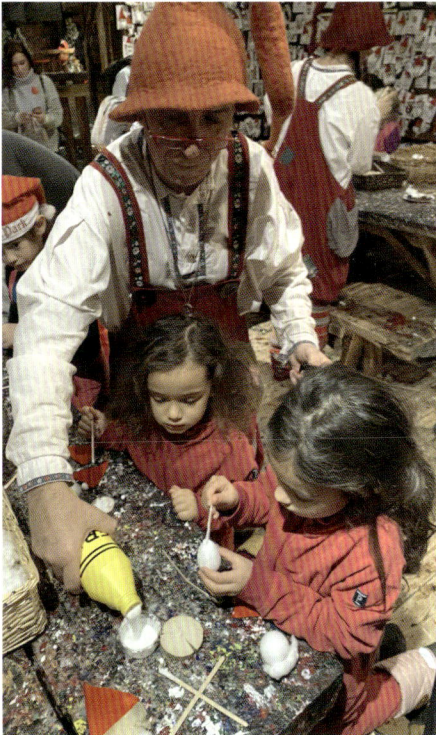

The girls making elves at SantaPark

Ditta disappears inside the Nightjet's mini-cabin

Passengers and a conductor buy hot dogs on the platform in Orlando

Stars twinkle above the *Andean Explorer* parked by Lake Saracocha

Monisha looks out at the Urubamba river rushing by

The *Andean Explorer* approaches La Raya mountain range, while Monisha makes notes in the bar

Monisha waits for Julian at Puno station

Photographs © Marc Sethi: page 3 (top and bottom), page 6 (top and bottom), page 7 (top and bottom right), page 8, page 9 (top).
Photographs © Collin Hughes: page 12 (bottom), page 13, pages 14-15, page 16.

were asleep and I was too exhausted to fight with the obstinate wench, knowing how much the French love a good row. There was only one guard in the vicinity and I had no way of calling him or hunting him down without leaving Ariel alone. To console her, I'd climbed into her berth and slept horribly, tangled in blankets and raging in silence. In the morning I saw that the woman had dropped her silk eye mask. Patterned with toile de Jouy, it was obviously expensive and I'd kicked it into obscurity, taking delight in watching her look for it later. Valérie gagged as I recounted the experience.

'I would have pushed them both out of the train,' she said. I didn't doubt her for a second.

My mum was deep in conversation with Valérie's partner. They were discussing organic gin, so I took the opportunity to slip away to our cabin for some private time. She was a master at chatting to anyone about anything, a skill she'd honed after decades as a GP. It was a trait I'd found annoying as a child – it took ages to leave a party – but as I'd got older I'd grown to admire her patience as my tolerance of others wore thin. I had no qualms about abandoning her as I saw her glass topped up.

The train was barrelling along towards Perth. Golden fields of rape whipped by, followed by forests flooded with lime-green light. I ducked as a series of branches whacked at the open window, twigs and debris cracking against the glass. As much as I liked hobnobbing with my fellow passengers, I needed moments alone and threw myself onto the bed, staring for a moment at the ceiling and enjoying the soundless sway. Our beds were positioned at a right angle, with mine facing the window. I flipped over and lay on my stomach, watching an S-shaped stream winding off towards a herd of cows wearing brown fringes, when the door opened and my mum climbed onto her bed.

'Very sweet man,' she said. 'He works at the UN. They went off for a nap and I got stuck with this boring fellow who wouldn't stop talking about his pelican exercise bike.'

'You mean Peloton?'

'Something.'

'Which fellow? I'll avoid him.'

'The Australian chap with the flowing blond hair, like Fabio. Gosh, how beautiful,' she said, looking across the purple moors, then wrinkling her nose in annoyance. 'I wish I'd brought my sketchbook.'

Soon the two of us were kneeling up by the window: together we watched as rabbits bounded around the grass, pheasants dragged their long red tails and a trio of deer appeared on the banks of the River Tay. A string of houses flashed by, towels and T-shirts drying on a broken football goal, and a workman paused his drilling to turn round and watch us beat past. From Perth we wound above the town of Pitlochry, looking down upon grey roofs and stone houses, the late afternoon sun warming my face. A growl came from behind and I turned to see my mum had fallen asleep, an elbow wedged under her head. For a minute or two I watched her. The once-grey hair was now white and her skin, while flawless, sat looser around her bones. I'd never considered my parents getting older or slower, but I now saw an ageing I'd wilfully ignored. I needed to travel more often with them while we still could.

That evening an informal dinner was served, with guests loosened up and chatting away over perfectly crisp sea trout and barley risotto. Unlike its sibling, the *Venice Simplon-Orient-Express*, life on *The Royal Scotsman* was a relaxed affair. The journey from Venice to Paris was centred on the train and its place in popular culture, powered by a healthy dose of nostalgia. In homage to the golden age of travel, it demanded cocktail dresses and black tie. Here, in my Converse and jeans, I felt no less pampered but much more at home. Passengers engaged freely owing to the long, communal dining tables instead of individual ones. Earlier in the evening we'd transferred from the main network at Aviemore to the private Strathspey railway, where we had now parked at the village of Boat of Garten for overnight stabling. After petit fours, I got down onto the platform to stretch my legs, enjoying the freshness of the cold. The sky was light enough to see the ridges of the Cairngorm

Mountains and I stood still, hands in pockets, listening out for the song of the River Spey. After the rock and thump of the train, the peace was overwhelming. Taking in a lungful of sweet air I got back on board and looked forward to a night of stationary sleep.

The following day was spent off the train, a coach taking us to the Rothiemurchus Estate, in the heart of the Cairngorms National Park. Scotland only has one other national park – Loch Lomond and the Trossachs – and at 1,700 square miles the Cairngorms was the UK's largest. Here, we split up for a mixture of clay-pigeon shooting, archery and fishing before a spot of lunch, followed by a visit to Culloden Battlefield in Inverness. This was the site of Scotland's last violent uprising, resulting in the annihilation of the resistance. The excursion was starting to feel a bit like a school history trip, with the group splintering off into factions: some drifted towards the gift shop for bottles of honey and Highland cow plush toys, while others went back to the coach 'for jackets', never to return. The train had moved on, picking us up at the town of Nairn, and as it journeyed east towards Keith, I sat down for a chinwag with Mark Tamburrini, the train's executive chef. Over the previous twenty-four hours I'd been spying into the galley, watching trays of cling-filmed pains au chocolat being prepped at 10 p.m. I was in awe at how his team managed to perform in the confined space, with the hazard of high speeds to boot.

A Glaswegian, Mark had been on the train since 2009. It had taken him six months to find his feet and to sharpen his spatial awareness, but after so many years on board he was in tune with the turns on the route, knowing what time the engineers would stop and shunt. I asked if disaster had ever befallen, and he rubbed his chin at one vivid memory.

'Sometimes when the train goes a bit quick round a corner, things fall in the fridge. One time I had a stack of lemon posset sitting there. There was a tree on the track and the driver spotted it, but the train braked really hard and it all hit the side.' He made a squelching sound in his cheek.

Travelling around the Highlands meant that fresh produce was easy to source and Mark made it a point to match the menu to the regions through which we passed, picking up scallops in Kyle of Lochalsh, kippers in Loch Fyne and beef in Aberdeen. Although he was always prepped for whims and fancies, his fridge stocked to the hilt. His own cabin was filled with eggs, canapé cups and other dry goods, so tight was the storage on board.

'I've done fish and chips for breakfast with a can of Irn-Bru,' he said with a wry smile. This was not a job for a chef with ego. I couldn't imagine the likes of Gordon Ramsay taking kindly to such requests, but Mark came across as measured, or perhaps experienced with the demands of the eccentric. 'It can be frustrating, but it's actually easier to go over and ask what they'd like instead of me trying to guess.'

'What's been the weirdest request?'

'Beef olives,' he said, leaning back to brief his sous chef, Rian, who was hovering gingerly at his side. We were nearing Keith and his team were preparing for arrival.

'It's a Scottish thing. You put sausage meat inside beef and then you roll it up. It was an American who came across it once and then he asked the manager for it.' He pushed himself up, draining his tea and handing his cup to Rian. 'We once arranged a helicopter. There were twelve of them I think – Russian – and they wanted to reroute the train to Liverpool to see the Beatles Story. It didn't happen but we got a helicopter. Flew them to Liverpool and flew them back later, in time for dinner.'

As Mark disappeared into the galley, I wondered what it would take to turn me into the kind of insufferable arse who would ask for fish and chips at breakfast. Perhaps it was boredom that pushed people to behave in this manner. Boredom and wealth. Fortunately, I had neither in abundance and was content to start my day with a fry-up.

Dinner felt different. After my chat with Mark, I looked around the table with a newfound appreciation for the salmon papillote, langoustine and caviar that was crafted and styled to precision. Tonight was prom night. For the only formal dinner of the journey, everyone had dressed in kilts and gowns, hair freshly tonged, the scent of many perfumes mingling. True to her signature style, my mum swept through in a silk sari that shimmered a peacock green, its gold brocade dusting along the carpet. Surrounded by sequins, diamanté and chiffon shrugs, hers was the most elegant outfit on board.

The train was running along the Shevock, a burn in Aberdeenshire that joined the River Urie. As expected, Mark had sourced local Angus beef, which was now gleaming pink beneath a peppercorn café au lait sauce, horseradish mash on the side. It sliced like butter, something I was never able to achieve despite my fancy pans, thermometers and timers. The food on board was flawless, cementing my belief that a dining car can make or break a journey. Around me, guests were thoroughly at ease, discussing the day's shooting and fishing, and I soon bonded with an American couple, Johnna and Jack. Fellow dachshund owners, they pulled out videos of their furball, Mr Hansel, riding on a train in Yosemite National Park. Louder after Chianti, passengers spooned up chocolate and almond tart as we sped along the grassy clifftop, twilight descending through the sea mist. There was an absurdity about the scene. Here we were, a group of forty strangers from around the world, dressed like a clan gathering and packed into a string of wooden carriages. I wondered how we appeared to onlookers, the workers at the Aldi supermarket we'd passed near the town of Montrose. Or to the cottage owners drawing curtains in the hamlet of Kirkton of Craig. Did they see the lights of a dinner party? Maybe they yearned to be on board. The likelihood was that the train was nothing more than a flash in the darkness. Perhaps therein lay the magic of train travel. Those fleeting moments. The ones that vanished as fast as they came.

'Oh god, just call them, Archie! Call them and then tell Daddy to call me.'

'All okay?' I turned to the woman standing next to me. She had one hand wedged into her back pocket while texting someone, a white silk shirt tucked into her jeans. Even in trainers she managed to look smarter than I did in my riding boots and skirt. She put her fists against her temples and clenched her teeth.

'We've got moths,' she said. 'My son found them. They've been at my husband's suits. He's got a whole stash from Gieves & Hawkes and I told him to get the lot out of there before they're ruined. He won't though. He and his brother just got back from school for Easter and it's impossible to get them to do anything.' Her phone rang and she turned away to answer it. 'No, I know! I've sent Peregrine a message but he's not bothering to reply to me. He's probably in bed.'

I leaned over the railing, watching the track tailing into the distance. As I sipped my tea I realised I'd been pronouncing it 'Jeeves' my whole life. I loved posh people. They were so wonderfully unaware of their poshness, wearing it on the sleeves of their Gieves & Hawkes suits. I waged a guess that she had at least two other sons at boarding school. Perhaps Hugo and Piers, certainly no Liams or Jordans in that household.

It was shortly before 9 a.m. and the sky was a perfect blue, the clouds whipped into peaks like small meringues. After a night of reeling and many not-so-single malts, we'd slept soundly for a second night, the train stabled at Dundee. Rumbling to life, it had set off after breakfast and I was savouring a last blast of salty air as it worked its way alongside the Fife Coastal Path towards Edinburgh.

'Gosh, aren't they quaint,' said the Moth Lady, joining me at the railing.

We were passing Kinghorn Harbour, where a row of mint-green caravans overlooked the sunlit surface of the North Sea. Walkers in wellies stopped to look up, dogs splashing off-lead. Others had now joined us, a group of around seven squeezing onto the observation deck for a last hurrah, my mum with them. She stood at my side, making a video of the tracks curling away, a curve of sand on one side and hillocks with lambs on the other.

'I can see why you spend your time here,' she said, as I stared at the line running away. 'What fun.' Where Indian friends of mine had been pushed into studying medicine, often against their will, I'd never felt anything other than support from my parents for what, at times, seemed a ludicrous career path. They might not have travelled with me, but I realised now that they'd always been on board.

We clattered back across the Forth Bridge, along the meadows, and soon the outline of Edinburgh rose into view. I'd made good enough friends on board to offer a couple of hugs and swap numbers, and as we drew into the station, I felt a space hollowing out in my gut. The train came to rest and we disembarked, the crew lining up by the carriages, an extraordinary group of cogs in a beautifully run machine. My mum was thanking each person in turn, holding their hands and chatting away as usual before gathering her things and boarding her train home to Birmingham. I waved her off, making a promise to myself to travel more often as a family. On the opposite platform, I saw the Lumo was due for arrival and I joined the crowd. And just like that, *The Royal Scotsman* was a thing of the past, and I was nothing more than another commuter waiting for a train to London.

THE INTERCITY NOTTE

A row of faces stared as we entered. One in particular stood out. Beneath a black birdcage veil, her eyebrows were pencil-thin, giving her a haughty air, red lips drawn into a pout. Next to her, a man's face was twisted into a grotesque expression of laughter. Heart-shaped, half his face was gold, the other red, the eyes empty. The smell of varnish was strong as I eased around newspaper-covered tables in Ca'Macana, a mask-making work-shop in the centre of Venice. Artists were spraying, buffing and putting final touches to an eye-catching selection of carnival masks: ribboned, glittered, feathered, comic and tragic, the masks featured a cast of characters from harlequins and pirates to cats, rabbits and the more sinister plague doctors, with their long, beaked noses. A group of professionals were sitting at the front of the studio and the three of us were handed aprons and guided towards the back, which reminded me of my old art room at school – a well-lit space with shelves stacked with pots of acrylic paint, an old radio playing on a stool.

It was the middle of the Easter school holidays and over the previous week I'd been riding across Europe with my daughter Ariel. Indignant that she'd missed out on the recent Scottish trip with her grandmother, Ariel had specifically asked if we could take some sleeper trains, which was music to my ears. This was now the third time we'd embarked upon a solo trip together since our previous year's journeys on the Paddington–Penzance *Night Riviera* and the train from Nice to Paris. She was fast becoming a pro at packing only a small bag of essentials and had clocked that night trains meant lots of pastries, hot choco-late and chaotic meals of her choice.

From Paris, we'd ridden down to the French Riviera, cross-ing over to Milan where her godfather, Ramin, had joined us, and we were now in Venice for a night. Our plan was to take the Intercity Notte to Rome, followed by a second sleeper to Palermo, where we would join Jem and my younger daughter, Maya. Where Ariel was quietly observant, kneeling up at the train window and counting lampposts, three-year-old Maya was what her nursery staff liked to call 'strong-willed'. Putting Maya into a closed compartment for a night was akin to throwing in a hand grenade and hoping for the best. For this reason, she and Jem were flying directly to Palermo. That way she could be harnessed and restrained.

On my last visit, Venice had struck me as a terrible place to visit with young children. It was overcrowded with too many bridges for buggies and too much breakable glass – not to mention a network of canals to fall into. However, now the girls were out of buggies, it was more than ideal. The streets were car-free and safe to stroll, with numerous corners and side streets to intrigue them. There were playgrounds and piazzas to tear around and the idea that the city was afloat (or rather, sinking) was thrill-ing to Ariel as we took a private water taxi down the Grand Canal, passing chandeliered but flood-marked palazzos. Now, she was sitting on a stool with her sleeves rolled up. With great care, she was stippling silver paint onto a papier-mâché mask, over-whelmed by the glitter and sequins. Ca'Macana was one of the oldest mask-makers in the city and had supplied numerous film and theatre productions, including Stanley Kubrick's *Eyes Wide Shut*. For almost thirty years they'd been running hour-long workshops where customers could select any mask and learn to blend and buff the paints in the Venetian signature style. Once the base layer was blasted under a hairdryer, the masks were ready for a top coat of gold or silver. I couldn't remember the last time I'd painted with the children, and it was intensely satisfying, my mind entirely focused on the sharpness of lines and swirls.

'Can I wear my mask now?' Ariel asked, pressing silver flowers into place. Unable to concoct a reasonable lie as to why not, I helped her tie the ribbon around the back of her head, and she sauntered out onto the street, purple feathers waving like antenna. Every day I was in awe of the girls' total disregard for what others thought of their appearance. Maya regularly turned up at nursery in ball gowns and Adidas, and I cheered her on, willing their indifference to persist into adulthood.

After pizza at Oke on the Zattere promenade, a twenty-minute ride by water taxi took us across the lagoon to the island of Murano, where we quickly felt the heat of blazing furnaces. Wearing jeans and trainers, the master glassmakers were holding metal rods in the fires. After a moment or two they'd retract the rods before blowing the molten glass into a bulb, rolling, teasing and nipping it into shape. Chandeliers hung around the factory. Like fragile fountains, they dripped with purple teardrops and green tendrils, candles sitting inside the mouths of bright red tulips. One of the glassmakers beckoned Ariel forwards as he began to roll a squidge of molten glass. He bent the tip up, then with what looked like a large pair of scissors, began to clip along the back as though crimping the edge of a pie. The mane finished, he swapped to a pair of metal tweezers, turning and nipping, turning and nipping, pulling out two legs, then bending the knees into shape. He then teased out the hind legs, stretched and cut the tail and placed upright a prancing horse. The sorcery took less than ninety seconds and, to her delight, he offered Ariel the pink horse to collect once it had cooled.

'Christ man, I need to get me a kid,' said Ramin, as we walked around the shop floors, agog at the gallery of blue jellyfish, floor-length mirrors and stringed instruments – including a lute, double bass and electric guitar – all of which were made from marbled glass. 'That horse has got to be worth something. Hey, Ariel, do you want to give Uncle Ramin your horse?' he said, squatting down as she rolled her eyes and wandered off to look at a troop of safari animals. Ramin reached up to read the tag twirling beneath a chandelier that bloomed like a wedding centrepiece.

'Holy shit, this is €475,000? Who buys this stuff?'

'Elton John? I don't know, they probably have a lot of Saudi sheikhs and luxury hotel groups who commission them for their lobbies and suites.'

'The sales guy kept following me around trying to show me sets of dining tables and chairs and I wanted to stop him and say "Mate, you've read me all wrong. I'm more of a keyring kind of guy."'

Dating at least as far back as the thirteenth century, the secrets behind the art of Murano glassmaking were passed down through families. Each new generation learned the techniques, which could take up to twenty years to master; I wasn't convinced that today's young people would be as willing to continue the legacy. Ramin wouldn't even take on his dad's launderette empire, preferring a career in acting and managing cinemas. The sad reality was that Murano's craft was suffering. Hit by the pandemic, glassmakers had already been struggling to recover when rocketing gas prices pushed many to shut their businesses, unable to afford the gas to fire the furnaces. Our visit felt bittersweet, and I made sure to pick up a souvenir pair of rose-gold earrings and a planet-shaped bottle-stopper for Jem before collecting Ariel's magical horse.

Much as he loved spontaneous travel, Ramin had a poor track record when it came to trains. Years ago, I had won a pair of first-class Interrail passes and with no time to travel before they expired, I had given one to Ramin to abuse. Happy to take anything for free, he'd swanned around Eastern Europe for three weeks and was reaching the end of his adventures when he'd fallen asleep on a late-night train from Zagreb to Budapest. When he woke up, he discovered that someone had stolen his suitcase. Only that hadn't actually happened and Ramin had fibbed to everyone concerned to cover for the fact that he'd got off the train, walked down the platform, taken a taxi and checked into a hostel before realising he'd left his bag on board.

'God, I'd forgotten about that,' he said, chewing the inside of his cheek and grinning guiltily as we taxied up the Grand Canal towards Venice's Santa Lucia station, moonlight bouncing across our wake. It was 10.30 p.m. and Ariel was lying across the seats, asleep beneath her jacket.

'I just couldn't admit I'd left it on board,' said Ramin, smirking as he recalled the incident. 'What kind of idiot does that? But I remember now what happened before, at the border. I woke up as all these burly men in coats came into the carriage. This one dude stopped by me, took my passport and then he called his boys over and interrogated me. They asked if I was Iranian and all the other passengers were looking at me.'

'Surely you had your British passport?'

'Yeah, that doesn't matter to them though, does it? It was so hostile. I was really shaken up and jumped off in relief when we arrived.'

'Did you ever get your bag back?'

'No! I spent three days at this hostel waiting for updates and didn't do anything but go to Burger King. On the last morning I got a phone call: "Is this Ramin?" "Yes it is." "Are you the guy who left his suitcase?" "Yes I am." "Did you leave it on the train to Budapest?" "Yes I did." "We've got an update for you." "Great, what's your update?" "We couldn't find your bag."'

The lights of the station came into view as we rounded a bend and I eased Ariel into her jacket, her sweaty head flopping around. With barely one day to spend in Rome before the onward journey to Sicily, we had decided to save time by taking the sleeper train, which departed at 11 p.m. and arrived into Roma Termini at 6.30 a.m. By day, the high-speed Frecciarossa would have taken as little as four hours and cost €10 less for the three of us, but this way we saved on a hotel and got to have fun along the way.

'I had a lovely encounter with a family on a train in Delhi though,' Ramin said, looking about for his bag. 'They treated me to my first McDonald's and let me crash at theirs. They even bought me a ticket directly to Agra to see the Taj Mahal. But then on that train I met a group of those eunuchs who go up and down the carriage asking for money.'

'Hijras?'

'That's the one. They put a curse on me. Which probably explains most of my thirties.'

The engine cut out and we drifted towards the pontoon. It was quiet enough to hear the slosh of waves against the wooden dock as we stepped out, Ariel slung over Ramin's shoulder. She was now awake, playing the cunning game of pretending to be asleep to be carried and I let her off. It was way beyond her bedtime and she'd done well to last the evening. I'd expected to find the station deserted but it was lively, a speaker playing dub music. Young people were sitting around the steps smoking, shifting along to make way as we climbed up through clouds of hash. Skateboards whacked the ground and touts sent neon toys spinning into the air, gesturing hopefully towards families milling around with gelato.

Inside the station the shops and cafés were shuttered. Travellers hovered in doorways checking phones and staying out of the cold. Others looked restless and bored, pacing the concourse, stopping to watch a screen showing the singer Alessandra Amoroso on MTV. During the day passengers came and went with a sense of purpose. At this hour though, they were vaping, stretching, yawning, looking at watches – willing time to pass until they could board and be on their way. After her power nap, Ariel was wide awake. As we looked for the platform, she spotted a homeless man wearing a duvet like a cape, his unlaced trainers revealing ankles grey and ulcered.

'Mama, why is that man wearing a quilt?' she asked.

I explained that he was probably cold and had nowhere to stay and she looked sad.

'Oh. What happened to his house?' she asked.

Having children was a bit like being on *Mastermind* – sometimes harder. (And I would know, having gone on the show with John Hughes films as my specialism.) From dawn until dusk, I was in the black chair, facing rapid-fire questions, thinking on my feet for age-appropriate answers while tossing out the occasional wild guess or white lie. Of late, I'd started to tell them plain truths, realising that airbrushing realities would only set them up for failure. Ultimately, I knew a lot more about *Planes, Trains and Automobiles* than why the world sucked. Turning back to Ariel, I admitted that I had no idea what had happened to his house. The man wasn't begging and his face was as down-turned as some of the masks we'd seen in Ca'Macana. Digging around in my wallet, I found a folded-up €5 note and told Ariel she could give it to him. I watched as he put out a grubby hand in surprise and she skipped back to me, his face transformed from tragedy to comedy as he blew her a kiss with a '*grazie bambina*'. Stations represent so much to so many. They're portals to a better life, symbols of history bearing witness to wars, but ultimately their openness spells safety, their arches, domes and corridors providing a place of warmth and refuge, their presence a constant in an unreliable world.

Fifteen minutes before departure, the promise of red lights flared at the end of the platform and the Intercity Notte drew to a halt, our carriage conveniently parked in front of us. Our compartment contained a smart triple-bunk with pre-made beds, a concealed sink and a stash of goodies piled up like a shopfront. In a clear indication that there was no dining car on this service, the staff had lined up six cans of mineral water, orange juice, croissants, wheat crackers and three boxes of Grisbi – old-school chocolate shortbread. Ramin seized upon his 'man deluxe kit', which contained slippers, a toothbrush, a razor, soap, hand gel and tissues, and Ariel went through the 'woman deluxe kit' which had the same items plus cotton pads and earbuds.

The Grisbi already ripped open, Ariel sat by the window and watched the platform glide away, happy to wave at other people's friends and relatives. On the lagoon, the lights of ships shone through the darkness and the three of us hunched over to observe them, until the train ran parallel with the motorway and Ariel asked if she could sleep. Unsure which berth to house her in, I did a quick risk assessment. The bottom berth left her too exposed. What if someone came in during the night and whisked her away? The top one was too high: if the train braked, she was slim enough to roll out through the harness. As a child, my friend Jane had travelled on a night train to Lake Garda with her family. In the morning her mum had woken up to find Jane had vanished from the bottom berth and she'd rushed up and down the carriage screaming for Jane in terror, turning out compartments in a frenzy. During the night Jane had rolled out of her berth and onto the floor. A heavy sleeper, she'd then rolled back under the berth, into hiding, where she had stayed asleep while her mum lost her mind. As a compromise, I tucked Ariel into the middle berth.

In the absence of a dining car, passengers had cleaned teeth, milled around for a few minutes then gone to bed, but Ramin and I flipped off the lights and stayed up by the window. It was midnight when we ran through Padua then on through the commune of Montegrotto Terme, where, to the right of the train, the Duomo of Saint Peter was shimmering through the blackness, gold lights trailing up the hillside. Shadows of forests fell onto the track before the train squealed into the town of Monselice. Ariel peeked over the side. She'd decided that she'd rather sleep in my bottom berth, which had more than enough space for us to top and tail, and it was time to call it a night.

'Ramin, I'm setting the alarm for sunrise,' I called up. 'Do you want me to wake you?'

'Yeah man, I'm up for that shit,' he said, flicking the lights on and off again as the train sped south to Rome.

———

He was not up for that shit. At 6 a.m. Ariel and I woke to a knock at the door and the aroma of coffee and hot chocolate. The sky was still a royal blue, a blur of golden moon shining in a corner. A magnificent mist enclosed the forest as we sat together counting the empty stations flashing by before my alarm went off, Ramin refusing to stir. In between warehouses and factories,

I could see the horizon threatening to turn pink and before I realised it, we were passing under loops of motorway, apartment blocks looming as we drew into Rome. Ramin was still asleep and stayed asleep as we pulled on shoes, packed the remaining Grisbi and climbed up to shake him awake. Only when the conductor passed through, rapping at the door and throwing them all open, did Ramin move. On the platform he realised he'd left his jacket on board and dashed back up to retrieve it, perking up when he saw rumples of cloud aflame across the tiled rooftops.

'It's beautiful, this shizzle, isn't it? Where we off to now?'

When travelling by myself it didn't matter if I arrived at dawn, the entire day stretching out ahead of me. I could leave my bags at the station then find a 24-hour bar or café and entertain myself until it was 3 p.m. and time to check in to a hotel. Accompanied by Ariel, I needed an immediate base and a loo. Fortunately, a bit of research had thrown up some useful information. I'd never stayed with them before, but the Hoxton group of hotels had a booking policy they called 'flexy time'. As long as guests booked rooms directly on their website, they could choose what time they checked in and out for free. In as little as ten minutes we'd taxied to the hotel and had checked in by 7 a.m. The Cosy Up room I'd booked wasn't quite ready but we were given a Shoebox – a single room – where we could take a hot shower and Ramin could snooze. Buoyed by a breakfast of Tuscan sausage, fried eggs and cannellini beans we were off into the city and by 8 a.m. were standing by the Trevi Fountain, tossing coins over our shoulders.

With just one day in Rome, we took Ariel to the Spanish Steps for gelato, then hired an electric paddle car at the Villa Borghese and spent most of the afternoon riding around its spectacular gardens. The sprawling park also contained a soft play area with bouncy slides, an arcade, a playground and fresh donuts – a win for everyone involved. Evening soon drew in and I knew from experience that it was wise to shower Ariel, brush her teeth and get her into pyjamas at the hotel to avoid wrestling her out of her clothes on the train. Collecting break-fast bags from reception, we taxied to the station for the 11 p.m. Intercity Notte to Palermo. It was a late train for anyone and poor Ariel fell asleep during the ride, waking up in confusion to find Ramin carrying her on board then jumping out and waving us off. To her deep disappointment Ramin was staying in Rome for a further night before heading to Manchester, where he had an advert to film about water pollution, playing the role of Pep Guardiola's body double.

For the first hour of the journey Ariel snuggled tearfully in my lap, munching through the Grisbi and watching the outskirts of the capital fall away, ivy-covered apartments flitting by. Eventually she cheered up as we played a game of count-ing people still awake. Their homes looked so inviting, warmed by retro lampshades and spotlit paintings. A number of houses had the libraries of my dreams, ladders hooked on one side and stairs winding up to galleries full of shelves. As factory chimneys twinkled against black skies, we fell asleep in the privacy of our two-person compartment, which was the same as the three-person compartment, with one berth locked into place – Ramin conspicuously absent.

It took the second thud to rouse me. Worried that I'd slept through it, I scrambled to the end of the berth and saw we were slowing into the Calabrian port city of Villa San Giovanni. Not quite 6 a.m., the last of the night's sky was reluctant to fade. Navy clouds drifted apart, a single patch of luminous pink firing up the ridgeline of the Peloritani mountains on the north-eastern edge of Sicily. Gleaming in the dawn light, the Messina Strait's waters lifted on the wind, and I knelt up to get a better look when the train jerked and travelled back the way we'd come. The carriages were uncoupling. I'd waited years to witness this moment. Little legs in striped pyjamas appeared on the ladder and Ariel hopped off.

'Are we riding on the ferry yet?' she asked.

'No, but nearly. Come on let's go and watch,' I said, pulling on my jacket and zipping her into hers.

The corridor was empty, and I looked around to find she was right. We had already been shunted onto the ferry. Jumping down from the carriage, which was bizarrely high without a platform to drop onto, we clattered up the staircase and onto the deck. Met by the slap of salty air and the cries of circling gulls, we stood at the railings and saw that we had already embarked upon the twenty-minute journey across the strait. A newly relaunched plan was in place to construct what would be the world's longest suspension bridge over the strait, but if it ever came to pass it wouldn't be operational until at least 2030. Looking down into the hold, we were greeted by the surreal sight of our carriages lined up side by side and locked into place. I spotted our window and Ariel started giggling when our neighbour drew up the blind, looking perplexed as he ran a hand through his wild morning hair. Most passengers slept through the crossing, unaware that it was even happening, but after a night of cramped space and dry heating, it was a treat to come up for a stroll in the sea air before we returned to the compartment for the final part of the journey. For all the positives of a bridge, it would be a huge loss to railway nerds if the train ferry ceased to exist.

Once on Sicilian terra firma, the train was recoupled and it set off along the northern edge of the island towards Palermo. It wasn't due to arrive until noon, so we dozed for an hour, waking to the sight of wisteria-covered houses. With a picnic of muffins and yoghurts spread out across the duvet, we watched a coastline of grey-sand beaches, upturned boats and giant cacti in backyards. It looked windy and cold, yet the Tyrrhenian Sea was an alluring blur of blue and green flashing between buildings, and I could just make out the humps of the Aeolian Islands on the horizon. The foreground was filled with lemon groves, stubby fan palms and Sicilian prickly pear. Unsure how warm Sicily would feel in April, I was relieved to see over the next hour that the clouds were evaporating and the sky cheering up.

Most people appeared to be in short sleeves as they emerged to hang out washing, work on boats and walk their dogs on pebble beaches.

In the final hour, the train climbed around the rocky coastline, and I looked down to where the waves crashed around Kalura beach in Cefalù. I'd considered coming here for a day trip, but changed my mind when I saw how rough the sea was, jetting spray across blade-edged boulders. All the same, a number of families disembarked at Cefalù station, fixing sunglasses on babies before waving off the train. Jem and Maya had reached Palermo the previous evening and were waiting at the station. Ariel was itching to reunite with her sister to debrief, and I checked my phone and saw that we were early, drawing into Palermo half an hour before schedule. Jumping onto the platform, Ariel hunted around then spotted the pair beneath the clock, tearing towards Jem's open arms. Maya ran at me full pelt, a vision in striped tights and leopard print, brandishing the contents of her British Airways Skyflyers pack. It would be at least another year before she'd be satisfied by Grisbi, crackers and a can of water.

According to everyone I spoke to, Sicily's railways were dreadful: delayed, old, infrequent, slow, and only to be expected once they drew into sight. Undeterred, we'd arrived on the Mediterranean island for a week of eating and trains – whichever came first – and on the first morning, after several strops, we called into the Mercato del Capo for breakfast. We followed our noses via Principe de Belmonte, where the smell of orange blossom sweetened the air, tiny white flowers settled between the leaves like snowflakes in spring. Clustered with fruit, the branches hung low, blood-red oranges split open along the ground. Elderly Sicilians wore flat caps and scarves in the heat, eating arancini from cupcake cases while cats twisted between their feet. At the entrance of Porta Carini the ground was wet and slippery, freshly hosed down around stalls stacked with strawberries and wooden crates of pears. For a couple of euros, the girls chose plastic cups of watermelon and kiwi, spearing most of their five a day, juice running down their jumpers. It was always in markets and wine bars that I felt the deep, smug pleasure of having booked to go home by train. With no restriction on liquids, I could shop with abandon, and I made my way from one stall to the next, plucking out wobbly bags of burrata and tubs of briny olives rolling around like marbles.

A handful of early-morning fruit-tasters had now grown to a heaving mass of Sicilians doing their groceries and tourists blocking their way. Those who'd come to browse were now sitting down to plates of hot, fried squid and potatoes, the scent of caramelised onions arriving with aproned servers. Over the fizz of deep-frying tempura, bargaining vendors and revving vespas, I could hear the pop of pesto jars being twisted open as I gazed longingly over tubes of bottarga, salted sardines and bottles of anchovies packed in oil. On the way downhill I noticed odd socks in the gutters and glanced up to see bedsheets drying overhead, racks of knickers and bras jauntily pegged into place. Fascinated by the slap of glassy-eyed mackerel on ice, the girls ran around blagging freebies, vendors plucking tomatoes off vines for them to taste. I realised then that Sicilians don't hate children the way the English do, and I relaxed, safe in the knowledge that the week would be a breeze. It was an opportune time to load up on snacks for our journeys and we emerged at the other end of the market with bags of pistachios, olives, and knobbly batons of salsiccia.

Home to highly distinctive palaces, churches and cathedrals, Palermo's four districts needed at least a week to explore thoroughly. But with little time at our disposal, we zeroed in on La Kalsa, the Arab quarter, and walked between alleys parked with mopeds, enjoying the quiet and the shade. A city of Phoenician origin, Palermo came under Arab rule from the mid-ninth to the mid-eleventh century, followed by a Norman invasion, all of which resulted in a remarkable, inclusive culture. Roger II, the King of Sicily, called upon Arab and Byzantine architects, farmers and advisers when it came to developing art, agriculture and science, and learned both Arabic and Greek, creating a society that was widely admired for its cultural harmony and envied around Europe. Many of what I had assumed were mosques were churches with domes. It was siesta time, and the streets were deserted as our voices echoed up the alleys, pigeons taking flight from emblems crumbling on baroque facades. Sandy and etched with the remnants of floral motifs, the buildings were tall and elegant with neat black balconies and potted plants stacked along the railings. Narrowing streets that appeared to lead nowhere would open onto piazzas or bring us face to face with walls covered in giant murals. Working our way out, we crossed through the Porta Felice, which looked like a baroque house sliced in two, and let the girls loose into the Parco della Salute on the promenade. As they ran around making friends in that incredible way that children do when no one speaks the same language, I realised it was the first time I'd ever seen an accessible playground. It was fitted with ramps in the playhouse, had a large swing to accommodate a wheelchair, and inclines on the merry-go-round. Palermo's history of inclusion was still going strong.

'*Ditt-a-ino!*'

'Perdono?'

'*Ditt-a-ino*... change... ah... bus... *sostitutivo*,' said the man behind the ticket counter, leaning towards his mic and passing me the tickets. We had arrived at the station in Palermo to take the train south-eastwards across Sicily to Catania. Even with my lack of Italian, *sostitutivo* sounded far too much like *substitute* and I sensed that we were doomed to take a rail replacement bus service for the last leg between Dittaino and Catania. Loath to be the harbinger of bad news, I kept this to myself in the hope that if I pretended it wasn't real, it might not happen.

From Palermo Centrale it was a four-hour journey across the island. Only three carriages long, the modern, air-conditioned service set off on time and I sat back as we sped past a slope covered in prickly pear, wisteria pouring over the fence between us. The slope dropped away, revealing a blaze of ocean, and the girls stepped up against the window, hands against the glass. Two iPads sat charged in my bag, but so far they'd had no interest in them, content to look into the backs of villas as we passed through Bagheria, its outline marked by one cove after the next.

'Is that Bagheria?' asked Jem, sliding up to the window and watching the water dipping in and out. 'I think that's where they filmed some of the second *Godfather*, at least it's supposed to be Bagheria.' In preparation for our trip, he'd gone back to his *Godfather* box set and together we'd watched the second series of *The White Lotus*, which was set in Taormina on the east coast. One particular episode of *The White Lotus* featured the famous scene at Castello degli Schiavi, where *The Godfather*'s Apollonia was killed in the car bomb meant for Michael Corleone.

'Can you imagine visiting the actual mansion,' said Jem. 'And sitting in Don Corleone's chair.'

'I've no idea where it is,' I said, as the train turned inland and descended into a valley of grassy meadows, buttercups and sheep. It was the ideal setting for a game of I Spy and we spent the next couple of hours passing hillsides brushed with blush-pink almond blossom and poppies growing between the tracks. Vineyards passed, followed by the silky hides of cows, then the medieval town of Enna, looming like a fortress. And rounding the corner, I spied with my little eye, something beginning with 'e', as Mount Etna rose into view, still covered in snow.

Few people remained on board and, as we drew into Dittaino, the train cleared and we were directed to the front of the station where a coach was already waiting to take us to Catania on the east coast, the second-biggest city after Palermo. To my relief it was a comfortable, luxury service with a constant view of the volcano and within an hour we'd pulled up by the station. An Uber-ride later and we were holed up in a noisy apartment overlooking a group of restaurants, where we spent the night listening to sirens, glass bottles being deposited and a group of English tourists fighting outside a bar.

Hot cones of fritto misto in hand, we set off the next morning up the coast to the town of Giarre. This train journey, too, was on a modern, air-conditioned service that arrived on time, departed on time and had wide seats, plugs and USB ports. The girls had eaten cannoli and I could feel a sugar-crash fight was brewing so set them the task of counting five red items on the ride, then leaned back in peace as they kneeled up on the seats with notepads. To my left were giant aloe vera plants, tall grass and poppies; and on the right, a hazy ocean.

In half an hour we were deposited on the platform and were wheeling our bags uphill towards a minuscule station to catch our final connection to the town of Linguaglossa on the Ferrovia Circumetnea – literally the 'around Etna train'. Sicilian trains had far surpassed my expectations but now I was concerned. My contact at Linguaglossa, Alfio, had sent me the most confusing timetable, a photo of a computer screen, and it was evident that he never rode the train. The departures were at 12:30, 13:50 or 16:26, and it was now 13:41 and we were the only four people standing by tracks that were narrow enough to run around our back garden. Sellotaped to the wall was a timetable from September 2020 that said Treno 24 departed Giarre at 13:54½, so I went to the little yellow machine to buy tickets. It was functioning until I pressed buttons at which point it chose to freeze with the message: *Macchina temporaneamente fuori servizio.*

'There's a guy here,' Jem called, as I started to lose faith. Waving me in through a side door, the station manager asked where we were travelling to and I handed him a €5 note, receiving change. He went over to a cupboard and took out a pair of orange tickets, writing in the date with a biro. Two teenagers in backpacks had arrived by this point. Three minutes before departure a square-faced, narrow-gauge engine drew into the platform and hissed to a halt, where it rumbled. The doors clapped open like a school bus, which was fitting as this was essentially a school service filled with children heading home for the day. Inaugurated in 1895, the three-foot-gauge train was originally built to assist farmers travelling around the region, which had made its wealth from wine and hazelnuts. Today it was used to ferry pupils up and down Mount Etna's foothills, which explained the infrequent service.

Comparable to some of India's toy trains, the half-hour journey was what trains were made for. With its windows slid open to let out the heat of tightly packed teenagers, the train rattled uphill, stone walls skimming its sides. While standing, I could see into the compounds of private villas, with their swimming pools and tennis courts, before we wound tightly into farmland, lemons thumping against the glass. Lavender was at arm's reach and at every turn Etna loomed, snow grazing its scalp. Today I could make out a single pipe of smoke hovering above its crater. The scent of rosemary was strong on the warm wind and the girls stood up to watch the passing olive trees and vineyards, chickens flapping away as the train wailed around corners. Cypress trees fringed the slopes, orchards bloomed and the stepped hillsides grew steeper until we slowed into the town of Linguaglossa.

'Mama, is that Alfio?' asked Ariel, as we stepped onto the platform. No one else was waiting to greet passengers and Ariel wandered up to a man who was wearing Balenciaga trainers and waving with both hands. Alfio Puglisi was our host for the next few days, and he led us down the cobbles towards his family home, Palazzo Previtera.

'Shit, what is that?' I tapped Jem, who groaned and moved away.

The noise started again, the howl of what sounded like an air-raid siren. I checked my phone. It was 8 a.m. After the recent Turkish earthquake I wasn't willing to take any chances with natural disasters and leaped out of bed, terrified that it was a volcano eruption warning. Wrestling with the wooden shutters, I gave up and hurried out of the room, the tiles icy against my bare feet. In the courtyard the parakeets were squeaking at full volume, the siren still going as Alfio appeared from a side door, two kittens at his heels. He was wearing a different pair of designer trainers and a new variation on the checked shirt from the day before.

'What is that noise?' I asked. 'It's not a volcano alert is it?'

Alfio started laughing and tucked his hair behind his ears. 'No, this is a tradition. It started somewhere after 1945 when the workers would start their shift and then you will hear it again at around 5 p.m., when it was time for them to put down their tools and go home.'

'Ah, okay, I had a heart attack thinking we needed to evacuate.'

'No, for that we get a text message. I'm so used to the siren I don't even notice it. Can I get you some coffee or do you want to wait for the others to have breakfast?'

'Coffee would be lovely, thank you.'

Pulling out a wrought-iron chair, I sat down at the marble table as the resident cats watched me from various hiding places. Two were tucked into a crevice by the parakeets, one was on an upturned flower pot, and another peeked out from under a stunning hedge of red camellia japonica. An archway covered by yellow Lady Banks' rose led into an adjoining pebbled court-yard and I finally felt at rest after many days on the move. Ariel wandered out and slid into a chair next to me as Alfio reap-peared with plates of sliced kiwi, peaches and figs, all of which were grown in the grounds. Spreading homemade apricot jam on freshly baked croissants, we sat in the morning sunshine, a sense of achievement between us as we mulled over our over-land journey from London to the foothills of Etna.

'Is this all Alfio's house?' Ariel asked.

'You can ask him,' I said, as Alfio returned with yoghurt, muesli and a pot of coffee.

'Well,' he said, 'I actually live here with my mum and dad, Mariella and Alberto, you will see them around.'

'Can I see the closed rooms?' she asked.

'Of course you can,' he said, 'you want to come now?'

Jem and Maya had surfaced and Alfio took us into the other side of the house for a tour.

Established in 1649, Palazzo Previtera had been in Alfio's family for 375 years. A former policy analyst and academic at King's College London, Alfio had spent the previous ten years restoring the family property which was, in essence, a museum with a library, and now a guesthouse with room for up to eight people in the main house and two cottages in the grounds, which spread across more than one acre. At first glance this should have been the last place to take children, with its recently upholstered armchairs, lace curtains and antique desks covered in trinkets begging to be picked up and played with. Yet Alfio remained indifferent to their nimble fingers and curiosity, opening drawers, handing them fountain pens and explaining the ladies in paintings.

'Is this Murano glass?' asked Ariel, pointing at the chandelier.

'Yes it is!' said Alfio. 'How do you know Murano glass?'

'I have a Murano glass horse, my godfather wants to sell it.'

The floors were covered in ceramic tiles from the 1820s, while the ceilings were painted with natural dyes in arabesque motifs. Nervous at the sight of jammy hands rubbing gold-leaf wallpaper, I sent everyone out to play hunt-the-cats and Alfio took me into the study, where he had dug out a series of yellowing documents, the thick black ink still legible. The pages smelled old and sour as he passed them to me, pointing to a paragraph of text.

'If you see here,' said Alfio, 'my grandmother's uncle, Cavaliere Avvocato Giuseppe Previtera, was directly involved in the founding of the Circumetnea railway.'

The document was dated 18 March 1882, and was an invitation for him to come to Catania five days later for the initial discussions around the creation of the railway. Sifting through the pages, Alfio found another document from 27 April 1885 relating to the line between Messina and Siracusa, which explained that some of the family's orange farms would have to be removed and cut through to build the railway.

'They ended up building the trains along the footpaths that the farmers were already using,' he said, 'they were smart.'

Jem poked his head around the door. 'I have a question, Alfio.'

'Of course.'

'How far is the *Godfather* house from here?' he asked.

'Not so far,' said Alfio. 'It's like twenty minutes or so in the car. But it's not open for the public to visit.'

'Ah, that's a shame.'

'The owner is actually a friend of my mum. I can maybe ask her if she can call him?'

The melancholy trumpet solo from Nino Rota's 'The Godfather Waltz' played in my head as we walked towards the wrought-iron gate of the castle. The sun was bright, the birds tweeting, as we crunched across the gravel behind the owner of Castello degli Schiavi. Alfio's mum had put in a good word and to Jem's delight, Baron Franco Platania had agreed to give us a tour of his home, which his family had owned since 1630. The famous balcony was straight ahead, the shutters open, magenta petunias flowering on the railing. And to the left, on the grass, exactly where he'd sat at the end of the movie trilogy, was Don Corleone's chair.

Leading us into a room to the left of the gardens, Baron Franco gestured for us to sit down in the row of chairs in front of a TV and dimmed the lights. In a surreal moment, the Paramount opening credits appeared on the screen, the trumpet playing through the darkness. Goosebumps from head to toe, I heard the gruff voice of Al Pacino and the opening shot of the castle appeared on screen, the building unchanged from then until now. The short film showed a compilation of shots from around the grounds and house, ending on the scene of the exploding car. It was futile to try and explain the cultural magnitude of the films to the girls, although they had disappeared with Alfio who was judging their game of musical statues.

Following the baron up the stairs at the side of the property, I felt like I was going backstage, expecting to find empty rooms and yet it was lain with faded carpets upon which stood sunken armchairs and busts on plinths. Even with the shutters thrown open it smelled of dust and old leather. The baron gestured for me to come over and stand at the top of a red carpet; when I turned I saw that it extended the length of the property, running through four palatial rooms of paintings in old tarnished frames and mahogany desks crowded with faded photographs of the Platania family, but also a number of royals and celebrities at the house, including one of Francis Ford Coppola behind the camera. Clearly a collector or hoarder, the baron had held onto original clapper boards from the set, along with sheafs of timings, directors' chairs, notes, old cameras and other paraphernalia, including a call sheet from the day they filmed the car explosion which listed all the notes from make-up and wardrobe, and was dated 1971.

In 500 years, the baron was the only person who had lived in the property on a full-time basis and I was curious about who might inherit it given that he had no children. I overheard 'Oprah' and Alfio quickly translated, telling me that Oprah Winfrey had apparently made an offer that, thankfully, the baron had turned down. Outside, the girls were still playing musical statues and I looked down to find Jem sitting in Don Corleone's chair, an expression of bliss on his face.

Back at the palazzo we spent the afternoon reading and playing hide-and-seek in the gardens, an expanse that looked like a childhood dream brought to life: olive trees, rose bushes and a century-old cherry blossom with branches trailing along the ground. The spring air was heavy with the scent of three different kinds of jasmine, and Alfio guided me around white tea plants, rubbing velvety petals of yellow and white magnolia. His mum was the whizz with the green fingers, growing pomegranates, pears, peppers, aubergine and fennel, and I surveyed the magnificent sight of nature in bloom, feeling sorry for the trio of frogs frozen in terror as the girls loomed over their pond.

The following day Ariel and I would make our way home by train. I stood beneath the blossom, watching Etna smoking quietly, the soft hoot from the narrow-gauge railway sounding out across the groves.

11

THE GOOD NIGHT TRAIN

The freight train came to a halt. Simon Gronowski sat up and listened. There were voices outside, followed by the sound of someone running the length of the convoy. It was pitch black inside the cattle truck where he lay on the straw-covered floor surrounded by fifty other people. A moment later he heard the crack of gunshots followed by shouts in German, but the train moved off again.

An hour later, eleven-year-old Simon was asleep in the arms of his mother when she shook him awake. The truck's doors were open. Leading him by the hand, Chana took her young son to the doorway where two other deportees were preparing to leap from the moving train. He sat down on the edge of the doorway, his feet dangling, before Chana lowered him by the shoulders; his shoes touched the steps between the ground and the truck. Simon was frightened to jump, but the train suddenly braked, and he took his chance, landing on the tracks. He looked up for his mother, waiting for her to follow – but she didn't. 'It's going too fast,' she called to him in Yiddish, and the train carried on.

Simon waited for her in the cold. It was 11 o'clock at night. In the distance he heard more gunfire and screaming in German, as the Gestapo began running in his direction. Simon turned and fled. Throughout the bright, moonlit night he ran through woods and fields, making his way back to Brussels by the next morning, where he would find refuge in friends' attics until the end of the war. Behind him, the steam engine had continued, puffing its way towards Auschwitz in Poland, where it arrived with 1,398 deportees. After three nights on the move across Europe, 877 Jews were immediately gassed, Simon's mother Chana among them.

It was the eightieth anniversary of Simon's escape and I was sitting across from him at his home in central Brussels. I had a train to catch in a few hours, but had rung up Simon and asked if I could visit after researching the history of night trains and stumbling across his extraordinary story. Now ninety-one years old – and still practising law – Simon gripped the left arm of his leather chair and stared at the desk sadly, his right palm pressed against his temple.

'If my mother wasn't going to jump, I would have stayed with her and I would have gone with her,' he said in French. 'She gave me the gift of life twice: when she gave birth to me and again when she pushed me. But my goal was simply to escape the Nazis... *they were not my friends*,' he added in accented English, his eyes brightening with a laugh.

Between 1942 and 1944 the Nazis deployed twenty-eight trains to transport the 25,490 Jews and 353 Roma who were detained at the Dossin military barracks at Mechelen, in Flanders, to Auschwitz-Birkenau. On 19 April 1943, Simon and Chana were two of 1,631 deportees packed onto a train comprising thirty trucks. Detained separately, his older sister Ita was held back. This train, known as 'the twentieth Convoy', would stand out in Holocaust history as the only deportation train to be stopped by resistance fighters, who ambushed it near the town of Boortmeerbeek. Together, Youra Livchitz, Robert Maistriau and Jean Franklemon arrived on their bicycles and placed a hurricane lamp wrapped in red paper in the middle of the tracks, which served as a red stop signal. Holding a pistol to the engineer's head, they bought time to cut open some of the truck doors with pliers, allowing 233 prisoners to escape; 118 of them survived, including Simon.

'The train ran at night,' Simon recalled. 'The Nazis wanted to avoid the chance of a train going through a normal Belgian station and for a worker or passenger waiting on the platform there seeing an arm coming out through the small hole or to hear someone calling for help.'

Although there remain no archival sources on the operational organisation of the deportation trains, including departure times, historians agree that the secrecy and security measures were tightly maintained to ensure the trains travelled unhindered – from using cattle trucks to banning Belgian civilians from standing on platforms when the trains passed through stations.

Boarding in stages from early morning until late into the afternoon, Simon and his fellow deportees had entered the trucks assuming that they were being moved to a labour camp. Casting one last hopeful look at his sister Ita, Simon watched the doors close with a metallic clang. He and Chana sat in complete darkness, nothing but the sound of crying and groaning around them. At ten that night the train finally departed from Mechelen.

A little over five foot tall, Simon's figure sat dwarfed behind an enormous desk piled with papers in a room filled with comical legal figurines, honorary doctorates and photographs of his grandchildren. For more than sixty years Simon had kept his story to himself, unable to even open a suitcase that was filled with family photographs, documents and letters. Five months after Simon's escape, Ita was also transported to Auschwitz and gassed on arrival. Only in 2002 did Simon break his silence and commit to bearing witness around the world to the horrors of the Holocaust.

'People have to know about the barbarity of yesterday so they can defend the democracy and freedom of today,' he said. 'Don't forget, Hitler didn't just kill Jews, he killed gypsies, Freemasons, the handicapped, homosexuals, Jehovah's Witnesses, not to mention socialists and communists and of course Soviet prisoners… poets. Hitler killed a lot of people. And now, I am struggling with the extreme right in Europe.' Simon eased himself up and shuffled around the room towards the window, beneath which stood an electric piano. He stopped. 'The extreme right is a cradle for racism and antisemitism and a breeding ground for hatred. Refugees aren't coming to us for pleasure, but because in their own countries they are starving or having political problems or they're at war. I am the child of immigrants myself. That's why I have a solidarity with migrants and undocumented people and we should treat them all alike.'

Simon straightened his blue V-neck jumper and pulled up a stool at his piano. During lockdown he had moved it to its current spot and thrown open the window to play jazz pieces for his neighbours in an attempt to lift their spirits, with many gathering on the streets or standing at their own windows to listen. Hunched over, he now placed both hands on the keys then looked across. He had the same look in his eyes that I'd seen when I had interviewed Sir Harold Atcherley. A former British soldier, 97-year-old Sir Harold had been taken prisoner by the Japanese and put to work building the Burma Death Railway. It was a look that conveyed unimaginable trauma, but there was calm within it brought about by a level of acceptance of that trauma.

'When I was running through the woods and the wheat fields, I was humming to myself,' Simon told me. 'I hummed "In the Mood" by Glenn Miller. It was my sister's favourite song and she used to play it on the piano, she loved jazz. She was a wonderful jazz pianist...'

And with that he began to play the jaunty tune.

After helping me put on my coat, Simon waved me off from the steps of his townhouse, smiling.

'Enjoy your train!' he said, as a taxi arrived to take me to Bruxelles-Midi station. During the ten-minute ride, I thought about Simon's deportation train running under the cover of darkness. The reality was that so many of the world's railways had monstrous histories. Often built by colonisers, trains were far from well-intentioned, but the stories behind them were vital to recount. I was for ever perplexed by travellers who shied away from brutal realities around them, opting for a sanitised experience that wouldn't evoke feelings of guilt – or taint their holibobs with inconvenient truths. Knowing their histories took nothing away from my enjoyment of riding the world's railways, neither did it fill me with guilt or shame. If anything, it only enhanced my experience by making me think. Besides, that was the point of slow travel: to understand how history had shaped a people and their homeland.

On arrival at Bruxelles-Midi, the rumble of engines and the hum of footsteps and announcements enfolded me like a warm cloak thrown around my shoulders. Something inside me came alive when I set foot on a concourse, the crossroads for thousands of stories and adventures. I was here to board the inaugural *Good Night Train* to Berlin. In 2021 a pair of sleeper-train enthusiasts named Chris Engelsman and Elmer van Buuren came together to found European Sleeper, a Belgian–Dutch cooperative aimed at putting night trains back on track. A Dutch engineer with a passion for sleeper trains, Chris had previously launched the *Jazz Night Express* in protest against the cutbacks to European overnight services. Determined to showcase the joy of night-train travel, he and a small team rented rolling stock and hired jazz musicians and DJs to play on three stages as the train set off at sunset through the Dutch countryside, passengers drinking, dancing and dining on Cajun-style meatloaf and shrimp jambalaya before arriving in Berlin at dawn. To Chris's dismay, the party train enjoyed one sell-out year before the pandemic brought it to a standstill. Refusing to accept defeat, he joined forces with Elmer, a former train guard on Dutch railways, and launched a crowdfund for European Sleeper. They raised €500,000 in seed capital by selling shares to more than 350 small investors, many of whom were no more than train enthusiasts keen to fire up the dying embers of night travel.

Chris and I had discussed his night-train dream in 2020, so as I watched the train drawing up to the platform, I felt a rush of excitement on behalf of him and Elmer – and for the future of sleeper trains as a whole. A hotchpotch of carriages sailed past, the first few in stainless steel, the next ones painted in the red and white livery of European Sleeper, limp blue curtains hanging at filthy windows. Cobbled together using German carriages from the 1950s and sixties, the makeshift service was a moving illustration of the problem facing the revival of sleeper trains: there was so little rolling stock available to lease, and to date, no one had committed to mass-producing brand-new carriages fit for modern-day needs.

Nonetheless, European Sleeper had fulfilled its goal of getting *The Good Night Train* up and running on schedule, and none of the passengers looked in the least bit bothered by its ramshackle appearance, too preoccupied taking photos with the train and eager to get on board. My friend Denny was joining me for the journey and I looked around for him then made my way up the steps, confident he'd find his way on board.

There was a tailback in the corridor as passengers waited for others to locate their compartments, breathing in and standing on tiptoes as neighbours squeezed past one another, getting carriage numbers wrong and tripping over bags. Yet the mood was a friendly one, an inherent understanding between us that we were now a team for the next twelve hours. On the whole, train people have a connection – one that is jovial, sympathetic and tolerant, a sense of community and collaboration established from the moment of boarding: everything that air travel is not. I'd concluded that this was, in part, down to the set-up of trains, which allows passengers to cross paths repeatedly during a journey. On an aeroplane, passengers are seat-bound unless using the loo. You could pick a fight while boarding, safe in the knowledge that the other person was unlikely to come in search of you later, and would at least have to clamber across other passengers to get to you. Trains, on the other hand, are designed for moving around, passengers strolling in and out of carriages at will, perching on armrests and lingering in doorways having chats. If you made an enemy of a fellow passenger on a night train, they could easily sneak in and stab you while you slept. From *Shanghai Express* and *Snowpiercer* to *The Lady Vanishes* and, of course, *Murder on the Orient Express*, it was why trains provided such perfect settings for thrillers and murder mysteries.

Once the queue had gone, I slipped into our stuffy sleeper compartment, which had no air conditioning. It was late May and the heat on board was intense. I listened to the reassuring sound of my neighbours rummaging around, shoving down windows and cracking open cans of European Sleeper's own-brand Weizen beer, shouts of laughter carrying through the walls. For a lot of people on board, night trains were still a novelty, many coming to them for the first time this evening and adjusting to the idea of clicking berths into place and sharing with strangers. Inside our compartment were three berths, the top one stowed away. The beds were pre-made with crisp, white duvets, upon which lay a flannel and a round of soap. There was one seat at a small table and a backpack was already wedged underneath it – Denny was on board. It was nearing 7.30 p.m. and I wandered out into the corridor, spotting his salt and pepper hair in the vestibule. He was leaning against the wall with one hand in his pocket and a naughty smile on his face. In his other hand was a can of Weizen.

'Hello, what have you got there?' I asked.

'Train beer.'

'Ah.'

'Train BEERS!' he said, reaching into his back pocket and pulling out a second can that he handed over as the train set off.

Adrian D'Enrico and I had been friends for almost twenty years, meeting through *Little White Lies*, a film magazine that he and his Chester school friends had founded when I was a journalism student, still naïve enough to write for free in exchange for mid-week Soho screenings and a glass of warm wine from a box. He was Maya's godfather, better known as Uncle Denny for his avuncular nature, and was first in line for any adventure, whether that was climbing Kilimanjaro, running an ultramarathon, or supervising a bouncy castle full of Haribo-fuelled four-year-olds. All the better if there was meat and beer available and the chance to skive off work. A dab hand at lining up gardening leave every two years – invariably just as summer started – Denny had recently left another job and had three months of freedom ahead of him.

He turned towards the evening sun, a look of pure happiness on his face until the train jerked then sailed off with a loud clank and a screech, apparently splitting apart. It was as though the carriages had come out of hibernation and needed a good stretch and bend to limber up for the journey.

'Got your EpiPen?' I asked, shielding my eyes from the deep orange light that was pouring through the windows.

'Yes, indeed,' he said, giving me an exaggerated nod.

'I don't want Gavin Henson making an appearance this weekend,' I added.

Denny had a nut allergy and on a holiday in Goa a few years ago, he'd devoured a plate of grilled sardines, not realising they were marinated in creamed cashew nuts. To his wife Emily's horror, he'd continued to eat them while announcing that although they were delicious, he felt a bit 'warm'. The following morning he'd knocked on the door of our beach shack, his eyes swollen in such a way that he'd developed a striking resemblance to the Welsh rugby union player. For £4 a nondescript injection from a village doctor had set him right, but I wasn't up for anaphylaxis on a night train.

'I'll be fine,' said Denny, as we returned to our compartment. 'There's no dining car to kill me anyway. Ooh, I missed this, is this a minibar?' he asked, pulling open a pair of rounded doors above the bin.

'No, it's not a minibar, it's the sink,' I said, closing them again.

'Should be a minibar. Get some ice in that sink.'

Although there were plans for one, there was currently no dining car on the train, which was disappointing to say the least. We'd eaten before boarding but there was a fun vibe pulsating through the train. It reminded me of Freshers' Week at university – with everyone going between the mini house-parties taking place in each compartment – and a dining car would have been the perfect place to congregate. Curious to see what the couchettes were like one class down, we wandered into the next carriage, which was even noisier than ours, and were invited into a compartment by Hugo, who was waiting for his friend Rick to hop on an hour later in the Dutch city of Roosendaal. Hugo was very blond with deep-set eyes, a beard and alarmingly red cheeks that made him look like an off-season Christmas elf. He let us nose around the compartment which had six berths in blue felt. There was no wash basin and less room to move around. Still, for a group of friends it was ideal, and I envisaged gathering a posse for a future weekend in Berlin. With the window pushed right down, a welcome breeze was flowing in, and I climbed up to inhale the summery scent coming off the fields, the sky still light.

'Where are we now?' Denny asked Hugo, opening another can.

'I don't know… yes, I do, we are almost nearing Mechelen,' said Hugo, joining me to look out.

I held my breath, my skin prickling at the realisation that this was where Simon Gronowski and his mother had been imprisoned. The train was running past meadows and forests in bloom. I checked the map on my phone, noting that we weren't too far from Boortmeerbeek, where the deportees' train had been ambushed. In a flash the trumpet riff of 'In the Mood' started up in my head as the train cut through what was an attractive suburban district, with farmhouses and cycle paths parallel. But all I could see was an eleven-year-old Simon, running beneath the light of the moon, running between these trees, running to stay alive, the swing music playing in his head.

Around forty minutes after departing Brussels, the train drew into Antwerp and a cheery, dark-haired passenger looked into Hugo's couchette compartment, where we'd made ourselves at home.

'Welcome, sit down,' said Hugo. 'You wanna have a drink?'

'Yes, I think I am going to sit down for a little bit,' the man said, wriggling out of his backpack and dropping it onto the ground. 'How long do we have until Roosendaal?'

'Er, I don't know?' said Hugo.

'Enough time for a drink,' said the man, who was also called Adrian. To Denny's delight, he pulled a bottle of Strongbow out of his back pocket and looked under the small table. 'This is disappointing, Czech trains have a bottle opener somewhere around here,' he said, feeling under the table then clipping the bottle top off on the edge and sitting down heavily.

'Czech trains sound fun,' said Denny, recognising a kindred spirit when he saw one. 'Do you travel there a lot?'

'Too much,' said Adrian.

'Which routes would you recommend?' Denny asked.

Adrian took a long sip of his cider, his hairline wet from running to board. 'The train to Rijeka,' he said, without hesitation. 'It's a wonderful experience because the city is right by the sea and Croatia is almost all on the coast. It's very sharp, it goes into the seaside and then... boom!' He turned his hand upwards. 'It goes up the mountains and then down a little bit and then you arrive in Rijeka. You're in the middle of the forest and then suddenly... wow!'

Hugo nodded in agreement. 'It's the same as Split,' he said, 'the approach to Split is beautiful, you are high up in the mountains still and you can see the city below and you see the coastline too.'

A passing train sent us tilting for a moment and as the three chatted, I made notes. It was invariably while on board one train that I discovered details of another, and I was in my element with fellow train geeks. Adrian was a member of Back on Track, the European network of volunteers campaigning to promote cross-border passenger traffic and night trains.

'Why did you join?' Denny asked Adrian.

'Actually, I just joined it a couple of weeks ago. I'm very active on social media about trains and they were doing good things. They did a film screening in Brussels, where they have the headquarters, and I went and I found they were nice people. I like night trains, it's my passion and I think it's quite fair what we ask for. We need long-distance connections between major cities, and also tickets should not be too expensive.'

A product specialist with Eurail, Hugo had once worked as a train steward while studying tourism, doing round-trips to Austria on sleeper trains at the weekends.

'I figured, you depart Friday afternoon and you are back on Sunday afternoon. It's really fun – tiring of course because you're working thirty hours, and then after the weekend you're completely broken.'

'Do you get to sleep at all?' I asked.

'Yeah, from 1 a.m. to 6 a.m. and then you start handing out coffee and people will say: "Hey mountains and snow!" and they're super happy. Then when the train stops you go into town, have some food, have some beers and then get back on the train.'

'That sounds pretty good to me,' said Denny as the train drew into Roosendaal and Adrian got up to leave.

'I wanted to check out this train, but I like it, I will be back,' he said. He turned to me from the doorway. 'Are you on Twitter by any chance? I am very active there. I tweet too much about trains. Ah, I follow you already!' he said, scrolling and looking back and forth from my face to my profile. 'In Spanish we have a word, *desvirtualizar* to "devirtualise". It's when you finally meet the people to whom you have spoken but you've never met and now they're real.'

Adrian waved as Hugo's friend Rick arrived at the door. The two had met through an online railways forum and often took train trips together. Once we'd moved off, I was wary of outstaying our welcome. Rick and Hugo were bound to want to catch up without us hovering about and we took our leave.

Back in our carriage the music had died down and the two women next door had already turned in. Their door was closed but we could still hear the occasional thump and laughter on the other side.

'Those two were steaming when they got on,' said Denny, standing at the window and admiring the beginning of the sunset. It was just after 9 p.m. and we were passing through Dordrecht, en route to Rotterdam. Windmills turned slowly and a solo cyclist rode at the edge of a field, the waterways blushing in the evening light.

'Really nice group on board,' he went on. 'Little railway community.'

Interactions were different from when I'd first started travelling by train. In the past I could chat for hours, often waving people off without knowing their names, the anonymity adding to the charms of our encounters. But social media had changed that, and within seconds it was easy to identify a person, locate them and follow their movements. I didn't mind. The world, while growing, felt increasingly isolating and it was reassuring to build a community and stay connected, knowing they were only a message away.

A handful of passengers boarded in Rotterdam and an hour later Amsterdam rose into view, a vision of neon and needle-sharp church spires. Neither Denny nor I had packed books and with no Wi-Fi on board there was nothing to do but watch one station approach after the other, savouring the sights of houseboat masts sailing into view and reflections rippling on canals. Tall and narrow, Amsterdam's houses looked squashed and skewed. Eventually we broke into a canter along a series of bungalows buried between trees, then into an affluent area of glossy apartments, windows thrown open, a woman working at a Mac desktop while her cat stalked across the desk. I saw that it was 11 p.m. and listened: the neighbouring compartments were quiet.

'Right, top or bottom?' I asked Denny.

'Oh, hello!' he said, giggling.

I rolled my eyes. 'Do you want the top or bottom berth?'

'Definitely bottom. I'll be up at least three times for a wee.'

'Why? Can you not just go for a last one?' I asked, climbing up to my berth and getting under the covers, looking around for a charging point that didn't exist.

'No,' he scoffed. 'I'm getting old, Monisha.'

'You're only two years older than me.'

'Yep, exactly, we're old.'

I always knew when Denny was pissed as he used my full name and blinked heavily. Having mentioned the loo, there was no way I could then lie in bed and think of anything else so went for one final visit, then got back into my berth. Drunk Denny was great fun. At my wedding he'd gently relieved me of my bouquet at the end of the night, telling me that his wife Emily was brilliant at drying flowers and that I should give them to her to look after. I'd handed them over only for him to return ten minutes later looking terribly concerned: 'Monisha… you've forgotten your bouquet,' he'd said, handing them back as carefully as he'd taken them.

I shuffled about for a bit, trying to get comfortable. 'Shall I flip the light off?' I asked.

'Yeah, sure. I'm going to stay up for a bit. Blind doesn't work. May as well watch the scenery with a beer.'

'You're going to drink in bed in the dark?' I asked, turning off the light only to find the moon beaming straight across our compartment.

'Yes, Monisha,' he said, the sound of a can hissing open below me. 'It's the best way.'

There was silence for a few minutes, then the gentle beat of the wheels. I heard Denny take a long sip. 'I could get used to this,' he said. 'It's like riding on the moonlight express.'

Just before midnight we made the final stop at the city of Deventer and I turned over, knowing that we wouldn't stop again until around 6.20 in the morning in Berlin. It was at that fateful moment that I noticed knocking. It sounded as though someone was tapping on the wall, and I realised it was our neighbours' ladder, which wasn't locked into place. And that was that. For the remainder of the night I lay awake, turning from one side to the other, pillow on head, kicking myself for forgetting to pack earplugs. To make matters worse, the ride was smooth — barely detectable — and were it not for the knocking I would probably have slept through the night. True to his word, Denny was up at least three times before I finally dropped off in the small hours, waking at 5 a.m. in the town of Peine in Lower Saxony. Giving up on sleep, I moved to the end of my berth and looked out to where an anaemic sky was beginning to turn orange, an icy-looking mist hovering above the fields. A passing attendant informed me that we were delayed so I crept back up to my berth and slept soundly for the next two hours, waking refreshed on the approach to Berlin.

Keen to swap details, I sought out Hugo and Rick, and came across Jonathan and his seven-year-old daughter Ruth, who had joined their compartment at Amsterdam. All Jonathan's family lived in Berlin and they had come for a weekend of birthday celebrations.

'This train has changed everything for us,' he said, 'I'm going to do it again this way.'

'How was Ruth?' I asked.

'She was okay, but getting on at 10.30 at night was quite tough for her, to keep her awake until then, and she didn't sleep all that well.'

'Well, that makes two of us,' I said, as Ruth pulled on her backpack and waited by the door. On a warm morning at the end of May, most passengers were off the train and straight into the city, cock-a-hoop at making it to the museums and galleries before the crowds. While I had no qualms about doing the same, I still preferred to offload bags and shower. Since my stay with Ariel at the Hoxton in Rome, the hotel group had introduced a new climate-friendly initiative called the Good Rate, which knocked £20 off rooms at either side if guests travelled between hotels by train. It wasn't a huge amount, enough for breakfast perhaps, but it was still an incentive and the new hotel in Charlottenburg also allowed guests to check in whenever they liked. By 9 a.m. we'd got our room and showered with a full day ahead of us. Denny and I had both been to Berlin before, and I'd previously visited the remains of the Wall at the East Side Gallery on the northern banks of the river Spree, so we decided to amble around in the sunshine and see where our instincts took us.

After a hiatus owing to the pandemic, the Carnival of Cultures had returned to the city and we noticed large groups heading towards the neighbourhood of Kreuzberg, so we joined them, the sounds of reggae and smoke from food trucks reminding me of the Notting Hill Carnival. Founded in 1996 as a response to violent racist riots in the Lichtenhagen district of Rostock, northern Germany, the Carnival of Cultures was populated by Berlin's immigrant communities: artists, performers and vendors whose origins lay all over the world. To the riffs of Anatolian jazz, Japanese fusion rock and mestizo music, we blended into the crowd, mojitos in hand, pulled along by the flow. Around us, kids sparkled in butterfly face paint, couples shared palm-leaf plates of pierogi and drummers thumped out beats, their skin glistening in the hot sun. The founders of the carnival billed it as a symbol of a free and pluralistic society, and I walked around absorbing the warmth and energy. Berlin had always been marketed to me as 'edgy', 'gritty' and 'cool' – clichés that could be applied to almost every capital city in the world. But for me it was the city's refusal to be defined that gave it appeal: the unpredictable architecture, the wariness I felt negotiating the uniqueness of each neighbourhood; the sudden emergence of gardens and lakes. More than anything, Berlin was a city that didn't seem to care what anyone thought of it.

The next day we biked around our neighbourhood, rewarding ourselves with a huge plate of pork knuckle, sauerkraut and dumplings in the Zollpackhof beer garden. It was a ten-minute taxi ride from there to Berlin Gesundbrunnen station and we arrived in high spirits, ready to board the new night train to Stockholm.

In September 2022 a EuroNight sleeper train had begun running from Hamburg to Stockholm. When I'd originally scribbled down my wish list of trains, there'd been rumours that it would extend to start from Berlin, and I'd hoped to tie it in with *The Good Night Train*.

For once, the stars had aligned and just a few weeks earlier the route had indeed started from Berlin. Run by Swedish Railways, our SJ EuroNight train arrived and departed promptly, gliding out of the station at quarter to seven in the evening. The twin sleeper compartments were compact and as hot as saunas, with not a lot of room to sit down. In the corner stood a vanity unit with a concealed washbasin and mirror and a large bottle of green-tea-and-ginger body wash fixed above the tap. The deluxe sleeper compartments had ensuite showers and toilets, otherwise there was a communal loo for us all. Fortunately the windows in the corridor could be pushed down for fresh air and most passengers were leaning into the wind as we ran along the river Spree. Kicking his trainers off, Denny threw himself across the bottom berth, a pair of warm stripy socks centimetres from my leg, which incentivised me to make my way down the train and see who else was on board.

While the scenery so far was unremarkable – sunlit fields and a few bends and twists of the river – it was still a joyful ride. Far from the party train from Brussels, this one felt more purposeful, with passengers politely chatting over drinks as they passed one another, but otherwise content to stay in their compartments, looking up from books and nodding as I wandered by. The train was whipping along through the borough of Spandau when I came upon a dad holding up his young son, who was clambering on the window trying to get a better view. The dad was wearing a T-shirt that said: 'Make Racism Wrong Again', and I hovered, desperate to ask him about it. A digital designer, Herman and his eight-year-old son Assar lived in Sweden and were on their way home after a weekend in Berlin. Herman's grandfather had started a travel agency in the 1950s, which his father had taken over and he reminisced with fondness about the train journeys he'd done as a child. Inviting me into their compartment to take a seat, Herman handed Assar a book as he climbed up into his berth, but he lay watching me over the side. His curious face and gangly legs reminded me of Ariel's and I waved up at him.

'I always travel in a couchette compartment,' said Herman. 'It's a gamble who you end up with, but usually it's people with the same sensibilities. It might be a bit of chaos, but overall you have to be forgiving, and it's usually okay.'

He chatted to Assar for a moment, who asked for his iPad, then Herman recalled an incident.

'I was recently on the Snälltåget train where the compartments are a bit old and a bit small. There was one loud guy who was talking so much that I had to leave, actually. And to be with a character of that magnitude during too many hours, I would rather be with that kind of character in this compartment.'

A private operator based in Sweden, Snälltåget (which translates as 'the Kind Train') had been running since 2007. A competitor to Swedish Railways, it refurbished old trains and also ran a night train connecting Stockholm, Malmö, Copenhagen, Hamburg and Berlin. They'd been my back-up plan in case I couldn't get tickets for this journey.

A familiar figure appeared in the corridor and I waved to Denny, who was now strolling past in bare feet. He joined us and Herman asked him how he was finding the sleeper trains.

'Are you a convert now?' Herman asked.

Denny explained how he used to travel regularly between London and Paris for work, getting up at 5 a.m. having not slept well the night before. 'If I could have gone to bed on a train and turned up in the centre of the city, I would have done this every time,' he said.

'That's it,' said Herman. 'The trains arrive right in the centre. You don't have to get a taxi in from the outside.' He snapped his fingers. 'You get off the train and in like fifteen minutes you can see a museum.'

A field full of deer passed by and all four of us sat up to watch them in a quiet moment of magic typical of railway journeys. Herman told us that he and his partner had mostly given up flying as a result of climate change. Assar also enjoyed hearing people speaking English and learned from observing his dad's interactions.

'He was actually really disappointed that there was no one else in here,' said Herman, looking up and smiling warmly at his son. 'For Assar, he's learning that people look different, talk different, smell different. Before we boarded, we were talking on the platform with this woman and he gave her a hug when we got on. He is learning to trust people he doesn't know, which is one of the best things I can give him.'

'For me,' said Denny, 'if they added a TV up here and I could watch it like this,' he said, stretching out his legs, 'I'd be… I think the phrase is "like a pig in shit". On that note I'm going to head back and grab a jumper. I'll catch you in a bit.'

It was starting to get chilly on board and I decided to ask Herman about his T-shirt.

'Ah, this,' he said, looking down at his chest. 'It's by a Swedish brand called Weekday. They do weekly prints to reflect the times. I'm not a slogan T-shirt wearer, but it's a conversation starter in so many ways.'

'I bet. Have you had any negative chats?'

Herman uncrossed his legs and took a deep breath. 'Not *nega-tive* negative. I've had discussions around it. I guess, right-wing people will go: "I'm not racist… but…" and I've had quite a few discussions with the "not-racist-but" people.'

'Do they assume your T-shirt is about them?'

'Yeah. Something like that. I am quite politically outspoken and I like having those conversations,' Herman said. 'And I think there are so many things in society that we need to be saying so that the world doesn't get fucked up. Most of the time bad people get to dictate, because normal people don't want to cause any trouble, but the bad ones will always want to talk and spread their opinion.'

I thought back to my afternoon with Simon Gronowski and his fears about the rise of the extreme right in Europe. 'It is frightening to see how emboldened people are now about their racism,' I said, aware that Assar was listening closely.

'In Sweden we have this right-wing government and they are building the power and they are free ruling. It's a battle now against proper UKIP right-wing, semi-Nazi people,' said Herman.

'He's very lucky,' I said, nodding up at Assar who was now playing *Minecraft*.

'How so?'

'To have a parent who is teaching him about racism.'

'It's important,' said Herman.

It was refreshing to hear and see how Herman was bring-ing up his child. More than anything I wished that white parents would teach their children about racism at a young age.

My heart sank when parents at the school gate would tell me: '*We don't want to expose them to anything awful before we need to.*'

'It's frustrating,' I told Herman. 'We have to teach our kids about the realities of racism from the minute they can talk. Racism starts so early that I wish white parents understood the need for allyship from day one… to teach their kids to stick up for their brown and Black friends and to not be part of the problem. But most don't bother because racism doesn't actually affect them or their kids. And then it's too late and round we go.'

I let out a long breath and felt something loosen in my chest. I was so tired of having stilted conversations with friends about race, that it was a huge relief to meet a stranger who had already got to grips with the task at hand.

'That's the thing about travelling,' Herman said. 'Being in different areas, it's good for Assar to see that people are just people.'

Assar looked sleepy so I thanked him and Herman for their time and company, and returned to our compartment to find Denny screaming with laughter with Wanjiku and Jules, a mother and son duo travelling by train from Prague to Stockholm. Wanjiku had been attending a conference in the Czech capital and Jules had wanted to fly home, but his mum had insisted they travel by train to give them some time to bond before he left home to study engineering at university.

'I wanted to talk to him properly about his decisions,' she said, as we drew into Hamburg and Jules got off the train to stretch his legs.

'And that's why he wanted to fly!' said Denny. Wanjiku wheezed with laughter and wiped tears as we watched Jules wind off through the crowd on the platform.

'He's not stretching his legs, that lad, he's flagging down a cab to the airport.'

Wanjiku and Denny had struck up conversation over their jobs, as she had founded a company that worked with marginalised children in Africa, helping them to rise out of poverty with vocational training schemes. Until he'd left his job, Denny had worked in social housing and the two were chatting away as I tucked into a microwaved bowl of meatballs and mash. Grudgingly or not, Jules found his way back on board and while the trio talked into the small hours, I took myself up to bed. I'd picked up a pair of earplugs in Berlin and, with a final glance out of the window to check I wasn't missing anything of note, I pressed them in and shuffled under my sheet as the train trembled over a bridge, lights scattered across the water.

The train had stopped. I sat up, plucking out my earplugs, and quietly jumped to the floor, which looked like an open bin, Denny's cans and empty tubes of Pringles rolling around. Checking my phone, I saw that it was 5 a.m. No one was up, every compartment door closed, as I nosed around for signs of life. Only a couple of breakfast boxes lay upside down in the corridor, jam splattered across the doorway, bread rolls strewn around after they'd fallen from a cupboard that was still swinging open. We'd paused at Malmö, not a soul on the platform, no other trains on the tracks. I pushed down the window and leaned out, the cold morning air stinging my eyes. It was only three days since we'd left Brussels yet I felt like I'd spent a month on the move.

First light warmed the sky, bringing with it the sense of hope that came with the newness of the day. I thought about my afternoon with Simon and his determination, in his nineties, to keep fighting against those who sought to hold others down. Then Herman, then Adrian and Hugo, pushing for climate-friendly travel and uniting with others to help them achieve their goal. Sometimes I worried that I operated inside an echo chamber, but I realised that there were people everywhere applying themselves to a greater good, you just had to ask them about it.

A short horn signalled that we were about to move. The sky was perfectly blue overhead, and as we set off along the canal and continued our journey towards Stockholm, I could tell it was going to be a beautiful day in the coastal city.

12

THE TRAIN TO THE MIDNIGHT SUN

Oslo was deserted. It was the second week of July when Marc and I drew into the Norwegian capital expecting to find noisy beer gardens, the streets filled with smoke from Go'Grilla food trucks and cyclists wobbling along the harbour promenade – but a ghost town awaited.

'Everyone leaves in July,' said Fredrik, a waiter at an empty bookshop café. 'Most people go to France or Italy or escape to their summer houses on the coast. For at least two or three weeks, it's dead here.'

In an ideal world I would have taken a train directly across to Oslo after my ride from Berlin to Stockholm, but the summer services were so popular that everything had been booked up until now. Besides, after our previous journey up to Narvik in the Arctic Circle, Marc was champing at the bit to accompany me again, because this time we would be travelling north under the gaze of the midnight sun. He had been to Oslo before, but this was my first time in the city and I was disappointed not to experience it at full throttle as we wandered around in search of a late lunch, stepping up to locked doors and tugging at the handles, peering inside to see stacked chairs and brooms leaning against the walls. To close down at the peak of summer seemed like suicide for the tourism industry, but considering that Norway's sovereign wealth fund had recently reported a record profit of $213 billion for the current year, its residents probably didn't care two hoots for cruise tourists moaning about shuttered microbreweries.

After finding little of interest in the city centre, we ended up at SALT, a nomadic art project built along the bay by the fjord. Styled on traditional coastal constructions, its wooden pyramids were strung with coloured bunting, and housed saunas, bars and hatches serving street food from truffle pizzas to globs of steamed gyoza. It overlooked the opera house and the Munch Museum – a huge, ugly building that towered like a metal slinky about to fall into the fjord. Wind skimmed across the water, and I zipped up my fleece, disappointed for the second time in an hour that it wasn't warmer. The sky was dreary, but a smattering of Norwegians were still out and about, mostly families with young children eating waffles in their buggies, ignored by parents sipping pints. I looked up at the sky again. In a few hours Marc and I would be bedding down on the Dovre railway, a 300-mile stretch from Oslo up to Trondheim. From there we would transfer onto the Nordland railway and ride the 500-mile line to Bodø – pronounced *boo-der* – just north of the Arctic Circle.

For several weeks, beginning in mid-May and ending mid-July, the sun doesn't set north of the Arctic Circle. Instead, it hovers above the horizon, offering no distinction between day and night. And in the luminescence of the landscape, Norwegians come out to play, biking between islands, kayaking across lakes, and hiking from one fishing village to the next, basking in the soft orange glow of 'night', with little care for the hands on the clock. Fascinated by the notion of 24-hour daylight and unable to conjure up an image, I wanted to take the night train to witness the natural phenomenon while on the move. Although 'night' train was technically an incorrect term for this sleeper service. The notion of moving around for days, in the absence of darkness, had an allure like nothing else. Over the previous few months I'd given much thought to my childhood aversion to darkness, when night wasn't a time for rest and recovery, only something to endure as I lay in bed, willing it to pass and for the comfort of day to return. But after staring into darkness night after night, adjusting my eyes to the movements of shadows and deciphering outlines, I was finding it easier to hold its gaze. All the same, the thought of spending the next few days navigating a constantly bright landscape was positively electrifying in its appeal.

Half an hour before the 11 p.m. departure, a short queue formed at the entrance to platform 4 at Oslo Central, where passengers in the sleeping carriages were checked in by a grandfatherly manager named Tor. Clean, with rubber flooring that squeaked, the twin compartment resembled a side room in a hospital ward, which was no bad thing. It was warm and smelled of detergent, with stark white bedding, a flannel folded on each pillow. The window was narrow, hopes of shuffling up to the glass dashed by a sink with a ledge that stuck out. One glance at the space and I knew that much of my time would be spent in the openness of the dining car. I was feeling out of sorts after a recent incident with a friend and needed to be around people, not stuck in here and ruminating.

The train groaned as it departed the station, thumping along walls covered with graffiti, bushes and vines. Ivy crept up the sides of apartment blocks and trees clustered between houses, an unusual proliferation of greenery for such a central location and one that hindered my ability to peer into people's homes. My brain was wired to expect dereliction as we sped through the outskirts of the city, but there was none. Veering east, the train ran through nothing but pristine neighbourhoods where the wealth revealed itself in the form of detached, multi-levelled houses, hot tubs on decking, and Teslas parked on driveways.

'This is where the oil money lives,' said Marc, pausing to admire the white timber properties as we sought out the dining car, the smell of frankfurters revealing the way.

The car was muggy. Two young women were sharing a bottle of chilled rosé, its surface sweating as much as they were. One by one they shrugged off cardigans and checked shirts until they sat in vests, rubbing damp necks and sharing stories of awful first dates, each worse than the one before. Pretending not to listen, I picked at a chocolate tart we'd bought at the station, giving silent thanks that I no longer had to negotiate the dating world, which sounded like an even greater hellscape of con artists and commitment-phobes than the one I'd left behind. At the table behind the young women sat an elderly couple sipping from bottles of Sol and reading their phones, their matching Merrell sandals touching under the table. They were the kind of couple I aspired to be like one day. A scuffle at the doorway drew my attention to dishevelled parents who had just boarded at the airport. Their twin toddlers were asleep in buggies, fat little feet bare in the heat. They were the kind of couple I was glad to no longer be: grey with exhaustion, snippy and weighed down by bags of nappies, toys and bottles. Looking round at the different stages of life, I sat back, exchanging a nod with a ginger-haired teenager reading in the corner.

'If it's okay with you I'm going to go meditate,' said Marc, 'then sleep I think.' We weren't far enough north to experience the ethereal skies, so Marc took himself off to bed. It was midnight and the young women retired too, stocking up on a second bottle of wine to see them through the ride. Their table now empty, I slid across to the right-hand side of the train for a better view of the Vorma river, which flowed alongside. The light had certainly dimmed, the clouds thinning to indigo ripples, but the sky above them cut through with snips of bright blue. On the horizon, a strip of orange refused to fade, eventually turning crimson and simmering for the next hour as I sank into my own meditation, my thoughts unravelling. Swathes of mist hovered above the river, a ghostly scene of lines and reflections, and I shuddered, watching it widen into Mjøsa, Norway's largest lake and one of its deepest. It appeared like a piece of silk in the gloam, outlines of the odd tiny fishing boat just visible on its surface. On most other nights this landscape would have withheld its secrets from my scrutiny, leaving my imagination to penetrate the space. But in the half-darkness I could see the curves of the shore, the forests kneeling at its banks, the homes trimming its edge. Mjøsa was alive and moving, its eeriness bewitching in the half-light.

Suddenly we braked into Hamar – a town filled with boutiques, Christmas trees and lavish apartments. No sooner had we arrived than we swept out again and I saw that people's outdoor spaces were furnished with futons, fairy lights and pot plants – not a washing line in sight. It was a far cry from the signs of cramped living in London, where every balcony was stacked with suitcases, bikes and boxes filled with junk. Tor, the train manager, was pottering around serving moose burgers, and I asked him if we might be able to chat when he had a moment.

'The train will next stop for four minutes,' he said. 'So I am afraid I have to eat my dinner then, but I will come back. The car is open throughout the night.'

At around 1 a.m. we pulled into the town of Brumunddal and my gaze settled upon a father bringing his son into the warmest embrace, having come to meet him on the platform. When they pulled apart, the father's palms clasping his face, I recognised the ginger-haired teen from the corner and glanced round to see that a tall man with a smooth, shaved head had taken his seat. A solo traveller, he was facing the window and in the reflection I could see he wore a thick goatee and an expression of contentment as the train moved off towards Lillehammer. Erik was a professor in medicine on his way to a conference at Tromsø, which sat on a splinter of island in the tip of the country. His was an extraordinary overland journey that would involve transferring onto the Nordland line at Trondheim and then disembarking at Fauske – forty minutes before Bodø – to take an eight-hour bus ride up to Tromsø. An avid fan of railways, Erik told me that Norwegians had a love–hate relationship with their trains. While Norway was home to some of the world's most spectacular routes, such as the Bergen and the Flåm lines, travellers were fed up with the constant closures, signalling failures and maintenance works that were always lagging behind, particularly in summer.

'I don't think most Norwegians realise it, but the night trains in Norway are very good,' he said. 'We have kept our night trains in a way that a lot of other countries haven't. The reason the day trains are slow is because we have challenging landscape. So that's why we don't have high-speed railways apart from between the airport and the capital. But when you're travelling on the night train it doesn't matter that the trip takes eight hours because you want eight hours to sleep.'

'And yet you're not sleeping?' I queried, checking the time on my phone.

Erik nodded. 'That's true, but I like the scenery. And in this region it's quite changing. You will have seen Mjøsa,' he said, tapping the window. 'If you happen to be awake, you will see people fishing early in the morning.'

We were nearing Lillehammer and the crowd was thinning.

'The valley from Lillehammer to the mountain top, that's called the Gudbrandsdalen or the Gudbrands valley; it's quite beautiful, but then you come up to the Dovrefjell and it's like a plateau and you can see the more spectacular mountaintops.' Erik took out his phone and showed me a video that he had taken in April of a herd of reindeer scattered around the snowy slopes on the Nordland line. He explained that they were owned and herded by the Indigenous Sámi people.

'Also – I don't know if you know – between Lillehammer and the highest point of the mountain top at Dovrefjell is the setting for the most famous classical piece of music written in Norway, about trolls living in the mountain, "Dovregubbens hall".'

'Trolls?' I frowned.

'*Gubbe*, that's the name for a conservative man and Dovre is the mountain, so he's living inside a hall in the mountain.'

'Oh, "In the Hall of the Mountain King"!' I said, looking at the woods whipping by the glass and thinking how the dynamics of Grieg's spooky composition were perfectly paired to the lie of the land.

'What other wildlife lives in this region?' I asked.

'The mountain is the only place in Norway where you get the musk ox,' said Erik. 'They used to be endemic in Norway but then they became extinct. They were reintroduced from Greenland in 1931. So they are now living in Dovre. You might see them from the train.' Erik waved his hands around his head. 'You would know if you saw it. It's like a massive cow with lots of hair. They have no natural enemies except humans, but the problem is that when the train approaches, they stand still. It's not uncommon that the train gets them.'

No wonder they'd become extinct.

The dining car had mostly cleared while we talked, Tor tipping out bottles and coffee cups as Erik recounted the history of the railway – which I found was a dark and bloody one. Of the two railways between Oslo and Trondheim, the first was built in the late 1800s and the second, through the valley, was built much later. It was only in the 1950s that the railway from Trondheim up to Bodø was constructed, an effort that was completed in segments until it opened in 1962. The project had been started before the Second World War, but it was the German Occupation that had ramped it up, an arduous task that involved going over Saltfjellet and into the valleys and fjords.

'The Germans used Soviet and Yugoslavian prisoners to build that railroad north of Mo i Rana,' said Erik. 'Slave labourers built both the railway over Saltfjellet and the road that accompanies it. It's called the "Blood Road" in Norwegian and that is some-thing that is not very well known outside Europe. The slaves were also building a railway from Fauske towards Narvik and Tromsø, but that part was never completed after the war. Today, only desolate tunnels exist as monuments to the many who died north of Fauske. I can't remember exactly how many died, but there were death camps,' said Erik. 'They were there to build the road and the railway and to die. There were a lot of executions and that's partly why it's called the Blood Road. It's a dark part of Norwegian history for the administration of the Norwegian state railways. They collaborated with the Germans during the war and organised the building of the railway over the moun-tains. The Norwegians were not innocent in facilitating that bit.'

The train crossed the Randklev Bridge at Ringebu, and as much as I wanted to stay awake to witness the first light, I was dying to sleep. I thanked Erik for his insights and wished him well with his onward journey, remarking that for all the tropes about Scandinavians being introverts and oddballs, they were chatty people once they got going.

'In Oslo you would never speak to anyone, but it's a different culture there,' he said. 'The further north you get it's easier to speak to people. They have had to survive doing different things in northern Norway. Life is more harsh in the north, with fishing and storms and threats from nature. Although, there are floods down here every year. We don't have to wonder about whether climate change is real. It's incredible that people pretend it isn't happening.'

Exactly four weeks after our conversation, the Randklev railway bridge slid into the Lågen river after Storm Hans swept across the country causing floods, landslides and mass evacuations. It would be nine months before the line would be fully running again.

Marc was fast asleep when I crept back into the compartment, and no wonder: the train was whispering along, not a jolt as I slid under the covers, marvelling at the smoothness of the ride. If only all sleeper trains were like this, they would fulfil the promise of delivering passengers refreshed and ready for the day instead of looking like we'd tumbled out the back of a bin lorry. I drew the curtain across the window then on second thoughts pulled it back. After my chat with Erik I was determined to wake before we entered the Dovre National Park.

———

Black coffee in hand, I stared into the waters of the Lågen – one of Norway's longest rivers – as it crashed through the Gudbrands valley. Like Christmas trees on stilts, pines trimmed its banks and a sandy islet rose up like a spine between the flow. The sky was baby blue now, soft light rising behind the hills, the clouds the colour of candy floss. Edging further towards the window, I could see a handful of people fly-fishing for trout, pike and perch, waders up to their thighs. Hikers appeared on a pathway and a group of cyclists glanced sideways as we swept by. My circadian rhythm going haywire, I looked down at my phone, which read 3.20 a.m. Was it even morning if night had never passed?

As Erik had described, we were descending into the Dovre National Park and I looked up in time to see a moose and her calves slipping through a hedgerow, startled by the train. Tor was still pottering around, cloth in hand, but he now had time to sit down on the edge of the table to describe the region's lynx, brown bear and elk. He'd been working on this route since 1997. His wife also worked on the railway, his younger daughter had recently joined and his elder daughter, a dentist, was currently on board with his baby grandson. He loved his job, in particular the night shifts when he was paid double and got to welcome all manner of passengers. I asked Tor about the Nordland line to come, and the precise point at which we would cross the Arctic Circle. He pulled out his official notes and ran a finger down.

'At 6.29 a.m. you need to be awake,' he said, smiling over a pair of smart Hugo Boss glasses. 'After passing the Dunderland Valley you are entering the Arctic Circle.'

By 5.30 a.m. the sky had deepened to a china blue, forests of spruce braced against slants of sunlight. Surrounded by meadows filled with buttery yellow flowers, the train swung wide to greet the Gaula river, where mist drifted like smoke. On less than two hours of sleep and with a headache circling one eye, I was beginning to wonder if constant light was such a blessing after all, and had almost forgotten Marc was on board until he appeared with his camera, annoyingly bright-eyed and ready to explore Trondheim.

We drew into the station and disembarked, the coastal freshness shocking me awake as we crossed the bridge over the Nid river which looped around the city. On first impressions Trondheim was awash with Scandi charm: the promenade was an eye-catching strip of six-storey buildings stretched out like a Dulux colour palette. Tethered sailboats rocked in the foreground. The city was soundless, but for the lap of water against decking.

There were no cars as we walked up the middle of the street, taking in the pastel-coloured fronts of shops and cafés that were yet to open. Known as Norway's original Viking capital,

Trondheim was a historic city dating back to 997, but cathedrals and Vikings aside, it was also known as the food capital of Norway – with three Michelin-starred restaurants – a key reason why we were breaking up the journey with a night's stay. Less than a ten-minute journey on foot, we arrived outside our hotel. Opened in 1870, the Britannia had been established with an unusually specific goal: to attract upper-class Englishmen and their angling skills to Norwegian rivers in the 1820s. Known as the Salmon Lords ('Lakselorder'), these posh boys brought with them the techniques of fly-fishing, which triggered the construction of a string of luxury hotels to encourage others to the Trøndelag region, home to some of the densest populations of salmon in the country.

A grand hotel with wonderful beds and a spa, the Britannia was an indulgence between two sleeper trains. After a power nap and a shower, we went down to find what resembled a wedding feast. Championed as one of the best in Norway, the breakfast buffet at the Palmehaven restaurant was a banquet of fluffy scrambled eggs, curls of shrimp in dill, and bowls of freshly pounded pesto. Cast-iron pots sizzled with shiitake sausage, and cartoonish rounds of local cheese sat on tiered cake stands alongside rumpled slabs of Brie.

With two full days to eat, roam and catch up on gossip in the hotel's sauna, Marc and I embarked upon the Midtbyrunden after breakfast, a four-mile trail around the city, following the bends of the Trondheim Fjord and the Nid. As we ambled across bridges, pausing to watch bathers yelp in the waters' chill, I could sense Marc was wrestling with something. He had been oddly quiet, meditating more often than usual. He had an opinion on everything, never afraid to share it, so I knew something was up. Eventually he told me about a longstanding friendship that was taking its toll, coming to a head with an exchange of emails. Chatting as we walked, he recounted the exchanges, watching my expression for validation as wet retrievers trotted around us. We were now a people who suffered from modern-day problems of communication. The irony was that it came down to the myriad forms of messaging available: texts, emails, WhatsApp, Instagram and Twitter to name a few. Relationships now hinged on guessing and assuming, scrolling likes, checking for read receipts, and the dreaded 'seen' that hovered without a response. Conversations in person had been replaced. We were left to infer intent, ruminate over replies, take offence to tone, and understand each other less instead of more.

Like Oslo, Trondheim had switched to summer mode and its Michelin-starred restaurants were closed, but there was no shortage of independent cafés with burly-armed chefs serving produce from the surrounding farms and orchards. Ice creams in hand, we slowed through the wharf neighbourhood of Bakklandet, where shops sold cashmere blankets, coffee and artisan soaps that cost a week's wage. Day drinkers played chess on barrels while others read in the sun. The timber houses looked empty, their walls concealed by blood-red rose bushes. I stopped to rub the petals, then unloaded my own woes. Someone I'd thought was a dear friend had recently let me down with what my gut knew was the most fantastic lie. We'd arranged to meet up, only he hadn't shown up, claiming he'd been rear-ended en route. He then went silent, dodging messages. At the time I'd been too nervous to unpick it or question it, afraid of confronting the reality that our friendship was over and wanting to ask why. But on the train I'd had time to reflect, unable to think of much else and I needed Marc's advice. We both practised Vipassana, he far more than me – sometimes sitting in silence for up to twenty days at a time – and I often felt like I was travelling with my personal Yoda.

As we walked along counselling one another, I looked around at the friends grouped on benches, dads closing their eyes against the warmth of the sun, and kids screaming with joy in the water. Couples nuzzled into each other's necks and my mood lifted. The scene embodied the Norwegian concept of *koselig*. Similar to the Danish *hygge, koselig* conveys the idea of togetherness and wellbeing that comes from nature and the simple things in life, and I felt consoled by the reminder that it lay all around us if we only chose to see it.

At 11 p.m. we were on the platform, ready for the ride up the Nordland line to Bodø. Above the horizon, the sun looked poised to sink, its body quivering as I stared into the yellows spreading across the sky. Faces warmed by the glow, passengers were basking in the radiance as though solar-powered. Summer was when Norwegians used trains the most and the sleeper carriages were full when I'd attempted to book our berths. I had, however, managed to secure seats in Premium Pluss class, where seats recline up to forty-five degrees and passengers are provided with blankets, pillows, breakfast – and unlimited hot drinks.

'Not got a berth this time?' said Marc, smiling towards the light. I noticed everyone around me was doing it, whether consciously or not, and I wondered if their Nordic constitution was somehow programmed to absorb vitamin D whenever they had the chance.

'Nope, it's an upright ride, I'm afraid,' I said, as the train appeared up the tracks.

There was nothing to be afraid of. It was the cosiest carriage and, to our excitement, Tor was in attendance again. He darted over, stepping around like a game-show host as he demonstrated how to adjust the electric foot rests, side tables and reading lights. The seats were enormous and it didn't take long for passengers to settle in, pull on bed socks and snuggle against their travelling companions. We were perfectly positioned at the tail end of the train and Tor beckoned us over to observe the tracks snaking behind. The Trondheim Fjord ran parallel, its waters the same colour as the sky's molten pinks and golds. A sense of in-betweenness got under my skin as I balanced across two carriages, watching the day not turn into night, the train running over land then water, water then land.

It was bedtime on board and Marc was preparing to meditate. Fifteen years of travelling by train together meant that we were finely tuned to each other's moods. He gave me a sideways glance.

'How you feeling about everything?' he asked as I sat down beside him with a sigh.

'I don't know. I think I need to get answers before I get closure. It's pretty raw and painful.'

'The closure comes from you,' he said, placing his headphones around his neck.

'Hmm, maybe if I sat in silence for twenty days it would… but I… just need to know.'

As the carriage lights dimmed, I looked out to where the fjord was playing hide-and-seek with the forest. A twinkle here, a shimmer there, it appeared then vanished, fields closing in then giving way to the waters once again.

'Remember that everything we've ever done has brought us to where we are now. We're supposed to be at this point. You and I were supposed to meet on the train in India. You and your friend are supposed to be at this juncture.'

From between the seats I watched a mother squeeze her young son's hand as he slept, the reading light shining on the roundness of his cheeks.

'Just sit with it,' he said. 'Pain can be a great teacher if we allow it to be. You've got all night, that's what these train rides are for. Your body will tell you what you need to know.'

With that he gave my shoulder a rub and leaned his head back, closing his eyes. I turned back to the window, the reflection of an iPad lighting up the glass. The houses were isolated, never in clusters or rows, but standing alone atop slopes or in the middle of woods. A herd of roe deer appeared, their fluffy white rears bobbing about in the twilight. Pulling out of Levanger station, the train ran obscenely close to the town, allowing me to see the pinboard in a taxi office, a dinner party on a balcony, a couple kissing on a sofa… and then nothing but woods. I stared into them and found myself back at the moment when my friend had texted to say he wasn't going to make it. Again,

I felt the nausea rise, my stomach fall away, the dampness in my palms. It hurt. My chest hurt. The murmur of the train sounded in my ears as I sat back and observed the pain taking hold.

———

The Nordland line crosses 293 bridges and runs through 154 tunnels, most of which I missed as I slept, waking at 4.30 a.m. to the sight of the Ranfjorden, its green waters bubbling with minerals and foam. Throwing off my blanket, I sat up and peered between its forested banks to where fingers of snow still crept down the mountains. Passengers were stirring, checking the time before turning over and going back to sleep. Determined to stay awake I fetched coffee and pulled out my book. Since Sweden, I'd become fascinated by Scandi literature and was almost at the end of *The Ice Palace* by Tarjei Vesaas, a slim but spellbinding novel set around the fjords as winter turns to spring. It was a deeply visceral and beautiful book about two young girls which explored, rather aptly, electric connections, friendship and grief.

'All good?' Marc was awake, and I nodded. The pain had lessened and I was now feeling lighter as the spirit of the new day took hold. He joined me to take up residence in the dining car, passing the family carriage on our way. It had a designated play area with building blocks, wooden xylophones and cubby holes in which to hide. A passenger was asleep there, stretched out across the seating beneath a mural of a little girl with a dragonfly perched on her shoulder.

Around us lay the Helgeland region, a salty, muddy scent entering through an open window. From on high it appeared like a jigsaw of river rapids, woods and slender beaches. The train was ascending and I looked down to where water tumbled over boulders, and patches of forest appeared on islets in lakes. Peaks rose in the distance, red cabins were tucked into the crevices and the morning light deepened, enriching the wilderness with warmth and colour. A bearded passenger in his thirties entered and sat down across from us.

'Isn't that the dude from the kids' carriage?' Marc whispered, as the man retied his pony tail and pulled both knees up against his chest. Determined to enquire about his odd sleeping arrangements, I struck up conversation with Ludwig. Originally from Stockholm, he was a chief mate for the coastguard and had been living in Tromsø for the past ten years. Like Erik he was getting off at Fauske where he would take a six-hour bus to Narvik followed by a four-hour ride up to Tromsø. For the last fifteen years Ludwig had given up flying unless it was mandatory. I asked him why and he gave a frustrated snort as though talking to a moron.

'When you see what's happening to the world – and I've seen it for a while now – I try to do my part and show people that you can do it if you want to. It's also really fun,' he said, breaking into a comical laugh that sounded like he was panting. 'One time I met this guy and he was an alcoholic, he really liked his drink and we shared a cabin. He didn't want to drink alone so he passed me beer and he had moonshine with him as well. He was a hunter-gatherer and he had a lot of reindeer as well... hearts.'

'Hearts?'

'Yah, he had a lot of meat, when you cure and ferment it?' Ludwig cupped his hands together. 'He gave me two reindeer hearts. It's really expensive food. But he just gave it to me because we had a lovely time together.'

'No one really gives you hearts on planes,' said Marc, from the next table. 'Just aggro.'

Ludwig started laughing again. His eyebrows turned up at the ends, giving him an intense look of concentration, but he found everything funny and had a lovely aura about him. For the most part Ludwig's adventures had centred on finding drinking buddies on board and carrying luggage for old ladies who gave him wine. 'I met some hooligans as well, they gave me beer.'

As a commuter, Ludwig had taken this route at least twenty times. In his opinion spring was one of the best times of year to travel for the scenery, revealing a wintry landscape on the brink of thaw; but autumn was also ideal for passengers wanting to see the Northern Lights, which he had witnessed once from the train.

'We have three months of summer now in Tromsø and you can have adventures around the clock: people are hiking, sailing, and you can still ski if you climb up to the glaciers,' he said. 'And then we have three months of total darkness.'

'I love winter,' said Marc. 'It's such a great time to be creative. It gives you the time to do things.'

'I hate it,' I said. 'It's so depressing doing the school run in the dark, not being able to take the kids to the park 'cos it's bloody raining all the time.'

'It's such a British thing, to moan about the cold every year when it comes round. We live in Britain, we know it's wet and cold. Why we moaning about it like it's something new?'

The mere thought of ninety days without sunlight was enough to have me reaching for Citalopram. But to my surprise, Norwegians living through polar nights didn't present with heightened symptoms of depression. It was a misconception and other than reports of slightly disturbed sleep, their moods and wellbeing barely wavered throughout the year. An American health psychologist, Kari Leibowitz, had conducted a year-long study in Tromsø which found that mindsets about winter were associated with wintertime wellbeing. More broadly, ten years of her research had found that the mental framing of seemingly stressful events had a powerful influence on how they affected people. Those who chose to perceive the situation as a challenge, with an opportunity to learn and adapt, coped better than those who chose to dwell on the more fearful aspects of it. Looking forward to the darkness as a time to catch up with friends in cafés, bake with children or be creative – as Marc had argued – was the way to turn the negativity on its head. Leibowitz also noted that mindsets don't just affect mood, but can also influence the body's response, such as changes in blood pressure and heart rate.

Around half an hour after passing Mo i Rana, I checked the time on my phone; it was 6.35 a.m. and I remembered Tor telling me that it was around this point that we would be crossing the Arctic Circle. It didn't look much different, but I felt like we were entering a new dimension. The three of us watched the scenery for a few moments before Ludwig spoke up again.

'The winter is long and it is dark, but we have a really nice twilight for four hours every day, it's pink and orange and you have the Northern Lights as well.'

'All the time?' I asked, sitting up.

'Most of the time,' Ludwig shrugged. 'It is special I suppose.' He looked thoughtful for a moment. 'We have this expression: *hemmablind*. It's a Swedish word, it's like "home blindness". You don't have it in English? It means when you stop noticing the beauty of something where you live.'

I couldn't imagine what was naturally so beautiful in the UK that I'd become used to it, but perhaps that was Ludwig's point.

The train approached the final two hours of its journey, and we arced around the Saltfjorden, its green waters lapping on rocky beaches where families were drying off in the sun. It was a clear summer morning, and a number of passengers were arriving for breakfast looking tidy and well-slept. Given that Ludwig was a seasoned train-traveller, I was curious as to why he hadn't booked himself a berth.

'We saw you napping in that play area,' I began.

'Yah! It was very comfortable,' he said, looking sheepish. 'Everyone in Norway has the time to travel in summer, so it gets very booked up. It's impossible to get a sleeper compartment because you can't just buy one, you have to buy both the berths.'

'Why is that? Is it for safety?'

'I think so. But a lot of people don't actually mind sharing with each other.'

Ludwig took out his phone and opened up the page of a Norwegian Facebook group called: 'Dele kupé på NSB', which had almost 9,000 members. It was a place where passengers could post their dates of travel and see if anyone was willing to buddy up.

'Still, I couldn't get one,' he said, glancing up in a panic as he saw we were drawing into Fauske.

Waving Ludwig off, we embarked upon the final stretch. In the last few minutes I tried to take it all in: the floral patterns on kitchen curtains, the deer skipping across fields, the church spire receiving a new lick of paint. And then it was over.

At 9 a.m. we pulled into Bodø and the train emptied along with stacks of fishing gear, mountain bikes and an extraordinary number of dogs, pleased to stretch their legs and pee. Much like Narvik, Bodø felt like a junction town for travellers wanting to sail to the Lofoten Islands, hike the glacier at Svartisen, or scuba dive at Saltsraumen, the world's strongest maelstrom. But this time Marc and I were content to embrace the concept of *koselig* and take pleasure in the little things by walking the marina, people-watching and sitting around in parks. That evening we sought out Lystpå, a fine-dining restaurant lacking stuffy airs and graces. By the time I was dipping homemade donuts into crème brûlée, a familiar orange glow had begun to sweep across my eyeline and heat the tops of my forehead. There was no simpler pleasure than smiling into the warmth of the sun and I knew that a short drive away was Keiservarden, one of Bodø's most popular hiking destinations. But hiking at 11 p.m. seemed like madness.

'There's no better time, it's when everybody goes,' said the restaurant owner as he cleared our table.

From the bottom of Veten hill, I could already see the skies were burning as though the horizon had gone up in flames. Runners overtook me in gusts of heat and sweat, and young children skipped over tree roots, carrying sticks and leaves from their hike. Marc had gone ahead, disappearing sideways through long grass that swished as he pushed his way into the undergrowth, twigs cracking underfoot. I kept to the path, reaching for the odd birch tree, the bark smooth like raw silk. To encourage people to take the trail, the path had been upgraded and paved by Nepali sherpas. The stones protected the terrain, making it easier to hop from one step to the next. I made my way up, ferns rubbing softly against my arms as I picked my way higher, suddenly aware that it was late and I was alone, with a total absence of fear.

My nose ran as I reached the top of the mountain plateau, my hair spiralling into salty knots. The wind whipped hard, my trousers flapping against my legs as I watched the outlines of Landegode island sinking into waters of liquid gold. It was midnight and the sun had come to rest on the horizon, the grass, rocks and clouds bathed in a rosy glow. Marc was quiet, staring into the light.

'I'm going to sit for a bit and meditate,' he said, dropping his bags and finding a soft patch of grass. 'Why don't you join me?'

Most people had left and I did a circuit of the summit before squatting down on a tuft of grass nearby. At its core, Vipassana teaches that everything in life arises to disappear and I realised that I no longer felt the intense pain I'd had at the start of the journey in Oslo. All I felt was the roughness of the grass, the cold ground against my legs and the presence of Marc a few metres away, a figure who represented honesty, safety and positivity – everything my former friend did not. Together we watched as the sun threatened to sink, then shifted sideways, casting rays out and over the island's silhouette. At 1 a.m. we stood up to leave. Throwing one last look at the sky, we turned to descend as the sun began to rise.

13

The Shalimar Express

Sandals slapped the ground as passengers leaped off, the train still sailing up the platform at Jodhpur Junction. Delighted, I peered from the barred windows, watching the same people now ambling along. As trains drew into stations the routine was always the same and I relished watching the familiar scene unfold. Passengers piled into the vestibule and crowded into the open doorway. Each one would lightly touch the wrist of the stranger in front or place a single finger in their lower back. These gestures were designed to goad with gentleness, but designed to goad all the same. At the first squeal of brakes, those in the doorway would jump off as though a fire burned under their feet, only to stand about on the platform sipping tea. Ever happy to go with the flow, I had no reservations about following local customs, but hurling myself from a moving train was not on my bucket list and I now searched under the seat for my trainers as the train jerked to a halt.

In 2010 I lost my heart to Indian Railways and being back on these clanking, dusty rails felt like a homecoming. With nothing but a withering rail pass, an outdated map and hopeless naivety, I'd spent four months travelling 25,000 miles – the circumference of the earth – reaching the four points of the country's geographical diamond. When I'd arrived in India, the trains were simply a means to an end, a cheap and cheerful way for me to get around the country with ease. But in between hanging from doorways, squatting on carriage steps and snoozing in vestibules on stacked-up bags of laundry, I'd realised that the railways were a microcosm of Indian society. Being on board the trains brought me face to face with everyone from diplomats to dabbawalas, and by the end of my adventure around India in eighty trains, I realised that the trains were the hero of my story: the lifeblood that kept the country's heart beating. There was nowhere like it on earth.

Of course, India was where I'd met Marc, on board a train. Now he was gathering his bags behind me, thrilled to be back in the homeland. Boarding at Jaipur that morning, we'd arrived at Jodhpur in Rajasthan. It was a couple of months after our journey into Norway's midnight sun, and we were on assignment for a magazine in honour of the 170th anniversary of Indian Railways. We'd finished a week-long trip from Bombay down the Konkan coast to Goa, travelling there on my favourite train in the world, the *Mandovi Express*, and we were now in Jodhpur to take another day train up to Jaisalmer then transfer to Delhi on the *Shalimar Express*, a sleeper service. Indian Railways had come a long way since I'd last travelled here, introducing bullet trains and electrifying almost all of its 42,000 miles of track. But I was sceptical about how much the new services catered to the average Indian traveller, most of whom couldn't afford the cost of high-speed rail. Instead of testing out what I suspected were vanity projects, I was curious to see the state of the clanking old sleepers.

I'd passed through Rajasthan on several occasions but had never spent more than a day in this princely state. Owing to niggly train timetables, I'd found barely enough time on my last visit to whip around Jodhpur's spice market, stocking up on cloth pouches of pepper and Himalayan salt that sparkled like chunks of rose quartz. I'd then hung around the rooftop of a heritage hotel, eating laal maans, smoking cinnamon beedis and – with the arrogance of youth – failing to see anything within the blue-walled city. The time had come to rectify that.

———

Mahaveer Singh arrived wearing a beret and a waistcoat embroidered with roses. A pair of black jodhpurs puffed around his thighs, tight from the knee to the ankle, but it was his footwear that set off the debonair outfit. The toes pointing upwards, his juttis were covered in suede leopard print. Of all the guides I'd ever come across, Mahaveer out-dappered them all with ease. We were now in Jodhpur's Old Town, which lay around the foothills of the Mehrangarh Fort. A jumble of indigo houses shaped like cubes, it looked as though someone had shaken a bag of blue dice and rolled them down the slopes where they'd scattered, coming to rest at different heights. Having only ever skirted the edges of the technicolour layout, I followed Mahaveer, who set off down an alley no more than four-people wide. Marc was somewhere behind, having stopped to scratch a one-eyed puppy and Jamie was slapping sun cream on his forehead, readjusting his trilby. Jamie and I had last seen each other in Türkiye. After I'd returned to London he'd carried on by bus to Tbilisi and then gone in search of a famous chonky cat in Poland. He'd found his way across to Nepal to interview a king-cobra catcher and had been working solo there for the previous four weeks. On hearing Marc and I were in India, he'd dropped me a line admitting that he was starting to feel lonely and suggesting we all 'catch up on the tracks', arriving the previous evening for a railway reunion.

Sweat beaded my upper lip as I hovered in the shadows, trying to avoid the wrath of the midday sun. Jodhpur was deemed the gateway to the Thar desert and the air throbbed with heat, so much so I swore I could hear it. Like a whisper. Steadying myself through passages, I placed my palms against each side, the walls cold, the blue paint electric between my fingers. Up close it had the patchy effect of watercolour, nothing neat or precise about the effort, pieces flaking off to reveal sandstone underneath.

'I'm amazed I haven't been bitten yet,' I said, expecting to be covered in welts by the day's end.

'The foul smell of indigo keeps mosquitoes away,' Mahaveer replied.

'How so?' I asked, stopping to admire a fresco. It featured a Rajasthani woman sitting on a swing that hung from a tree, peacocks and parrots in its branches.

'Indigo is a herbal plant that produces the pigment,' he said, rubbing the nearest wall. 'And the name comes from the Greek word *indikon* which means "from India".' At that moment, I felt the same satisfaction as when I'd learned 'dungarees' originated from the coarse fabric manufactured in the textile mills of a town called Dongri, north of Bombay. Sanjeev Bhaskar and company weren't wrong. Everything really was Indian.

A single moped put-putted round the corner and Mahaveer steered us to one side, his deep voice carrying over the engine. In the past the city had been largely inhabited by members of the Brahmin caste, he said, who painted the houses blue to distinguish themselves from lower castes and to keep the heat at bay. However, the neighbourhood was now much more diverse, the residents sitting in circles, playing cards in the shade of an old banyan tree.

There was a strong sense of community and trust here, peppermint shutters and front doors left open, the aroma of pan-fried paratha drifting out of kitchens. Solitary walkers stopped to clean and dress deities wrapped in silk, and stray dogs were granted shade on private porches. Every now and again I heard the gurgle of fat pigeons, looking up to see them tucked into cubby holes, their feathers ruffling at our presence. Sometimes it was the *chip-chip-chip* of palm squirrels hurrying along walls painted mauve or turquoise. Other than the sudden clang of Hindi dramas playing out of darkened living rooms, it was peaceful. From the shade of an archway, I observed a Marwari woman sifting rice, framed by a doorway carved with foliage. She wore a marigold sari, the pallu pulled over her head, as though painted into the scene. Marc raised his camera and she turned slightly, giving him a curious smile then going back to sifting rice.

Convinced we'd wound back on ourselves, I saw we'd arrived at an unfamiliar junction. One wall was decorated with a series of painted Coca-Cola bottles that had been cut in half and filled with carnations. Mahaveer stopped.

'I am going to show you one of the best views of Jodhpur,' he said, leading us up a staircase so steep it had to be taken sideways.

Shoes kicked off, we entered a home that smelled of ginger and cardamom. The low wooden furniture and slow-turning fans reminded me of my grandparents' old flat in Madras, and I warmed instantly to the grey-haired owner, Chandrakala, whose husband – a colleague of Mahaveer – had died during the pandemic. Her son had moved away and her daughter had got married and left, so she'd opened up her home to offer masala tea to visitors along with access to her terrace. My feet burning, cup in hand, I darted across the stones to Marc, who was lingering in the shade of a bedsheet, his hair slicked to his neck. Together, we took in the panorama of packed homes, the fort rising in the background like a butte of the Grand Canyon.

'Actually, the most beautiful viewpoint of the city is on that hill,' said Mahaveer, pointing to a sandstone stack opposite the fort. 'But they have stopped allowing visitors to go there. There was a Chinese guest here and he was busy with his photography and he slipped.'

Stairs ran up the outside walls of most houses, flags fluttered in the breeze and pot plants lined the balconies. Looking down, I could see now that not all the buildings were painted in the signature shade, a handful of peach- and mustard-hued havelis were wedged in between, their latticed windows setting them apart. Saris flapped on washing lines, their mirrorwork flashing in the sun, and a storm of lemon emigrant butterflies blew around like snowflakes. The Dhuhr call to prayer began, a soulful call that gave me pause. Even as an atheist I could feel the significance of the reverberations and the way the call calmed my thoughts.

'It's very quiet here,' I said after a few minutes. 'What do people do?'

Mahaveer raised a different finger for each point. 'They play cards, they gossip, they know everyone. They feel safe, they don't want to move anywhere else. Their children get married and go to the big cities, but they will stay.'

'And how about you?' Marc asked, as we regrouped on the street.

'Me? I'm born around Jodhpur, never left Jodhpur, never feel like leaving Jodhpur,' Mahaveer said, smiling beneath his moustache and guiding us onto a main road that suddenly appeared, throwing off my wavering sense of direction. I could no longer resist and squinted at Mahaveer, shading my eyes.

'Can I ask about your moustache? It's very typical to Rajasthan.'

Mahaveer gave the end a little tweak. 'If we go deep into mythology, then only a few Hindu gods were depicted with moustaches as they might look impure. But when the caste system seeped into the Indian subcontinent then the moustache became a symbol of purity for many of the upper castes. In this kingdom moustaches are seen as a symbol of masculinity and strength as a cultural significance.'

'That is a very masculine moustache,' Marc said.

'I am from a warrior clan and the moustache is an essential part,' said Mahaveer, stopping outside a shop where packets of popcorn, crisps and namkeen hung in strips, like a savoury curtain. 'If today I try to shave my moustache on fashion grounds my father will give me such a good thrashing. I will shave my moustache only once in a lifetime and that will be the day when my father will leave this world for eternity.'

Outside the Old Town, the regular noise of cycle bells and horns was coming back into play as we walked towards Sardar Market, dodging auto-rickshaws crowded with school children.

'Come this way, I will show you your Omelette Man,' said Mahaveer, pulling out a pair of sunglasses from his breast pocket.

Despite an iffy tummy from an ill-advised box of train rice, I had asked Mahaveer to help me track down a street vendor known simply as the 'Omelette Man'. The more I travelled, the more I realised that my needs were few and basic. Warm weather, a comfortable bed – maybe a temple or two – and fine cooking. Standout food could mean the difference between returning to a city or drawing a line straight through it. Certain meals were seared into my memory. I could still taste the buttery flesh of the fish amok at Chanrey Tree in Siem Reap, the wobble of bone marrow at Arzak in San Sebastián, and the crunch of gai lan in the basement of the now-defunct Daimaru shopping centre in Singapore. Little could divulge as much about a people as observing their predilection for food, preparation – and consumption. From the dhabas in Bombay and truck stops in Kerala to the bylanes of the Jama Masjid in Delhi, Indian food would take a lifetime to discover. Parsi surnames, like Peppermintwala, often denoted the snacks their ancestors hawked. Delhi's street grills were aflame at midnight, and guests judged weddings by the catering. In a country where 'Have you eaten?' was a common greeting, it was safe to assume that food was life.

Since we'd begun our walk, I'd lost at least half my body weight through sweat and was famished, longing to find the vendor I'd read about on blogs. In spite of the odd rumble and twinge from my gut, I followed Mahaveer as he entered the gate by Shri Mishrilal Hotel where customers queued up for glasses of creamy makhaniya lassi. A splendid clock tower stood like a sentinel in the centre of the bazaar, one of the least aggressive markets I'd come across, and I hung back watching young Indian women haggle for leather handbags as Jamie disappeared to buy trousers. Mopeds beeped around shoppers and cloth merchants called out to no one in particular, their scarves, shawls and throws vibrant with vegetable dyes. Onions rolled out of sacks, ancient scales banged under the weight of potatoes, and cyclists stopped to sip clay cups of tea, their friends riding side-saddle in flip-flops.

The Omelette Man was on the opposite side from where we'd entered, surrounded by towers of eggs. From the signs beneath the awning, his stall was also a one-stop shop for sim cards, memory cards, cigarettes, USB sticks, camel safaris and 'flying fox' – which I'd assumed was some kind of wildlife tour, but turned out to be a ziplining experience over Mehrangarh Fort.

Ghanshyam Gawlani, the Omelette Man, was sitting on a stool when we turned up. He jumped up, slapped a towel across a cast iron pan and lit the flame, which roared as he whipped eggs, dipping a teaspoon into mismatching pots of cumin, chilli powder and salt, shaking, flipping then folding over the fluffy mass, laying it between two squares of sweet bread. Set up by his father, Ram Kishan, in 1974, the shop was mostly manned by Ghanshyam who cracked more than a thousand eggs a day. I bit into the sandwich, feeling the instant gratification of hot Amul cheese oozing from the sides with a burst of green chilli and onion. Omelette sandwiches are an Indian street-food staple, usually known as 'bread omelette', a healthy, grab-and-go snack, but the stall represented more than that. It was an excellent spot for exchanging gossip, a valid reason to duck out of work for a bit, and a unifying force. For the vendors, their snacks marked out the identity of a region, sustaining the flow of local suppliers, showcasing ingredients and ensuring that the origins and stories of families and their recipes would stand the test of time, as high-end restaurants embraced fusion food, tailoring classics to modern tastes. Gone in four bites, my sandwich was one of sixteen variations on offer and I ordered two more to go before a crowd of young and old began to gather.

'Manforce?' I stopped beneath an advertising hoarding and looked up at the image of a woman in a tight dress next to a box of super-thin condoms. *'Feel Nothing But Extreme Pleasure.'*

'Doesn't sound pleasurable,' said Marc.

'Jesus, Manforce is so...'

'Brutal?' Marc offered.

'Yes!' I said, stepping back for a better look. We were on the platform at Jodhpur Junction waiting for the train to Jaisalmer. While it was a relief to see safe sex being promoted in a notoriously prudish country, the choice of Manforce as a brand name gave me the ick.

'Force sounds so... violent,' I said, wincing.

'Or macho?' said Marc. 'You're probably not the target audience. Some young, virile dude in tight jeans is probably who they're appealing to.' He looked up at the woman again. 'Isn't she a porn star?'

'How would I know? Actually, I think it's Sunny Leone.'

'Well, then you're definitely not the target audience,' Marc started laughing. 'But I know who is.'

'And what's going on over here?' I wondered out loud, walking round to the front of a huge pink vending machine.

'I could do with a bag of crisps,' Marc said, coming to stand next to me. 'Oh no, that's not crisps.'

To my amazement, we were face to face with a Femikare machine, vending sanitary towels. And not just one type, but at least eight different ones.

'That is quite amazing,' said Marc.

'Isn't it? It's not even hidden in the toilets; it's bang in the middle of the platform for anyone to use.'

The machine had been installed at the beginning of 2022, a handful of other stations around Rajasthan receiving their own machines in an attempt to make life more comfortable for women travellers. India had a long way to go to achieve a just and equitable society for women, who faced gender discrimination, endemic violence and abuse, particularly in rural areas. The presence of this machine was a glimmer of hope that women's needs were slowly being addressed.

Our train to Jaisalmer was due and we were back to being a twosome. Jamie had gone to the tailor to collect his new trousers, deciding to join us by road. Taking advantage, we'd offloaded our backpacks and sent them along with the driver, freeing us up to stroll about inspecting the station, which had a book stall and a pharmacy selling everything from nappies and Vicks inhalers to Dettol and packets of bourbons. The main hall was painted with murals of desert life, labourers leading camels, and courtesans dancing for kings, which were best observed while lying down on the floor alongside waiting passengers, their heads propped up on bags.

'It's so clean,' said Marc, looking around. I stopped and did an about-turn. Not a sweet wrapper in sight.

'Possibly the cleanest Indian station I've ever seen in my life,' I said, veering off to peer over the platform edge. 'No paan stains, no rotting fruit.'

'No crows pecking about piles of rice,' said Marc.

On my last visit this was certainly not the case. Train tracks were characteristically filled with empty bottles of Bisleri water, carrier bags and shoes, a goat or two chewing up paper packets. After talking to a few passengers on the platform, I discovered that Jodhpur Junction often received accolades for its cleanliness. Toilets had been built in the parking lot and staff were armed with whistles to blow at miscreants who dropped litter. Nearly 150 workers were on site, working in shifts to maintain top levels of sanitation with the help of machines, and each worker was assigned a particular spot to take pride in. They were currently being briefed, sitting cross-legged in two lines. The women were dressed in tulip-red saris trimmed with gold borders, the men in indigo shirts trimmed with the same gold. All were wearing protective face masks. An impressive set-up.

'I wonder what's changed?' Marc said.

Above the workers hung a poster saying 'One Station One Product', featuring an unsmiling bearded man wearing a sleeveless jacket.

'Modi,' I replied as the train drew into the station.

When Prime Minister Narendra Modi came to power in 2014 he launched the Swachh Bharat Mission, a national movement designed to bring about a cultural and societal shift in attitudes towards cleanliness and hygiene, with the key objective to end open defecation within five years. The government posted videos of the PM sweeping, and invited the nation to join in under the hashtag #mycleanindia. Although much had improved, the government had failed to meet its targets. When placed under scrutiny it presented misleading data about the number of new toilets being built, with rural areas and lower-caste workers bearing the brunt of the shortfall. I couldn't speak for 1.4 billion people, but as the special service drew out of Jodhpur Junction and began to clatter through villages, I noticed an undeniable change in the landscape, which was free from the usual mountain range of waste, wound through by rivers of open sewage.

My own misgivings about Modi had roots in darker ground. His rise to power had seen his Bharatiya Janata Party (BJP) pursue a right-wing religious nationalist agenda which was in conflict with India's secular origins. He was increasingly accused of rhetoric and policies that targeted and discriminated against India's 200 million Muslims, the largest minority group. What cemented Muslim fears about Modi were the Gujarat riots in 2002, when he was the state's chief minister. In February that year the *Sabarmati Express*, carrying Hindu pilgrims from Ayodhya to Ahmedabad, was set alight near Godhra. Four carriages went up in flames, killing fifty-nine people.

Numerous narratives have since emerged about the origins of the incident but at the time the fire was attributed to a Muslim mob, which in turn sparked revenge attacks from Hindu groups across the state. According to a report by Human Rights Watch, saffron-clad groups had arrived in trucks not long after the train fire, armed with swords and explosives and rampaged through neighbourhoods, guided by printouts listing Muslim homes, restaurants and hotels. Women and girls were gang-raped then burned to death. Parents were forced to watch their children being slaughtered. Mosques and graves were destroyed. After many months of violence, official records listed 1,000 deaths, the majority of whom were Muslims, but the actual number is thought to be closer to 5,000. More than 100,000 Muslims were pushed into refugee camps and forced to live in squalor. As Gujarat's chief minister, Modi was accused of complicity in the pogroms, allegedly encouraging police and authorities not to intervene. Eyewitnesses testified that the police had participated in the violence. Modi denied playing a part and twenty years after the events the Indian Supreme Court dismissed charges of criminal conspiracy against him. However, in India that meant very little. Someone had once said to me: 'In India you either pay a politician or you become a politician. And the latter is cheaper.'

Ten minutes after departure, our train slowed into a small station and a handful of passengers hauled themselves up, among them a vendor selling earpods, toy cricket sets and packets of moisture-wicking socks made in China. Although tempted to liven up the journey with a game of cricket down the carriage, I settled on the socks instead: sockless feet in trainers was never a good pairing, least of all in desert heat. Marc went to inspect the other carriages and I shifted towards the window. Abhishek, a 24-year-old Indian Air Force engineer, was sitting opposite me. He was travelling from home in Ayodhya to the base at Phalodi and, for security reasons, refused to tell me what his work entailed. This was a regular commute for him and he liked meeting people on board.

'On aeroplanes you have someone on laptop, someone on phone. Here you have different views, different culture, different states, different food. On an aeroplane all you are seeing is cloud. This is not good. This is my view.'

You couldn't buy hot onion pakoras through the window either, I noted, as we came to a standstill again and a vendor shoved a packet through the bars.

'Tourists are not travelling on this long, hot train,' said Abhishek, accepting a pakora. 'You are unusual. Also, it is better up here.' Checking that the berth above was empty, he climbed up and lay there watching a film on YouTube, but not before asking me for my Instagram handle. Two friends, Ram and Mohan, sat on the other side of our compartment, both staring at their phones and working their way through a carrier bag of pistachios and banana chips. They were visiting Jaisalmer for no reason in particular, at least none that I could fathom. It was not a busy train. The majority of passengers were members of the air force, lying around in khaki and heavy boots.

Last time, I did this route on a sleeper service, shivering under a cotton sheet in third class as trains screamed past all night, the horn clanging louder than usual. At one point there'd been so much dust in the corridor I'd worried that the train had caught fire. This train's horn blared non-stop too, and I realised it was a warning to anyone who might be emerging from the fields that flanked us. Butterflies scattered like confetti, hot wind blowing sand in through the bars, leaving a red layer on every surface. I pulled a hat down to protect my face and squinted at camels tethered in backyards. Groups of women hoisted trays of bricks on their heads, their nose studs glinting in the sun. Suddenly I saw the *Maharajas' Express* tourist train pass by, just as Marc strode up the aisle.

'I've ripped my fucking trousers,' he said, stopping in front of me. 'And I've not got anything else.'

'Ah shit, our bags are with Jamie,' I said, sitting up and trying not to look directly at the bright patch of inner thigh that was now on display, along with more than a hint of boxers. A neighbour's head appeared around the corner, a coffee vendor drifted over, and Abhishek swung down, elated by the commotion. Two teenage girls ran up, clapping their hands to their mouths and giggling.

'Do you have Insta aunty?' one of them asked me, holding out a Samsung Galaxy phone.

'Did she just call you aunty?' Marc asked.

'Maybe,' I replied as he threw back his head with laughter. 'Look, I'm not the one with my cock hanging out of my trousers.'

'Yeah, that would be weird, aunty,' said Marc, still laughing at me when Mohan unzipped his bag and wordlessly handed him a pair of his own black sweatpants.

'Can I borrow these?' Marc said, sitting up.

Mohan nodded.

'Ah man, that is *so* kind.' Marc placed a hand against his chest and thanked Mohan, who shook his head and smiled, staring intently. 'Let me get you coffee,' he added, noticing the vendor standing idle, still enjoying the scene. 'Can you imagine someone in London lending me their trousers?' Marc said as he pulled out some notes then went to change. I wondered for a moment if our foreigner vibes had made Mohan more inclined to help, but overall Marc had a point. There was a unique spirit of generosity about Indian train travellers. Whether it came to sharing food, shifting up to make space, or offering advice – unsolicited or otherwise – the railways usually brought out the best of human nature.

Six hours was a long time on board a desert train, much of it spent in the doorway as we passed through fields of flowering millet that appeared like corn on the cob. Looking up the corridor at the kids napping in mothers' laps, an elderly musician playing a stringed instrument, I thought back to the origins of these railways, built 170 years earlier by colonisers motivated to centralise their rule. Our schoolbooks had been blank when it came to truths about empire and I'd lost count of the number of times I'd heard 'but the railways' from apologists for the British Raj. The building of the network was no benevolent act. It was a means for the British to govern more efficiently, speed up the plunder of loot and line their pockets at the expense of the Indian taxpayer, who funded the railways' construction even though Indians weren't initially permitted to travel in the same carriages as their overlords. So many countries had built their own railways without suffering the indignity of being colonised and I wondered for a moment what India's would look like had the British never set foot on our land.

On the approach to our destination the ground turned gold. Shadows of cacti grew longer as the sun began to drop. The birds chirped wildly and a pair of peacocks scarpered up the dunes, their tails raking tracks in their wake. Then, for a moment, everything turned gold: the air, the light, the sand. And through it, like a mirage, rose the ramparts of Jaisalmer Fort.

Once a trade hub on the Silk Road, the Golden City of Jaisalmer was founded in the middle of the twelfth century by a Rajput king, Raja Rawal Jaisal, and its charm still centred on the fortress, a sprawling sandcastle in the Thar desert. Unlike India's other forts, which were mostly converted into luxury hotels or museums, Jaisalmer's was considered the largest living fort, owing to the fact that it was still inhabited by a 4,000-strong community, its spaghetti-thin passages leading up crooked steps to where a number of homes had been converted into cafés and rooftop restaurants. Bazaars sold all manner of handicrafts, from embroidered handbags and mirrored pens to block-print fabrics, bedspreads and camel-leather goods that smelled faintly of manure. On my first visit, drawn towards the enchantment of pushcarts clattering, merchants selling silver and the amber glow at sunset, I had stayed in a haveli within the ramparts, curled up on a four-poster bed with a puppy I'd rescued from kids who had tied its tail to a brick. Together we had fallen asleep in the breeze flowing through the holes in the *jharokha* windows and woken to soft gongs from the nearby Jain temples.

It was now unethical to stay within the fort: illegal construction and an improper sewage system were cracking the foundations, exacerbated by tourism. Climate change was also contributing; abnormally heavy rainfall had caused walls to collapse. All things considered, we checked into Sonaar Haveli, a boutique hotel just a ten-minute walk from the fort where Jamie was waiting.

—

Over a breakfast of masala scrambled eggs and roti, Marc received a message from Sweatpants Mohan that read: '*I really miss you brother.*' Jamie laughed into his chai. He'd received a flurry of texts from his auto-rickshaw driver, Ali, and I was starting to feel left out as we walked up towards Jaisalmer Fort with a strict schedule in hand. It read:

1 nose around Jain temples
2 lunch
3 blanket shopping for Marc/bhang lassi for Jamie
4 camel ride into the desert
5 night train to Delhi

Jamie had run out of deodorant and was scanning the side streets for a supermarket or pharmacy.

'They sell everything everywhere. You could probably find some at a bakery,' said Marc, stopping to scratch the soft forehead of a cow that was chilling in the middle of the road.

'Try that one,' I said, crossing over to a shop that displayed a dartboard in the window, along with toy tractors and a collection of Avengers action figures.

'That's a toy shop,' Jamie said, looking irritated, but following all the same.

The owner, an affable chap wearing a fake USPA polo shirt, pulled out a box of magnetic chess as we entered. 'Chesssssss,' he said, in greeting, tapping the box. 'Crossword game?'

'Do you sell deodorant?' Jamie asked.

'Yes, sir.'

'Yes!' said Jamie, doing a small fist pump.

'For man or woman?'

I watched Jamie's shoulders drop. 'Man,' he muttered as the owner presented him with five cans of aerosol, each with Arabic script labelled 'oud'. Content that Jamie would at least smell like Dubai airport, I went back to Marc and his cow just as a Royal Enfield rumbled to a stop alongside him. It was driven by Mohan with his friend Ram riding pillion. A short exchange took place and yet I still couldn't fathom what they were doing in Jaisalmer except driving about looking for Marc. With a wave they revved off as Jamie rejoined us, smelling like Dubai airport.

'Do you reckon Mohan dropped a tracker in my bag?' Marc asked.

'Wait, was that the guy from the train?' Jamie said.

'The one and only.'

On cue, Marc's phone beeped. '*Miss U*' read the message, along with a red love heart.

'How's he sending that while driving?' Jamie said as we entered the fort's carved rosewood gates, above which was a wall of sleeping bats, wings folded as though they were cold. We immediately drew the interest of vendors who closed in, flapping at us with a collection of coloured patchwork wall hangings. The more persistent salesmen walked alongside until we were at least around the corner before giving up, honing in on fresh blood arriving through the gate.

Everywhere evolved, it was simply the cycle of life. Cities went up, built on the hope of birthing communities, commerce, culture and education. At times they fell, brought down by invaders, fires and earthquakes, but they gathered themselves together, rising from the flames, grouting the cracks and persisting, changing faces, names and direction. Nowhere stayed the same, I could see that as I stopped at the top of a passage and scanned a section of wooden wall carved with floral motifs, war horses rearing up over the doorway. It had recently been painted from the ground up, obscuring the most delicate craftsmanship in a frightful egg-yolk yellow, a slapdash effort by someone who couldn't even be bothered to ruin the whole wall, just some of it. In spite of its deep fissures, mass of wires and satellite dishes, the fort retained its mystique, the ground rubbed smooth by millions of feet over centuries. The sun struck the sandstone at angles, its midday ferocity muted through blood-red saris stretched taut overhead. In open spots the rays bounced off the mirrorwork of clothes and rugs, a deliberate design from the past that would alert desert wanderers to life within the fort. Whether or not the fort could persist in its current persona, it was destined to survive in one form or another.

Between the twelfth and sixteenth centuries Jaisalmer Fort was considered the safest place to build seven Jain temples, in the hope that they would escape the destructive force of Islamic invaders. We were outside the entrance of one, covering shoulders and legs, jostled by crowds in the courtyard. Inside the air was scented with the smokiness of sandalwood and rosewater, a deep gong announcing visitors crossing the threshold. The stone ground was cool against my feet, fossilised shells marking the floors. Along the walls were carvings of the apsaras – heavenly dancers – the rounds of their hips and breasts hung with heavy jewellery. Coming to stand inches from the pillars, I saw how each was engraved with needle-like precision, as though the entire complex was cut by laser. In among the army elephants and horses stood dragons representing the Chinese influence that had passed through from the Silk Road. A quartet of tiny bells hung from the top of each dome, now tinkling in the breeze; a gentle sound to accompany my circuit. As ever, I was in awe at the ability of human hands to create such a spectacle.

On my way out, I found Marc admiring the gleam of a black onyx statue, its eyes wide open, sitting in a full lotus position.

'This is just reminding me that I need a blanket for my meditation,' he said as we wandered out into the blast of hot air, where Jamie had all but melted to a puddle topped with a trilby.

After lunch we happened upon the Bhang Shop in Gopa Chowk. It was buried in a turret that had pigeons camping in the slots, and had smiley emojis drawn onto the signs. Government authorised, the Bhang Shop was probably the country's most famous purveyor of cannabis-infused food and drink. Before I realised what was happening, Jamie was up the steps, pushing aside the plastic curtain. Like Marc, Jamie had given up booze and was keen to try out some edibles. As he turned the laminate pages of cookies, cakes and shakes on offer, I looked up at the walls of what reminded me of a private clinic. 'Dr Bhang' was sitting in a chair, a framed photograph of Anthony Bourdain looking over us. It showed the gentle chef deep in conversation with a member of staff. Within the pitiful genre of TV travel shows, overcrowded by white male presenters deeply uninterested in travel itself, Bourdain was a gift. His humility and integrity made him the perfect guide to unpicking the human psyche through food, and his death had left a gaping hole.

Jamie was holding a cup of lassi piled with crushed cashews, almonds and coconut, and bejewelled with jellied fruit and jaggery that I could smell from atop my stool.

'The same for you ma'am?' Dr Bhang asked. 'Or would you like the super-duper, full power, 24-hour no toilet, no shower?'

'Ooh, hell no,' I said to Dr Bhang. 'Perhaps a tenth of what he had, maybe less.'

'I will make it *veeeeeery* mild for you,' he said, writing on a prescription pad and handing the note to his colleague. If the Bhang Shop had the Bourdain stamp of approval, then it had mine.

My only dabble with edibles had been in Goa ten years earlier. I'd travelled to Anjuna with my friend Jeet who'd bought a pair of brownies from his friend's café. Not realising they were to be picked at, I'd wolfed it down and within half an hour the voices in the bar had thinned to distant echoes. Paranoia set in and I convinced myself the diners at the next table were a Russian pimp, a sex worker eating chicken wings, and an English punter who looked like a skull. After observing a cash exchange between the bedsheets drying behind us, I'd realised I wasn't wrong about the trio, but I was now panicking that everyone was looking at me.

'*Alriiiiiight...* It's kicking in!' Jeet had said, smiling in recognition as I wobbled down to the beach, running away from the waves then begging him to let me lie down. To his amusement I'd spent the next four hours foetal on a cushion in a place called Curlies, hallucinating kaleidoscopic visions. He'd reassured me that no one was looking at me and the majority of the people in there were also foetal on cushions, hallucinating kaleidoscopic visions. After his conker-smooth head turned into an alien's I had tried to sleep, eventually giggling, then attempting to eat a plate of chips, only I'd forgotten how to swallow and gagged for ten minutes as Jeet tried to re-teach me.

That afternoon everything was terribly funny, but mostly to Marc, who was enjoying watching me and Jamie drift around with dopey smiles. We wandered the streets outside the fort, enticed by the fizz of frying jalebis, and loading up on bottles of ayurvedic hair oil, camel-hair blankets and snacks for the night train to Delhi. Both Jamie and Marc stopped for wet shaves, reappearing with haircuts and neatly trimmed nasal hair before one last jolly: a camel ride into the desert.

A half-hour before sunset, we moved off in single file, the camels grinding their teeth like cokeheads as we lurched into the dunes, only to find a dumping ground for broken bottles and plastic. The more I moved around the world, the more I questioned our place within it. Our guides needed income, but tourists were ruining the land – domestic tourists, they explained. They came to party at night then left at dawn, their waste still smoking in heaps. Here, the Swachh Bharat Mission was an abject failure.

For the first time in years, I had booked a first-class compartment. Trains in the north were notoriously dirty and unhygienic when compared with those in the south, despite train maintenance following standard practice across the country. It boiled down to passengers and their habits, and on my first adventure around India, I'd observed first-hand how the state of carriages deteriorated the further I travelled north. Yet I couldn't help but find a weird charm in it all. It was 10.30 p.m. and the *Shalimar Express* was the only train at the station. Jamie had a visible spring in his step, so excited was he about the prospect of travelling in a swanky compartment. At first glance of the interiors, I sensed the excitement would be short-lived.

'Is this the right carriage?' he asked as we clumped through, checking the numbers of each berth.

'Think so,' I said, taking in the ripped covers, grubby windows and torn curtains. 'Marc and I are in a twin one and you're next to us.'

Worse than I'd expected, the train looked as though it had been repurposed from a scrapyard. Hospital lighting did little to lift a rapid onset of depression.

'Could have at least sprayed the table,' Jamie said, pushing a finger through the greasy layer. 'I was expecting something a bit different. Anyway, this might help,' he said, pulling out an edible cookie from Dr Bhang and taking a large bite. The trains had reached a sorry state of affairs if they were only tolerable while stoned.

Assuming we were sleeping in the main first-class carriage, we discovered that our tickets were actually booked for one of three compartments with doors that locked. A family of three had settled into ours, their child asleep under her mother's sari.

Two suitcases blocked the door and my heart sank. I was loath to make them move, but we had no choice. The ticket inspector arrived and scanned his clipboard, moving them to the four-person compartment next door – which included Jamie, whose berth had been assigned with them.

'Erm, okay,' said Jamie, climbing onto his berth still wearing his trilby and shoes, his legs sticking out at the end, like Pete Doherty lying in state. Helping the couple to shift their suitcases, I saw Jamie pull out a paper bag and take another bite of his cookie. At least the child was still deeply asleep, and I waved to Jamie as a family member arrived from a different compartment, sat down at the end of the lower berth and started talking at the mother so loudly I wanted to cry for everyone concerned. For a second or two the woman watched me standing in the corridor. She picked her left nostril with her right hand and then reached across and yanked the door shut in my face.

'Well, that's that then,' said Marc. 'Hope Jamie has a good night with aunty in there. Want to go for a wander? The compartment's a bit claustrophobic.'

The train was starting to move, so I went to the door to look out. The fort was shimmering like a palace, golden in the darkness. I watched it shrinking, listening to the drum of the wheels before picking my way back into the corridor. Passengers were unrolling bedding, laying out glasses and tablets and plugging in phones. Some were already asleep. Halfway up the carriage a young man sat propped up against his pillow making notes. He was listening to music and gestured for us to sit down.

'It's been good,' Marc said to me, reflecting on our time in India. 'Got a lot packed into a short space of time.'

For a few moments we sat back listening to the wheels thumping as we jerked sideways and barrelled into the desert. In two weeks we'd travelled more than 2,000 miles by rail and I wanted to carry on, to go back to Bombay and Goa, to continue down to Kerala... but home beckoned. A bearded blond man wearing a maroon hoodie and cargo pants stopped by the compartment and we both sat up.

'Sorry, man, are we in your seat?' Marc asked, leaning to get up.

'No.' He raised both palms to tell us to stay put. 'I just wanted to see how the other half lives,' he laughed.

'Which carriage are you in?' I asked.

'Like 2A or something?' he said, looking into the neighbouring compartment.

'Not much differently then. We've got a doorway, that's about it.'

Marc offered him a seat and the usual exchange of traveller stories kicked off. Daniel was at the tail end of a three-month journey around the north of India which had largely centred on the Himalaya. He was on gardening leave before starting a new job in Pittsburgh and was now recounting how he'd tagged along into the Thar desert with a gang of students from Gurgaon.

'Did you go into the desert?' he asked me.

'For the sunset, yes.'

'Oh, so we actually stayed overnight. With like a fire and those beds.'

'Charpoys.'

'Yes! Charpoys,' Daniel pointed at me. 'I mean you're Indian, right, so you know how it is, these guys wouldn't let me pay for the ride and they bought all the beer and the food, and honestly, I've spent like, literally no money this whole trip. It's like everywhere you go, people just want to know everything about you,' he said, scratching something out of his beard and examining the underneath of his nail.

'Did you want to know about them?' I asked.

He flashed me a vague look then carried on chatting to Marc for the next few minutes.

'Anyway, I better get back in case someone tries to steal my shit,' he said. 'Maybe catch you guys on the other side?'

Watching Daniel walk back the way he came, I sincerely hoped we didn't. I'd grown weary of wealthy white Westerners traipsing around the Global South, exploiting the kindness of strangers to boost their dinner-party chat. A few years earlier I'd met someone whose entire schtick was travelling without luggage. Nothing more than a toothbrush and credit card to hand, he navigated his way around the world by blagging and borrowing, allowing people to put him up and pay for his meals, while he turned up as a 'chief guest' at their weddings and sometimes funerals.

'That's so dark, man,' said Marc.

'I'd haunt him if he came to my funeral.'

'I bet he had way more money than everyone else as well.' He thought for a moment. 'It also sounds like quite an unsophisticated ploy to get laid.'

The young man whose berth we were sitting on had taken out his earphones and was now listening to our conversation. Karthik was a postgraduate student from St Stephen's College in Delhi, a prestigious university. He'd been in Jaisalmer celebrating a friend's birthday but had left early to sit an exam.

'What you reckon?' Marc asked him.

'I bloody hate these people,' said Karthik.

'Oh wow, mate, tell us what you really think,' said Marc, clapping his hands, bent over laughing.

Karthik adjusted his T-shirt and sat up. 'A lot of young people in India, not just young people, but people in India still have this way of worshipping the white man,' he said softly. 'Racism is still a huge problem here. Huge,' he said, fanning out his hand for emphasis. 'And people still feel that the lighter your skin or the closer you place yourself to white people, the more likely you are of success.'

Marc was listening to Karthik with a look of resignation etched across his face. 'That's really grim.'

We chatted for a while about Karthik's plans to stay in Delhi after he graduated. In the past, young people couldn't wait to flee abroad but, according to Karthik, there was so much opportunity that there was no longer the same impetus to escape.

I looked around. The bodies were still, humped under thick grey blankets. Midnight had come and gone and I too was desperate to sleep. I promised Karthik we'd find him in the morning and he tipped his head to one side, wedging in his earphones and turning back to his books.

Two hours into the journey it was too dark to see anything but the lights of passing trains. I tried to get comfortable but the berth was hard, the air-conditioning set too high. Turning onto my back I wondered how Jamie was faring, wishing I'd asked for a cookie. I had thought this was what I'd wanted. It was why I'd come back, to be bounced around on a rickety old train, reminiscing about my first adventure around India. But as the train lurched along at speed, I could feel my stress levels rising at every bump. I'd ridden more than a hundred of India's trains, juddering across some of the highest bridges in the country, winding up precarious mountainous tracks and inching through jungles known for severe landslides and floods. Invariably I did so just days before the bridges collapsed, the tracks came apart and burst rivers swept away the lines. Safety had improved on India's railways but when an accident did occur, the death tolls were staggering, and I was now being flung around like a rag doll, convinced the train would derail. Anxiety was my new travelling companion, and a part of my brain was always focused on my children. Before their arrival I owed nothing to anyone. No one depended on me, no one needed me, hell, no one missed me when I was away. I thought of all the male travel writers who disappeared for months at a time, leaving young children behind with their partners, and I wondered how they did it. I knew the girls were safe and well, but I still missed them deeply.

A *chaiwallah* boarded at the town of Borawar and I woke to the melancholy drone of his call. Sipping the milky tea, I looked around wondering where Marc had gone. From the vestibule I watched a couple of children waiting under an awning, their school ties reaching down to their waists. It was just before 8 a.m. and the morning light made everything feel safe again, my anxiety long forgotten. The train was now running along the body of Shakambari Jheel, India's largest inland salt lake, which fluctuated between shades of purple and orange depending on the concentration of the brine. In winter it saw thousands of migratory flamingoes flock to its wetlands, but for now it was green and still. An elderly man came through to wash his hands and neck, and we struck up a conversation. Jayanth worked for the Ministry of Defence and since the early 1990s he'd been travelling by train around the north of India for work. He made a clicking sound with his teeth as he slicked back his hair with water.

'These northern trains, they haven't really got better in terms of conditions. People have learned bad behaviour but it's now more clean on board. Old, yes, but cleanliness is there and improvement in service is there. Fifteen years back I went to Dibrugarh in Assam and the train was 102 hours late. Now it is maximum ten hours in winter due to fog. Modi has made our India proud,' he added.

From what I could tell, Indian Railways' priority was to invest in brand new trains which created an illusion of progress. Money was being poured into semi-high-speed rail and Vistadome specials, which included glass roofs and rotatable chairs to enhance views of the scenery. Glamorous Vande Bharat Express trains were being introduced with the intention of replacing the daytime Shatabdis and plans were afoot to put on long-distance versions of the Vande Bharat trains, but with sleeper cars that would include better-quality berths, floor lights, designated luggage racks, staff cabins and even a space for pets. But I still felt that the pressing needs of the average Indian traveller were being ignored. Few could even dream of riding on those unaffordable new trains. Overcrowding on board was still a huge, sometimes fatal problem and what the government really needed to do was invest in more low-cost sleeper-class coaches for the working classes who made up the majority of ridership.

Jayanth sniffed and looked out at the villages sailing by. 'Modi is a good PM. He is my PM. If my PM tell me you jump for me, I will jump,' he held up his fist. 'I have blind faith in my PM.'

This was emotive rhetoric and I asked Jayanth why he felt so strongly.

'There is no corruption any more. He does maximum things for poor people. He gives food for poor people. He has given free gas, free houses, free medical care for the poor. If you have single girl child, you can get education.'

'Is there anyone who doesn't like him?' I asked.

'Muslims. Other political parties.' He held up his hand. 'All the fingers cannot be equal.'

'Why don't Muslims like him?'

'They are always fighting someone. If they don't fight Hindus then they are fighting among themselves.'

Jayanth went on to ask if I was married and I explained that my kids were at home with their dad.

'My wife was a school teacher but I asked her to be at home with the children,' he said. 'When they're small it is not good to work or they will go here and there.'

'I work and my children are just fine with their dad,' I replied, filled with indignance.

Jayanth smiled demurely in response. He leaned his head to one side in an infuriating gesture, at which point I decided to take leave and head back to the compartment.

Marc had reappeared and was dealing out the Kama Sutra-themed playing cards we'd bought while buzzing in Jaisalmer. I sat in a corner watching him teach Jamie how to play Shithead and pulled out my diary, which was covered in sand from the desert. Dusting off the cover, I turned to my original bucket list of trains, most of which had satisfying scores through the middle. While fingering the stuffing coming out of my berth, I thought back to the comfy compartments on the *Dacia*, the dining car on the *Doğu Express* and the double bed on the *Caledonian Sleeper*. European sleepers were sleek, comfortable and, in comparison to Indian trains, quiet. As I listened to a hawker crowing up the aisles selling samosa, I realised that for all the positives of Europe's night trains, I still found an unrivalled charm on Indian Railways. I looked at the trains remaining on my list. In a few weeks I'd be riding the *Silver Meteor* in the US, then the *Santa Claus Express* with the girls at Christmas. The name of the final train still looked at me, taunting me. Giving it no more thought, I shut the diary and turned to enjoy the view.

An abundance of recent rain had replenished a thirsty landscape, and the meadows were flourishing. Buffalo wallowed in deep lakes and perfect lines of saplings stretched out like fields of cocktail umbrellas. Solitary farmhouses popped up, solitary shepherds keeping watch, their bright orange *pagaris* like tiny flames in the fields. Haystacks were tied into bundles, and I noticed new tracks being laid, girders piled high. On the approach to Jaipur a fight broke out at an intermediate station, and everyone rushed to the windows to watch the *tamasha*. No one threw punches here, but tight slaps were dealt out in the style of Hindi movie villains. I observed with admiration as someone in the middle of the brawl managed to maintain a phone conversation while limbs flew all around him. Just a few metres away from the ruckus a child was imprisoned inside an orange sari fashioned into a hammock. His mother continued to thread flowers in spite of the noise, and he was trying his best to escape.

At Jaipur we hopped out for coffee, Jamie nailing three in succession as an officious type drifted over and began to narrate his thoughts unprompted. Everyone had an opinion in India, especially when it came to how other people ought to live their lives, and it didn't take long for the man to bemoan the onslaught of smartphones among young people.

'They are causing havoc in rural India,' he grumbled, gesturing at passengers scrolling as they waited for the train to sound its horn.

'In what way?' I asked, enjoying the warmth of the sun.

'They have the world on the phone. Anything and everything is there. They join groups, debating this and that, very different from how they have been brought up.'

'Surely that's a good thing?' I said.

'No. Rural children grow up in a traditional society here. Now they are exposed to Western ways of life where live-in relationships are normal, there is pornography. They are questioning religion, social structures. You can't rebel against it.'

Jamie flushed. 'It is a difficult balance though isn't it,' he said. 'I mean it is good to question things per se, and find your own sense of mind and question authority.'

'No one is asking you not to question, but don't oppose it for the sake of obsession,' said the man, sniffing deeply then pulling out an enormous handkerchief. 'You can't have everything, feminist rights, all of that, you have to understand the deeper reasoning behind many of the structures. They see certain things happening at home and then they find arguments against it on YouTube and they start opposing what happens at home without stopping to think why it happens.'

The train let out a long and sonorous horn and we clambered back up the steps for the final few hours.

Back on board, the three of us sat in a row like a still from *The Darjeeling Limited*, but minus the garlands and bandages. In less than twenty-four hours we'd established that the woman's place was still in the home, colonialism was alive and well, and that the rural poor had no right to question structures of oppression. Throw in the fight on the platform and we'd had a mighty fruitful journey. Nothing at all out of the ordinary for a regular old Indian sleeper. Little did I know that we were some of the last riders on the *Shalimar Express*, which would be permanently cancelled the following year.

At around four o'clock the train passed between high-rise apartments and woods, and under a tree I spotted my favourite sight: a group of elderly men cross-legged on a blanket, dealing out cards. Two others were leaning over the game, hands behind their backs. The brakes began to creak and the *Shalimar Express* slowed into Delhi Cantonment station. The three of us disembarked, pulling bags along a floral path as the train rumbled to life and continued on its way.

14

THE SILVER METEOR

'My god. Why would you do that to yourself?'

Such was the response from a friend in New York when I explained that I wasn't flying into JFK or Newark but taking a sleeper train from Florida that would run all the way up to his city via Georgia, the Carolinas, Virginia, Maryland, Delaware, Pennsylvania and New Jersey, arriving into the brand new Moynihan Train Hall at Penn Station.

'And you're getting on in Orlando?! Jesus, that's a shithole,' he added.

Whether or not Orlando was a shithole, it was certainly hot and humid – normal for October – as I walked around the station's waiting area, tickled by the metal gumball machines, wooden telephone booths and the peg letterboard that detailed each arrival and departure. Like a portal to the past, the 1920s building on Sligh Boulevard was an example of Mission Revival-style architecture – one that adapted elements of Spanish colonial churches including a corridor of arches, a parapet and twin bell-towers. Huge, tiled floors made it perhaps feel cooler inside, where curved hardwood benches were filling up as passengers arrived to board Train 98: the *Silver Meteor*.

Originating in Miami, the *Silver Meteor* was one of three Amtrak services that passed through the station, branching off into variations that all terminated in New York. On my last adventure around America, I'd used a thirty-day Amtrak pass to ride some of the country's most iconic trains: the *Sunset Limited* from New Orleans to LA; the *Southwest Chief* from LA to Chicago, and the

Empire Builder from Chicago to Seattle, to name a few. At the time there were no Amtrak services running east of New Orleans, owing to the destruction that Hurricane Katrina had brought to critical railway infrastructure, so I'd marked this as a region to return to. Even though I'd spent a sizeable chunk of that month on board, befriending everyone from runaways and aid workers to guitar-strumming veterans, teachers, convicted felons and German Baptist Brethren who deep-fried squirrels for dinner, I'd not spent much time *off* the rails. Many of the services took between thirty-five and forty-five hours to cross the country, so tourists often booked separate legs, hopping down for a couple of days to explore towns along the way. For the first time I was breaking up my journey with a long weekend in the Georgian city of Savannah before carrying on by sleeper to New York.

Long-distance Amtrak is not for everyone. Certainly not for upper-middle-class Americans who balk at the idea of riding anything but the Northeast Corridor's high-speed Acela. I could see that my enthusiasm for American trains confused them, as I recounted stories of sharing stacks of French toast with mechanics from Idaho, fights breaking out at bedtime and drink-drivers condemned to ride the rails to visit their kids. A magnet for the unhinged (what did that say about me?) Amtrak could often be delayed and gnarly, but it lit a fire in my belly, bringing me into the folds of Middle America in a way that nothing else could.

Inside the station I took a seat and watched a woman sit down heavily against someone else's bag, her Hawaiian shorts riding up to reveal thighs covered in bruises. The bag owner cursed as bottles of conditioner and deodorant fell out and rolled around the ground in a circle in time for a large man to wheel his shopping trolley over the top with a crack. Expressionless, an elderly Black couple watched the circus, the woman catching my eye and breaking into an impish smile. This station had once been racially segregated with *a separate waiting room with ticket windows and restrooms for African American passengers on the south side of the building* – such was the information on a sign outside the station which had brought me up short. I wasn't used to seeing open acknowledgements of racism and its ugly truths, but the US seemed more willing to confront its past, in a way that Britain wasn't.

Intensified by the humidity, the scent of fried onions was now wafting in from the platform and I looked around for the source.

'You going to get a hot dog?' my travelling companion asked, his eyes shining with amusement.

Jeremy was a humanities professor from Orlando and a skilled photographer. He hosted a travel podcast and on a trip to London he'd extended a flippant offer to look him up on the highly implausible chance that I came to Orlando. Somehow he had now been roped in as my photographer, guide and sidekick for a weekend of eating soul food in Savannah before he returned home for his wife's antenatal scan. They were due a baby boy in a few months and Jeremy had been asking me a number of questions, seemingly casual but underscored with the fear that children might destroy their lives. I looked at my watch, more for performance than anything else. It was lunchtime – but even at ten o'clock in the morning I would have made room for a foil-wrapped frank from a cart.

Before I could reply, a bell began clanging and we followed the sound outside to where a steel body was curving into view, its front shimmering in the heat. From food portions to political scandal, everything in the US was huge, and the trains were no exception. As the monumental engine pulled into the station, I could feel passengers shrink back in its presence, some of them no taller than the wheels. With little time to spare, I darted across to the Hot Corner, which was run by Maria, a petite Colombian woman with black gloves and a sweaty hairline. She already had a queue, at the front of which was a conductor who had disembarked to buy a box of hot dogs for his colleagues. Next in line was a family. The teenage daughter carried a fleece blanket that was trailing along the ground and her young brother wore a neck pillow and a Spider-Man backpack. They were in for the long haul, stocking up on Gatorade and packets of Haribo, each more lurid than the next. As I unwrapped the chilli-cheese dog, passengers were invited to make two lines: solo travellers in one; families and groups in the other. This was a new set-up since my last trip, and we were assigned seats by destination and invited to climb up using a footstool to reach the steps. Once we were on board the manager came along and wrote SAV2 (2 for Savannah) in black marker on a piece of card, slotting it overhead. Amtrak, it seemed, was determined to retreat as far into the past as possible.

'Wow, this is so… spacious,' said Jeremy, looking up the carriage. 'And clean… and comfortable?' he added, sliding into his seat and stretching out his legs, propping up his Converse on the footrest. Jeremy couldn't remember the last time he'd ridden Amtrak – decades ago at a guess. He'd taken trains as a child, 'but like a little novelty during the holidays'. Oddly pleased by an American's approval, I took my seat as the bell for the railroad crossing began to clang again and we rolled out of the station. Within a minute or two the door between the carriages started to slide back and forth, slamming with increasing fury until the passenger behind got up and hauled it shut.

'Thank you,' I nodded.

He stared down at me for a moment, swaying in the aisle in a flamingo shirt. 'I'm like with seven people and I don't know where they're at!' he yelled, holding up six fingers and falling sideways, the stench of beer on his clothes. Jeremy adjusted his flat cap and gave me a sideways look as the man swung towards the window then sat down, pressing his face into the gap between our seats.

'Good to be back?' Jeremy asked.

———

Savannah was six hours away and the bright Floridian landscape was a welcome distraction, creeks and ribbons of river catching the light. From the window the ground appeared as one great, moving wetland. But while the other passengers tore open sweets, adjusted headphones, or rambled to anyone who would listen – the door still slamming – I searched between the ridges and reeds, spotting sandhill cranes, egrets and leggy herons preening in waterways. Lakes widened into view, many of which were former sinkholes that families swam through in summer. As the train drummed across Lake Monroe Bridge, I looked down to where the surface was glossed with lily pads on blooms of blue-green algae. An hour or so later we were belting past Baptist churches, neat white spires poking up behind squat sabal palms, their bodies like overgrown pineapples. Live oak bent overhead, lichen hanging off like ripped lace, magnolia buried in between.

Not known for its views, the *Silver Meteor* had nonetheless fulfilled my needs and I dug out my copy of *Midnight in the Garden of Good and Evil* by John Berendt. A mixture of true crime and memoir, it was a fabulously louche portrait of Savannah's rich and crazy, featuring beauty queens, divorcees, pianists, thieves, antique dealers, old women punching out their neighbours' windows, and Berendt revelling in the madness of it all. Savannah was a city I'd yearned to visit since Forrest Gump had sat on a bench in sunlit Chippewa Square. In my mind's eye it was a gourmet's haven, home to Italianate mansions with wrought-iron balconies looking onto cobblestone streets. I imagined strolling across its garden squares, the mist from fountains reaching oak trees draped in Spanish moss. Berendt's book touched on all the tropes and I had just encountered Chablis, whose 'mama got the name off a wine bottle', when I overheard the passengers in front bickering over the best spot for blue-crab bisque in Charleston.

Two hours up the coast, Charleston was my alternative choice of stopover on the *Silver Meteor*'s route, but Savannah had appealed to me in a way that its sister city had not. Charleston had long been sold on its colonial charms, beckoning visitors to stay on antebellum plantations where they could imagine themselves as Southern belles sipping mint juleps on a porch swing. Nothing was less charming than colonialism and slavery. The fact that Charleston's plantation houses were graveyards for the Black slaves who'd built them and were then raped, tortured and killed on them, did little to entice me to stroll between the weeping willows of their grounds, no matter how manicured. To my horror, many white Americans still insisted on plantation weddings, akin to celebrating love at the site of a concentration camp. It had taken until 2018 for the city council to formally apologise for Charleston's role in slavery, and after centuries of oppression, Black-led tours were finally correcting history, righting wrongs in museums and filling deliberately empty gaps. Long overdue, a number of privately owned plantations now publicly recognised their legacies, rebuilding slave quarters and documenting the stories of those their ancestors had enslaved, but until they shared their wealth as reparations, nothing would ever feel enough. One day I would make my way up there for ribs and red rice, but not this time: I had a special food story to unearth in Savannah.

A cheery voice announced that the café car had reopened, so Jeremy and I took ourselves up the carriage, eyes flicking from one row to the next, taking in the assortment of passengers. Despite being chilly, the air was as ripe as a post-game locker room, the floor strewn with Funyuns and Air Jordans on their sides. One passenger slept in mirrored sunglasses, a towel wrapped around his head, while his neighbour painted her nails with glitter. *Frozen* balloons bumped overhead, their young owners exhausted from Disney World and napping across the seats. At the end of the carriage, a number of walking frames were parked by passengers in various degrees of decay, bandages and slings on show. In the café we found Flamingo Shirt. He still hadn't located his friends but seemed content to work his way through a pack of Corona as we got talking to the train managers, their radios crackling in sync. Delivering a huge blow, they revealed that the main dining car was closed to passengers in coach class, owing to staffing problems. Furthermore, this wasn't limited to the *Silver Meteor*, but affected a number of Amtrak's services.

'The dining car was out for a while,' said Matt, pausing to relay numbers into his radio, 'but now it's all new and upgraded and they're once again doing chicken and steak back there. It's only for people in roomettes and bedrooms though.'

Mortified, I told him how I'd loved sitting down with random riders and he nodded. 'Right, you sit with somebody else and it was neat. But I think the short answer is that it's a staffing issue.

There used to be two waiters and two chefs. And now it's one chef and one waiter. The capacity of the train is 180 in coach class, they can't handle that quantity.'

Like a great class-divider, the dining car lay between our three coaches and those travelling in roomettes and bedrooms, which ranged from $550 to $1,400 for Orlando to New York, a steep curve up from the $120 fare in coach class. Although private, roomettes were a claustrophobe's worst nightmare: two window seats facing one another that folded down to make twin berths at night. Bedrooms could sleep two to three adults and came with ensuite showers and toilets. Tickets for both included meals in the dining car, but Amtrak was on track to lose its last vestiges of charm by closing off the car to other passengers. It was over sour coffee and pancakes that people came together, people of all colours, classes and creeds. Subdued, I asked Matt who his average passenger was on the other side.

'So it's folks who have the means to swing those tickets and not worry about it. Quite a few older folks back there and folks who don't want to fly. They want the romantic bit of the train, looking out of the window, the nostalgia, there's definitely a demand for that. We're always fully booked.'

When Matt revealed that there were a lot of young families in both bedrooms and coach class, a young father wearing a Baltimore Fire T-shirt turned around, his baby, Viola, climbing over his shoulder.

'It was $400 for us to take the train from Jacksonville home to Baltimore or $1,000 to fly. And driving wasn't worth it either,' he said. 'It was like 400 bucks for gas and then more for motels and food along the way.'

'How have you found it?' I asked, as Viola secured a fistful of my hair.

'Flying with a baby is not fun. Even getting on a plane, six months old, it's the wild stage.'

I looked at Jeremy who was listening intently.

'But this is nice, the babies have a little more room to move around, more to see and people are just less bothered on the train.'

To the fury of the dining-car attendant, Matt let us troop through to have a look at the new car, which had floor lighting, red and white roses on the table, and white linen. Glass dividers separated each table, which took away the fun of twisting around and interrupting other people's chats. Overall the upgrade was impressive and only served to depress me more that it was off-limits to us great unwashed, stuck with the café's Hebrew all-beef hot dogs, Asian noodle bowls and microwaved cheeseburgers – the last of which was strangely delicious so long as it was eaten before it hardened like a brick.

The train crossed the St Marys River, the easternmost border between Florida and Georgia, and I looked out of both sides of the carriage to where coral-coloured light was breaking through the cloud. The flatness induced a numbness, no peaks or troughs of joy from hills or valleys. Level, uncomplicated and predictable, the steadiness of the landscape brought my body to a place of calm when Matt pointed out of the window.

'This area attracts a lot of rail fans. Some of them like to rent a caboose here and photograph the trains as we pass.'

'What's a *caboose*?' I asked.

'The caboose was what they used to have on the back of the train. It had a cupola up top with windows, the engineers would stop and eat back there and sleep in these cars maybe fifty or sixty years ago? Then the conductors would sit at the top and look down the train for sparks shooting out of the wheels and things.' Matt paused, then pointed again. 'And if you look right out there, that's the Okefenokee Swamp – I wanna say it means "trembling earth".'

Home to black bears, bobcats and alligators, the wetlands were anything but steady. They were the very opposite in fact – moving, complicated, unpredictable, the water levels fluctuating, thousands of species trying to survive an endangered world. In seconds the landscape had transformed into one of vulnerability, instilling me with unease.

On time – no small feat for Amtrak – the *Silver Meteor* drew into Savannah at 7.40 p.m. and Matt waved us off. 'Y'all have a nice night now,' he said as we disembarked along with the smokers, one of whom was pacing in a pair of duckling pyjamas and Crocs. The train would carry on to New York and arrive the following morning at 11.20.

'Shame about the dining car,' I grumbled to Jeremy as we darted through the rain into the station, 'but it was interesting to see the fancy end of the train, mainly elderly and wealthy...'

'And white?' he added, laughing.

Enforced segregation might have been a thing of the past, but the starkness between the haves and the have-nots was all too clear to see on board.

In Savannah's North Historic District, Dottie's Market was in full swing – literally. Lindy Hop music played beneath the hiss of frothing milk, and the sizzle of bacon emanated from the open kitchen. Over a plate of sausage patties, cornbread, grits and greens, I looked around at contented diners cutting into wodges of blueberry cheesecake, while others thumbed through preloved cookbooks or shopped for tubs of quince paste and packets of bourbon sugar tea. Soul food is central to Southern living, and before I'd left London I'd searched for the top restaurants in Savannah, only to find celebrity chefs such as Andrew Brochu, Sean Brock and Paula Deen repeatedly popping up as specialists of Southern fare – white chefs excelling in food rooted in Black history. There was nothing unusual about this – and chefs are free to cook what they want – but what struck me was the scarcity of Black names. Digging deeper, I came upon what appeared to be a nascent group of Black chefs and restaurant owners reclaiming African-American cooking – which was largely down to a woman named Mashama Bailey, executive chef and co-owner of the Grey, an upscale diner round the corner. The first Black woman to win America's prestigious James Beard Award for Outstanding Chef, Mashama had spent her career reconnecting with the heritage of Black food and turning it into a fine-dining experience that had inspired others to follow in her footsteps.

As Jeremy slunk around taking pictures of the diner, I finished my breakfast and sought out Ericka Phillips, who was wearing a headscarf and large hooped earrings and sitting at the chef's counter. Together with her husband she'd recently opened Dottie's in homage to her great-grandmother. A recreation of the 1900s, it was designed to feel like grandma's house, with mismatched crockery, jars of pumpkin butter secured with bright linen tops, and Gullah sweetgrass baskets once used to separate rice grains from husk. Pausing between clangs and shouts from the kitchen, Ericka explained why she'd relocated from Chicago, where she had grown up alongside Dottie – the 'gatherer' and matriarch in the family – from whom she had learned to grow tomatoes and cucumbers, and make pickles and apple sauce.

'She was very connected to the earth in a way that wasn't common in the city,' said Ericka, scrolling through her playlist. 'I grew up in Chicago in a community of people who had migrated from the South, but as you know the migratory patterns followed the train lines so lots of us had family from Alabama and Georgia and Mississippi. They moved north for better opportunities but also…' Ericka paused and pulled at her earring… 'to escape the terrorism that they saw and felt every day.'

Ericka took slow breaths as she spoke, but continued unprompted.

'It was remarkable to me that Dottie reflected on her childhood in such an idyllic and beautiful way. There was a love and joy and longing in her eyes when she told me those stories of growing up on a farm. Being a Black person in America is complicated in general, but with that is also that deep connection and investment in this land and I see more people of my generation wanting to reclaim and investigate that. I see myself as part of that.'

Ericka described how many Black people – including members of her own family – refused to visit the South, but that she felt tied to it through Dottie, along with a spiritual energy that had pulled her to Savannah and the profundity of its history.

A waiter passed with a plate of steaming hot chicken-biscuit, gleaming with grits, greens and spicy chilli sauce, and Ericka gestured towards it with a dimpled smile.

'Black American cuisine has shaped American cuisine at large. The history of our food tells the truth and tells a much more interesting story about the foundation of America and how our history has played out.'

I asked her what she meant by the 'truth', and she let out a deep but strangely beautiful laugh; I could hear frustration inside it.

'So, there are these stories that you get in history books and you become indoctrinated as a child. But when you look into the culinary history, it doesn't lie. It tells a rich story about America, like grits or cornbread: both are things I grew up eating. And these grains? These seeds and technology and techniques were things that our ancestors brought to this country.'

While I made notes, I could feel Ericka scanning my face.

'Why is this story important to you?' she asked.

On the train I had questioned if I had the right to tell Black people's stories on their behalf. I'd felt indignant that there weren't scores of celebrity Black chefs hosting Netflix shows and, as I'd tracked down Ericka and others to speak to, I felt an obligation to amplify what they were doing. Out tumbled my thoughts as I explained to Ericka how I'd felt detached from India as a child. Born and bred in the UK, I was comfortable in my identity, never needing to trace my roots, but recently, as the scourge of racism had come to the forefront of British politics and onto the streets, I'd started to reconsider what it meant, being born in the country that had colonised my people. It mattered that Ericka trusted me with her story and, as we sat together on bar stools, I recognised a woman also melding her past and her present.

Savannah was experiencing an unprecedented boom in development, hosting more than 17 million tourists in the previous year. New housing was attracting thousands of residents, there was now an annual film festival, and a recent surge in hotels. Yet it was astonishing to me that in a population of 150,000 – predominantly Black residents – there was not one Black-owned hotel or guesthouse.

'There's been a lot of changeover,' said Ericka, 'the whole gentrification thing, but we have to be careful in this moment about conscious versus unconscious development. We have to make it a point to uplift and highlight and acknowledge local creators and artisans and not just erase a whole group of Black vendors who have always been here and are still here.'

With that, she wrote down a list of old favourites for me to visit and sent us on our way.

The evening was pleasantly muggy as we wandered through the Starland District to the Garage at Victory North. Diners were here for gumbo and deep-fried chicken, but with a difference. Foie-butter grits gleamed with a Jackson Pollock drip of plum-balsamic reduction, crisp flatbread was spread with hot blue crab and mascarpone, and the fried chicken drumsticks were twice-cooked for crunch, with the sweet tang of Gochujang glaze. Jeremy and I had little to say to one another as we bit into steaming crawfish-and-coconut beignets that collapsed and dripped through our fingers, and a wagyu beef and bone-marrow wrap leaking lime and salsa roja. It was an extraordinary elevation of comfort food that gave away the Michelin-starred training of the chef–owner, Todd Harris. When the rush had died down, he emerged from the kitchen in a checked shirt, a bald-eagle T-shirt underneath, and joined me and Jeremy outside. Todd placed a clog across one knee and pulled down his beanie as we talked about his reasons for also leaving Chicago to come to Savannah.

'Soul food is such an interesting food,' he said. 'For example, take mac and cheese, it's such a Southern thing, but Thomas Jefferson, he sends his slave to France, and he comes back with mac and cheese and starts cooking that on a plantation in Virginia.'

Much of Todd's vocational training had centred on French and Italian cooking – how to make a velouté, for example – but what he had never learned was how to make a brown roux.

'It was giving that respect and voice to food coming from the South that was important to me. And so much of Southern food is about what you can grow,' he said gesturing around at the ground. Todd described his little garden, where every week he'd find forty pieces of okra on six plants. 'Okra was tied into the hair of slaves when they were shipped to America so they had the seeds to start their gardens. Now I can see why they cooked it so much, you can't stop it from growing.'

Jeremy asked Todd how much the success of Mashama Bailey had influenced his decision to come to Savannah.

'Mashama?' he repeated. 'She was a key reason. Watching her story was interesting for me as someone working in fine-dining, and being the only Black person in the kitchen – at least the only Black person cooking.' Todd gave me a rueful smile. 'You might have a Black dishwasher but in the world of fine-dining there's not very many of us.'

On Broughton Street, in the tourist hub, I'd barely seen Black people on the streets or in shops and Todd nodded with the same frustration I'd recognised in Ericka.

'It's crazy to think Savannah is half Black. During the day, it's just white. I think there is a feeling in the Black community that places like that in those neighbourhoods just aren't for them, 'cos we don't blast about the fact that we're Black. So sometimes Black people will say you know, "*Oh this is bougie*", and then they find out that it's me back there and I come out, and they're a little bit more disarmed.'

For a few minutes we listened to the sound of a hen party falling out of a Hummer, the street lamps lighting the top halves of our faces in the dark.

'A hundred years ago, the three of us wouldn't be freely, casually sitting here,' Todd said quietly. 'And it's still very white and parts of it are segregated, but there is a sense of pride in being here and having the freedom that I have to do what I want in a place with such a history.'

Less than a year after we met, Todd left the Garage and set up his new venture, named Red Palm, cooking food that would bring the history of West Africa to twenty-first-century tables in Savannah.

Halloween was a couple of weeks away and the South Historic District was prepared: flower beds of pink azalea were marked with mock gravestones and black cats, bloodied hands reaching up from the soil. Bales of hay were piled with pumpkins and the grandest houses had bats on their facades, skeletons dangling from wrought-iron balconies or hanging off the shutters. Even the avenues that were free from decoration looked as though they were dressed up – swathes of Spanish moss hanging like cobwebs from the painfully twisted branches of live oak. I'd expected the moss to feel as soft as cotton wool, but it was rough to handle, like thicker threads of rosemary. During the American Civil War, Savannah was spared the flames that engulfed much of the South, which explained why its mix of Victorian, Georgian, Greek Revival and Gothic architecture stood out from the drabness of surrounding cities. The most fabulous mansions had stairs running up to entrance porticos with columns on either side, while the older, smaller residences were made from wood, no more than two storeys high, with gabled roofs.

It was our second afternoon in the city, and while Jeremy and I walked from one square to the next, listening to church bells over the treetops and the clip-clop of horses leading carriage tours, I remarked on how I felt safe among Savannahians, who had a warmth I'd only experienced in New Orleans. On the approach to Montgomery Street, I paused before a black truck with an Alabama licence plate slowed to let us cross, and something caught my eye: a Confederate flag on the bumper.

'Was that...?' I asked, in disbelief.

'Yeah, it was,' said Jeremy, entertained by my reaction. 'A lot of people think the flag is about Southern pride and Southern heritage. And you know, they're probably perfectly decent people who would be nice if we talked. They just like to argue that the Civil War was about "states' rights" instead of slavery.'

Walking through what seemed like someone's backyard, and probably was someone's backyard, we arrived at a small door that opened into a darkened tearoom, so dimly lit that it took a moment to adjust as the door banged shut on the sunlight and the scene inside emerged like a developing photograph.

Agatha's Coffee and Tea House was new, and co-owned by a Black woman named Taía, who appeared like an apparition wearing pearls. Around us I could now see customers reading murder-mystery books taken from shelves lined with Agatha Christie and Nancy Drew. Some wrote in notebooks while others played chess on an old marble board. After raspberry iced tea and a long-needed sit-down in velvet armchairs, we followed Taía around into an adjoining space that looked half-dressed. The soon-to-be 'King Oliver's Creole Jazz Bar' smelled of fresh paint from its recently touched-up murals, the soundtrack to *The Shining* playing quietly.

'This used to be a funeral home, pool hall and video-game arcade,' said Taía, her hands clasped in front of her. She had a voice like caramel, soft and sweet as though it belonged to a child.

'Funeral home?' asked Jeremy, touching the pillars. 'Any ghosts?'

'Oh yeah,' she said. 'We've seen a lot. It feels calmer lately. I don't know if it's just because the weather is colder.'

I looked across at Jeremy whose face gave away nothing.

'Usually it's kinda jittery in the morning,' said Taía, who hadn't moved, her hands still clasped. 'You walk in and it feels like someone's going "How you doin'?" Can't say for sure. But yeah, sometimes you can tell.'

'Who do you think it is?' I asked, suddenly aware of the chill in the room.

'King Oliver used to work in this building. He was Louis Armstrong's mentor and as his fame died out, he came to work here as a janitor in this building. He worked here until about 1938.'

'Do you think it's him?'

Taía shrugged. 'I have a theory that some things are just trapped in a moment in time, so sometimes you can feel that. But yeah, the city is haunted.'

'Sorry?'

'The city. It's haunted.'

That night, with Taía's words echoing in my head, I had my first night terror in months. No doubt Savannah was spooky. It offered a number of ghost tours and stays in supposedly haunted hotels, though I couldn't imagine why anyone would pay to lie awake listening for footsteps of the dead. Snapping the lamp on, in the very un-haunted Thompson Savannah hotel, I slept in fits and starts, waking late to find Jeremy had gone. He'd risen at dawn to take the *Silver Meteor* back to Orlando, boarding before 7 a.m.

My own train in the opposite direction was departing at night so I made my way down to Mashama's place for brunch at the Grey. There was already a queue of around thirty people when I arrived, the majority of them Black families from Atlanta, and as far up the coast as Raleigh, all of whom were in Savannah for Mashama's food. Seated at the bar, with tiny bottles of bitters, cocktail shakers and stirrers for company, I tucked into a plate of chicken, hoe cakes and syrup, enjoying the double bass from a live jazz band. Housed in a formerly segregated Greyhound bus terminal, the diner still had gate numbers on the wall, and I started to think about Ericka's family not wanting to visit the South. Everywhere was a reminder of the horrors of the past. While some needed to untangle their history, I understood why others were happy to leave theirs in knots.

The diner busied and I was about to leave when a pretty blonde woman named Malia – 'like Maria with an "l"' – took a seat next to me. An estate agent from Oahu, she had wide-set eyes like Jackie O, leaning in so close that I could smell her perfume as she whispered: 'I was here last night for dinner too.' As two solo travellers, we got chatting about safety and she picked up her phone to show me NomadHer, tapping it open with sparkly nails. It was a travel app for women wanting to buddy up, organise trips and share advice. Knowing a number of middle-aged women too nervous to travel alone, I was heartened to see the confidence that travel apps offered, even if I found no need for them myself. Leaving Malia to her poached eggs and potato rösti, I slipped out of the diner and went in search of Forrest Gump's bench on Chippewa Square, where I planned to finish reading my book. Sadly, the bench had taken up residence in the Savannah History Museum and as I ambled around aimlessly, I heard chants rising in the air. A significant crowd of pro-Palestine protesters passed by with a megaphone, the majority of onlookers filming and joining in the calls for a free Palestine. Only eight days had passed since the Hamas attack on Israel and both the attack and Israel's scorched-earth response against Palestinian civilians in Gaza was already reverberating around the world.

Before heading to the train, I bought a blanket then took myself off to Shabazz seafood restaurant on Todd's recommendation. Unmissable, it was housed in a bright yellow building in the middle of a parking lot by a busy junction. Through an old bank-teller's hatch with bars on the window, I was handed a Yasmin crab burger by Yusuf Shabazz himself, whose fish sandwiches, spicy crab patties and Styrofoam cups of fries were all named after members of his family. Burger in hand, I parked myself at a picnic table alongside two elderly men in Nike tracksuits, looking for a way to insert myself into their conversation and resorting to the worst chat-up line.

'Do you come here often?' I asked.

'I been comin' here thirty years,' said one.

'Is it the best fish sandwich in Savannah?'

'To me,' he said, slurping red juice through a straw. 'You live around here?'

I explained my business in Savannah, listing where I'd been, and they nodded to each other. Val introduced himself, curious about Dottie's.

'What's the name?' he asked.

'Dottie's.'

'Say again?'

'Dottie's.'

'Spell it for me.'

'*Dah-dees*,' I said.

'Oh! Dottie's! And that's Black-owned?'

I nodded, sauce spilling down my wrist.

'You knew about that?' said Val, turning to his friend, who shook his head.

'So where else you been?' Val asked.

'Agatha's?'

'That's that tea spot on MLK,' said his friend.

'514, 515?' asked Val.

'516,' said his friend. 'You remember, that used to be a funeral home one time. They had a horse and buggy to carry the casket.'

'Well, you have a beautiful time,' said Val, tying his crinkly fries into a plastic bag and standing up. 'Oh lord, everything hurt. I was playing tennis today and I'm too old.'

'Nice to meet you,' I said.

'You be careful, you gone get fat by the time you get back,' said Val, breaking into a large smile.

'It's worth it,' I replied.

Val's friend balled up his wrapper then wiped his mouth on a napkin. 'You go to the House of Prayer?' he asked.

'Where?'

'The United House of Prayer! The church. They got some real good food. They got *soul* food. Like turkey wings, ox tail, pig feet, you know. It's on Ogeechee Road and 34th, they got *real* soul food there. You get yo' belly full there real quick. But you gotta be quick 'cos they sell out. You eat everything?'

'I do.'

'You try any of the rib spots?'

'Nobody told me about them.'

'When you leavin'?'

'Tonight.'

'Ah, you missed that. You gotta come back. One is called Tricks and one is called Randy's. One used to work for the other then they had a little spat. Anyway, you be well. You a brave lady. Riding on those trains.'

———

Like Floridians bracing for a storm, I was ready. Armed with a silk wraparound eye mask, silicone earplugs and a pillow that worked like a neck brace, I got in line to board the *Silver Meteor* to New York. Eight years had passed since I'd spent a month sleeping in coach class, but I remembered only too well how the lights barely dimmed, passengers argued until the small hours and the air conditioning was set to arctic. The temperature had dropped over the weekend and I was glad for my hoodie and knee socks under jogging bottoms frayed at the edges. Fashion was redundant on a night train. Comfort was at the forefront when it came to making it through the ride, which explained why most of us looked like hobos. Not Susan though. Susan looked ready for a day at the office, her long ginger hair plaited down her back. In both hands she clutched a vintage case. Susan was from Savannah and had been taking the sleeper to DC for almost fifteen years – in a bedroom of course.

'I do it for work,' she said with a gentle drawl. 'It's so convenient. I can literally get here ten minutes ahead of time and then walk on. If I was flying I'd have to get myself to Atlanta.'

'Do you genuinely enjoy being on the train?' I asked, spotting headlamps approaching up the tracks. Susan gave me a guilty look as though caught with her hand in a cookie jar.

'I do,' she said, clenching her teeth together and giggling. 'Once I get on the train, I have all this time and I can do anything. I've often woken up and thought "Thank god I'm going to take the train" because I'll have like a big presentation to get ready and it's like nobody's going to bother me, and I can do a bunch of work or go to the café car and use my computer. I get a couple of naps, I do my stretches, I read some magazines or my book-club book.'

The train drew into the platform and, soon to be separated, I told Susan that I was leaving with a good feeling about the city, and she beamed and squeezed my elbow.

'Savannah is just so different from all the Southern cities. And it's so inclusive, you know. We got all the L-G-B-T-Q-I-A letters. And it's been this way for ever. For. Ever. Since the fifties. There were never any issues.' She waved a hand back and forth across her forehead as though struggling to get her thoughts out. 'I hear these conversations now and I don't understand it. Nobody ever debated it. You don't have issues here. You don't have problems. We have a huge gay pride, it's just… it's just a really nice place to live.'

As she waited at the bottom of the steps, I could picture a young Susan wearing daisy headbands and hippy skirts. She turned apologetically. 'Thank you for making this fun. I hope I see you again,' she said, as the train manager welcomed her up, recognising her from past trips and steering her to the right.

Assigned a seat, I turned left, straight into the scrum where passengers were already in each other's spots and refusing to move, much to the chagrin of the staff. My own seat was taken by a man wearing headphones who wouldn't even make eye contact as I tried to explain. Moved by the manager towards the middle of the carriage, I took a new seat next to a woman reading a copy of *The Hunted* by Gabriel Bergmoser. She turned to face the window as I sat down. In the row in front, a group of friends was sharing a box of Popeyes fried chicken, the smell reassuring in its familiarity as I settled in, tugging my blanket across my lap.

'I like your nose stud,' said the woman across from me, tapping her own nostril where a delicate pin shone. 'I want a big one. Where'd you get that?'

'From India,' I replied, touching the diamond which I often forgot was there.

'Damn, girl. I can't go to India,' she said, pursing up her mouth and rubbing her hair, which was purple with a few months' growth at the root.

'Where are you heading?' I asked, as the train set off through the rain.

'I'm from New Jersey. I got on in Jacksonville,' she said, shifting in her seat and pulling out a bag of Haribo from under her. She told me that once a year her son and his wife went away to celebrate their anniversary and paid for her to come down to Florida to look after their baby, giving her 'sweet time' with her nineteen-month-old grandson.

'They don't trust nobody to look after the baby,' she said, the sugariness of raspberry Goldbears on her breath. 'I think the baby is okay, it's the parents. You can't do nothing effectively if you don't know that someone is there who you can trust. You can work at peace when you ain't got nothing to worry about.'

She raised her shoulders and looked up and down the aisle, shaking her head at a pair of friends who were watching *John Wick* without earphones. 'This is the last time I'm catching the train; this is too much. I'd rather take the plane and be done with it.'

'Why didn't you fly?' I asked, glancing across to where Keanu Reeves was throwing knives at someone's head.

'I'm scared to get the plane but I'm going to have to suck it up. It's a lot quicker – and quieter,' she added, rummaging in her handbag and pulling out a packet of earplugs. 'When I was small – and I travelled with my daddy in my younger days – I would catch the plane, but as I got older I realised I had a choice. So I took the night train.'

One by one the woman had pulled out her earplugs, blanket and eye mask and was evidently ready to sleep. Aware that the lights were starting to dim, dissuading none of the loud talkers, I decided to leave her alone.

'What's your name?' I asked finally, kicking off my shoes and pulling on a second pair of thermal socks.

'Monique.'

'Oh! I'm Monisha.'

'Monisha? What?' Monique leaned away, then leaned forwards and placed her hand on mine. 'We special… we special. It's nice meeting you, Monisha.'

With that, Monique pulled down her eye mask and reclined her chair, pressing prayer hands against her cheek.

Around me there were towels over heads, duvets across couples and a number of N95 face masks. Strapping on my neck pillow, I adjusted my eye mask, pulled my hood over my hair and lay back, pressing in my earplugs. Not an inch of skin visible to the human eye, I sank my chin into my pillow and went to sleep, the train jolting through the darkness.

At 6 a.m. I woke and pushed up my eye mask to find an orange glow lighting up the carriage. Dotted around, a few passengers were sitting on the armrests, watching the sun come up over the Potomac River. From what I could tell, a number of rivers created natural boundaries between states, the Potomac worming up towards the capital with Virginia on one side, Maryland on the other. Whether or not I was ready, morning had arrived, and I bundled up my blanket and went to the café car for a cup of horrible coffee. To my left the sunrise was giving the water a mythical lustre and I crouched by the window to photograph the moment, just as a man in a sweatshirt tapped me on the shoulder and moved me to one side so he could vomit into the recycling bin.

For the final couple of hours, I did not move from the window. Time and again I'd been told this was not a scenic route, no oceans, canyons or mountains to please the eye. But scenery conveyed more than the natural beauty of landscapes. There was humour in graffiti on bridges towards Baltimore, joy in the Philadelphia zoo murals, and hope in the solitary fisherman boating on Pennsylvania's Van Sciver Lake. As we thumped and bounced towards New York, I tried in earnest to lose my thoughts to the surroundings. I'd woken to the news that Wadee Alfayoumi, a six-year-old American boy of Palestinian descent, had been murdered in his home in Illinois – stabbed twenty-six times by his landlord Joseph Czuba in a hate crime. My social media was filled with scenes from Gaza, bodies without limbs, limbs without bodies, a father carrying his child's remains in a plastic bag. Israelis mourned their dead, their faces frozen in anguish, some holding images of some of the 250 people taken hostage by Hamas. Now as I watched smoke unfurling from chimneys, I saw only the smouldering from bombs, car cemeteries piled high with metal corpses, and autumnal trees engulfed in flames. Around me passengers were chatting about basketball, comparing iron levels, laughing in a hum of superficial human interaction. As the *Silver Meteor* approached New York, it descended towards Penn Station and I watched the tracks fork, strangled by the fear that beneath the veneer of normality our world was about to crack in two.

15

THE SANTA CLAUS EXPRESS

Yes, this is a Finnish elevator.
So try to keep quiet like a Finn, please…

With unease I read the sign, then looked down. In shocking pink base layers and matching boots, the girls were a woollen-clad picture of cuteness – until a single glance or word of provocation could spill blood. This was a new stage in their relationship and I'd recently spent an afternoon in paediatric casualty after a five-second fight over a pencil had resulted in teeth sinking into an upper arm. 'Wow, through the jumper as well,' the on-call registrar had commented as I flushed with shame at the bite marks.

Jem, Ariel, Maya and I had just arrived in Helsinki and I was starting to question whether Finland was such a good idea for our debut sleeper train as a decidedly non-quiet foursome. Since the trip to Sicily, Maya had started school and I felt confident that she was ready for her first overnight journey, but the girls' volume and propensity for physical fights still made me nervous. An Indian train would perhaps have been a wiser choice.

As we walked towards the station, ice crunching underfoot, I looked up 'Finnish silence' and found an article in the *Wall Street Journal* about Finns taking classes in the art of small talk which 'does not come naturally'. It suggested that one of the reasons for their aversion to chitchat was the sub-zero temperature: no one wanted to stand around making inane comments about the weather while their hands turned blue. Further on,

one interviewee remarked how surprised he was to have someone once talk to him on a train.

Far from a deterrent, the revelations made me more determined
than ever to strike up conversation with these introverted souls.
My journeys through both Sweden and Norway had revealed that
Scandis were talkative after bottles of wine and a nudge here and
there, and I was hoping to find the same from the Finns.

Christmas was a few days away and the Finnish capital was
ringing with Yuletide cheer. Markets sold mugs of hot, fruity
glögi; spruce trees sparkled up and down the streets; strings of
golden orbs reached from one rooftop to the next. A cold front
had brought an unexpected amount of snow and it was packed
into shoulder-high peaks, the temperature now an eye-watering
−8°C. The wind left me breathless as we crossed the road to
face Helsinki Central, a rare beauty of a railway station. Built in
1904 by a Finnish-American architect named Eliel Saarinen, the
Art Nouveau edifice came about after Saarinen won a compe-
tition, but his National Romantic designs – typical of Nordic
architecture – were met with disapproval by his colleagues who
felt the new station should represent the modern era and the
expansion of global travel. Saarinen took off around Europe to
gather inspiration, returning to completely overhaul his plans,
eventually opening the station in 1919.

We came to stand beneath the pink granite facade, admiring
the four statues that flanked the arched frontage. Known as the
Lantern Bearers, these muscly chaps stood in pairs, each sporting
a pageboy haircut and holding an illuminated globe. From time
to time, they were manipulated for fun into mascots, the globes
turned into footballs to support the Finnish national team, or
the figures dressed in the Eurovision entry's signature green
bolero. Today, with the snow piled upon their heads and necks,
they looked like a quartet of old British barristers.

Inside the station I had flashbacks to journeying around
America, so grand was the space with its arched ceilings and
neoclassical chandeliers hanging from black rope. Shaped like
paper scrolls ringed with brass, the frosted glass lamps had been

casting their glow through the atrium since the 1950s. For all the wizardry of modern stations around the world, this one felt like the real deal. It echoed with footsteps and announcements, wooden doors swinging as passengers charged in and out, some carrying little more than phones and satchels, while others were loaded with luggage for the long haul. Lost in a moment of pure pleasure, I felt Ariel tug my hand.

'Come on, Mama, I don't want to miss the train.'

Salted and grey with ice, platform 8 was crowded with passengers wheeling spinner suitcases. A glass roof zigzagged overhead, yet the tracks were still filled with snow and brick-sized chunks of black ice. In between fur-trimmed boots and dogs wearing jackets, small children trudged around, their breath twisting up on the air. Our train was almost twenty minutes late to arrive and as each new pair of headlamps shone at the spaghetti junction of tracks, little hopes soared then crashed as the green trains turned into every platform but ours. A young woman with pink hair and clever eye make-up stood behind us in a VR railways uniform, her eyes turned upwards, giving her the look of a shrewd Disney fairy. She was checking her phone and I stepped back to ask if she had any idea when the train was due. A dining-car attendant, Saara revealed that it was outside the station and would be pulling in soon. I watched Maya staring up at the pink hair with admiration as Saara bent down to ask her which carriage we were in.

'You should move further that way,' Saara said, pointing down the platform, 'it is going to stop there.'

'I like your pink hair,' Maya said at last.

'Don't get any ideas,' Jem said, wandering over.

'If you're going to eat, you should come early to the dining car as it will get very busy,' Saara said, with an accent that reminded me of flute music.

'We've not eaten, we'll be there for sure,' Jem replied. 'Are you going to be on the train the whole night?'

'No, I live in Tampere, so I'll be working until around 10.30 p.m. and then I will get off and go home,' she said. As an afterthought I asked her what the most popular dish was.

'The meatballs for sure and also the salmon soup. On the routes that have a lot of tourists more people order pasta and omelettes as well; I believe that is because it's more approachable for foreigners rather than our traditional foods. A lot of tourists do want to test them also though.' Saara checked her phone again and then pointed to where a double-decker train was now coming into view. 'Your train is here!' she told the girls as the crowd galvanised into action. 'See you soon.' She flashed them an impish look then disappeared.

At 7.45 p.m. the *Santa Claus Express* roared into the station, its red tail lamps burning as it reversed in through the darkness. As a child this train would have fulfilled my every dream; in fact, as an adult it still did. Departing nightly from Helsinki, the year-round sleeper service was Finland's flagship ride. Over a leisurely twelve hours, it wound its way north into the Arctic Circle, arriving at 7.30 a.m. at the city of Rovaniemi, the heart of Finnish Lapland. The terms 'Lapp' or 'Lappish' were now considered an ethnic slur for the Indigenous Sámi people who called the region Sápmi, though Lapland was still the official name.

Although the train continued to the eastern town of Kemijärvi, most passengers disembarked at Rovaniemi to meet the big man at Santa Claus Village, spending a couple of days taking husky rides and hunting the aurora borealis. A Father Christmas emblem swept past as I scanned the carriage numbers, gripping Maya's hand. She looked sad.

'What's up, buddy?' I asked, straining to hear over the engine.

'I need a wee wee.'

'Please be joking. Can you wait until we get on?'

'No, I need to go now.'

'Shit.'

'No, just a wee wee.'

'Jem, quick, pass me a pull-up,' I said, scooping her up under one arm and frantically tugging at her boots as passengers queued behind us. Yanking down her leggings, I glanced around before whipping off her knickers, much to the horror of a Korean couple in matching white parkas. The train was now coming to a standstill as I coaxed Maya to wriggle into the nappy pants, holding her socked feet off the ice. With seconds to spare, she relaxed her bladder with a satisfied look.

'It's nice and warm,' she smiled as I breathed a sigh of relief. She'd not worn pull-ups for months but at the last minute I'd packed a few just in case.

'Never apologise for your kids,' said an Australian woman as the doors hissed open. 'We've all been there.'

Giving silent thanks to Saara for directing us, we boarded the train and clambered upstairs to our compartment, the sound of boots running down the corridors amid hoots of purest joy.

To guarantee a place for dinner, we dumped our bags and bolted to the restaurant car, where a large family was already crowded around an iPad and watching *Elf* dubbed into Portuguese. Saara was carrying out steaming plates and gestured towards a table by a window sprayed with snow. Tinsel spiralled up the brass bars, mistletoe peeking out from the backs of banquettes. Leaving the girls to fight over packets of salt, I wandered through to find the kiosk and joined the queue behind two young Chinese women wearing towelling slippers, a bold move given the slush brought in on people's boots.

'Can we get McDonald's?' asked the first woman.

'I'm sorry?' said the attendant, frowning lightly.

'McDonald's. Is there McDonald's here?'

'No, this is just our dining car,' she replied, suppressing a smile.

'There is only one restaurant?' queried the second woman.

'There is just one restaurant car.'

Dismay etched across their faces, the two women muttered to one another, stepping aside as I scanned the menu and found two key items: 'meatballs and mashed potatoes' and 'bigger portion of meatballs'. For an extra €2 I opted for the latter in the hope of averting any kind of dispute. I then noticed the specials featured a bowl of smoked reindeer stew and added one on for good measure.

Next door the windows had fogged up from passengers crowding in, most of whom were turning away in disappointment now that the tables were filled. Through the glass I could barely make out where we were, towns flashing past, woods drooping under the weight of snow. It was like being in a gastropub with the smell of stews and bubbling carbonara. Pints of pale ale left rings around the tables as passengers drank, laughed and made small talk – there were no Finns in here.

In a matter of minutes, we were spooning up hot meatballs and buttery mash – a blob of lingonberry jam on the side.

'Mummy, what meat is this?' Ariel asked, batting away her sister's spoon with stealth. I stared at a meatball, cutting one open to inspect it.

'I'm actually not sure.'

'And what's this one?' she asked, dangling a piece of smoked reindeer into her mouth like a Roman, then giving me a nod of approval. This was a moment I'd been dreading. How to explain that they were devouring the protagonist of their favourite Christmas song?

'Well,' I said, 'in Finland they eat lots of different things depending on what they can grow and farm, and this is… reindeer.'

She shrugged and finished the bowl. According to the railways' statistics, more than 80,000 portions of meatballs were consumed every year on board, and I could well believe it, so delicious was the hearty meal. Our food was served in large ceramic dishes, not a plastic tray in sight, and I looked around wondering why it was so hard to replicate this model around Europe. Enjoying the clamour, we spotted another young family hovering for a table, and reluctantly returned to our carriage.

Our compartment was a warm and comfortable space with bunk beds and an ensuite toilet that converted to a shower. The water was hot, the floors heated and there was enough space for us to top and tail with the children. Up to the age of ten, children travelled for free, as long as they shared a berth with another passenger. So far, this was the finest overnight train I'd found. Worn out from excitement, Maya slept immediately while Ariel sat on my lap on a pull-down seat by the window watching snowflakes fly at the glass. Eventually she too began to yawn and I watched as Jem patted her to sleep, vindicated by the sound of other parents yelling at their kids through the vent. Then she started to cough, a dry cough exacerbated by the central heating, and I felt a familiar sense of panic as she sat up, Jem rubbing her back. There was only ever one conclusion to her dry cough. Sure enough, Ariel vomited onto the duvet then burst into tears.

'Don't worry,' I said, 'I'm sure you're not the first child to puke on this train.'

It was, however, a sleeper-train milestone for me. Darting out into the corridor I hunted down one of the train managers, who directed me towards the unoccupied accessible room.

'You take whatever you need from there,' she said, patting my shoulder. 'It is very normal, with the movement and the excitement and everything. There is usually one. Often two.'

By the time I returned to our compartment, the woman had already removed the soiled cover and Ariel was now smiling with relief in a fresh pair of pyjamas as I made up the bed.

Once she had fallen asleep, I resumed my seat by the window. Silent but for the lightest drum of wheels, the train cut through forests closing in like an army of white ghosts. Slim-bodied lakes flashed by, their black waters glinting under street lights. Buried in the deepest thickets were golden stars hanging in porches and nativity scenes aglow. Humming over one bridge after another we soon belted into national parks filled with rowan trees, firs and larches. I glanced up in the hope of spotting some sign of the aurora borealis but, mottled grey, the sky revealed nothing but the North Star. After my sighting back in the Swedish city of Kiruna I hoped so much that the girls would be lucky this trip. Travelling here with children felt different and I found myself looking into the night-time scene with a sense of magic and wonder that I hadn't previously experienced.

I took out my diary and flicked through the pages, coming across my conversation with Ludwig about the polar nights in his home of Tromsø. As much as I wanted to learn to embrace the cold and darkness, genetics dictated that my body needed heat: I thrived in sunshine, something we would not find much of over the next few days, with sunrise at 11 a.m. and sunset just three hours later.

Snow drifts flew by, blankness followed by wilderness, then a flash of light from a single farmhouse window, followed by more darkness and woods. With a population of just 5.6 million spread over 130,000 square miles, it wasn't surprising that Finns weren't so forthcoming, given that there were so few people to talk to. In the north, there were more reindeer than humans. Soft orange light fell across the berths and I saw that we had stopped at Hämeenlinna, a city laid out along the shores of Lake Vanajavesi. It was from Helsinki to Hämeenlinna that the first railway had run in 1862. Only a handful of passengers boarded here, carrying skis and snowboards, a fox darting through the car park as we departed. The girls were in a deep sleep and Jem was reading by the nightlight. Stepping around our luggage, I opened the door carefully, slipping into the corridor to go back and find Saara.

Eight people remained in the dining car, Finns who had come out to play once the noisy foreign families had retired to bed. Even so, none spoke to the others, each leaving a space of one seat between the next as they drank Jameson whiskey and stared straight ahead. Relaxed, now the rush was over, Saara wiped her hands on her apron and came over to talk.

'The trains are popular because they are an easy way to travel,' she said, 'but at the same time it's eco-friendly. I would say it's a very Finnish way to travel, as we as a nation are very big on public transport and you can bring your car on board.'

'I hadn't realised.'

'They are parked below and you can take it at the other end and go. Finnish weather can be quite tricky from time to time so the passengers can avoid having to drive all the way to Lapland and just relax.'

I looked around to where two teenagers had entered and were now setting up a chess board.

'What do you enjoy most about your job?' I asked.

'The people. Finns are not ones to open up to strangers but I have noticed that a lot of our customers love to tell about their trip – where they are going, who they are meeting, etc. I have heard some great stories while working.'

There it was: the admission that Finns don't open up – from a Finn. More curious than ever, I thanked Saara and decided to turn in until I saw the conductor emerge from downstairs. I had more questions about this train and figured he might have many of the answers. Tailing him to the conductor's cabin, I tapped on the wall outside and he looked up, beckoning me in and shoving a pile of papers to one side so I could sit beside him.

Kimmo – 'like *chemo*therapy' – had worked with Finnish Railways for sixteen years, most recently on the Allegro high-speed train from Helsinki to St Petersburg and the *Tolstoi* sleeper from Helsinki to Moscow. Since Russia's invasion of Ukraine, sanctions on Russia had ended both routes and he'd moved across to the *Santa Claus Express*. At my request, Kimmo turned off the light so I could enjoy the view of wintry forests lit up by the train's headlamps. He waved at his two colleagues who kept poking their heads in, amused by the sight of us conversing in the dark. I asked Kimmo if there were many Finns on board.

'During summertime there are lots of Finnish people on board, but not at the moment; it's mostly tourists and families on this particular train because Lapland is for SantaPark and whatnot. It's a convenient way to travel, you sleep for the night, you have some beers. It's fun. If you fly it's only half an hour or a one-hour journey but this is nice.'

Neither Kimmo nor his colleagues could remember how long the *Santa Claus Express* had been running, but it sounded like the train was a cornerstone of Finnish Railways, one that could withstand any future threats to night trains. With the exception of departure and arrival, there didn't seem to be an enormous amount for train managers to do while everyone slept and I took the opportunity to probe further.

'What's the best part about working on a night train?' I asked, distracted by the lights of a bridge approaching.

'On the day trains people are in a hurry and they have to go to work and after work they are in a hurry to go home. So they are more upset if we are running a little bit late. They are much more annoyed during the day. But at night they are asleep and they wake and say "Oh we are late by two hours" and they go back to sleep.'

There was infinite truth in this. After many a rocky night there had been nothing more wonderful than hearing a train was running behind and that I could turn over and snooze for another couple of hours in the warmth. Kimmo explained that delays were sometimes down to snow, but with warmers on the track, it was never a huge hindrance. Occasionally old locomotives broke down and he'd once encountered thieves trying to steal copper wires, but instead they'd cut the information cable for the train, delaying the train by fourteen hours.

'There are nineteen tracks out of Helsinki, with the bay in between and lots of ships,' said Kimmo. 'So it can get quite bottlenecked. When they built the railroads, they didn't believe there would be this much train routes. Finnish Railways is 160 years old, built by the Russians, as you know, and we have the same rails. But now the European Union wants us to have the same gauge as the rest of Europe. That's why when we go to St Petersburg and Moscow it's possible. But I don't know who will build the whole new network. It's crazy. It is costly and lots of work.'

'From what I've seen so far, I think Finnish trains are great,' I said, as we skimmed across another bridge.

'Yeah? Tell that to the Finnish people. They believe that we are always late.'

I looked out of the window to where the forests were no more than a blur of feathery branches.

'Do you get a lot of wildlife up here?' I asked.

'Yeah, you get reindeers all the time.'

'Do they ever cross the tracks?'

Kimmo paused as if piecing together what he could say to me. 'So, you get money if the train kills your deer. So some people, they will put some hay on the tracks.'

'My god.'

'Yeah, if your reindeer get hit, you get easy money from the government.'

'How much?'

'Oh, I don't know,' Kimmo said, looking dejected. 'You'd have to ask the local people. I believe it's really hard to be a farmer for the reindeer. It's not that often, but we hit mooses also. Once we hit the moose with the Allegro train... at 200 kilometres per hour.' He closed his eyes and wiped the top of his head. 'We had half the moose inside the train, because the train is only plastic.'

We were approaching Saara's home city of Tampere and Kimmo checked his watch.

'Were you glad to finish the Russia route?'

He sat upright. 'No! That was *the* best job I have ever had because I like the Russian conductors and it was really nice to go to St Petersburg. You check the passports and visas and it was an interesting job – and an international job. The Russian people are nice, but the politicians... yeah. I liked those trains. It's a weird country, things are so different. You have to find out and see.'

I started to wonder if I was missing a trick with my career choice. Almost every railway worker I'd met on sleeper trains had spent years on board the same service, with no desire to leave or reduce their hours. I thought back to my conversations with Elisabeth on the Nightjet, Arthur on the *Caledonian Sleeper*, Mark on *The Royal Scotsman*, Harun on the *Doğu Express*, and Tor on the Dovre and Nordland lines. They knew their passengers by name, understood deeply their needs and took such pride in their jobs – and they were clearly well-loved in return. The community on board a sleeper train was truly akin to family, sometimes closer.

Jem was asleep when I tiptoed back into the compartment. We'd just left Tampere and I bent down for one last look outside. I was often asked how scenic a night train could really be, everyone sleeping as the train pushed on through the darkness. Even though I couldn't decipher details, I could see that Finland was fragmented, a mass of islands and forests held together by waterways and bridges. During day rides I was spoilt by big blasts of ocean, sunlight sweeping across meadows, mountains dominating the landscape. It was all there, doing the work for me as I sat back trying to take it all in. But at night I had to scour the landscape, a labour of love to spot the candles burning on kitchen tables, the berries in handwoven wreaths, the dogs asleep by the fire – each a tiny reward for my time. Tomorrow there would be no sun to wake us, so I left the blind up and climbed the steps into bed.

A mere seven minutes behind schedule, the *Santa Claus Express* reached Rovaniemi just after 7.30 a.m. It was pitch black, the snow bright yellow beneath the street lights as we taxied to our resort on the edge of the city. A village of igloo-style cabins built around the curves of Lake Olkkajärvi, the resort looked as though it had been designed from a child's imagination. Moomin-shaped ice sculptures were dotted around, torches burned outside *lavvu* and a row of sledges were lined up to transport luggage to and from the cabins. I could smell the reindeer before I could see them, stamping by sleighs piled with fur. But it hurt to breathe in, each inhalation chilling my brain as I adjusted to the temperature which was now hovering around -17°C.

By 10 a.m. the skies had lightened to ashen, and the grounds were now alive with the sound of five-year-olds revving snowmobiles. Huskies barked in the forest and bells tinkled as reindeer rides took place across the frozen lake. Panting uphill, tugging red-cheeked children in toboggans, most adults had regressed and were now pummelling each other with snowballs and screaming, nipping off to the side to where cups of vodka nestled in the snow. Whether or not the sun was due to visit was anybody's guess and by 2 p.m. it had already set behind the clouds as we crowded around a fire, fat marshmallows browned and dripping off sticks. From afar I noticed that the trees weren't just piled with snow, but that they had taken on a strange bone-like structure that extended all the way up to the stems and twigs. It was as though the trees had an outer coating of coral formed by thickened ice. The phenomenon was known as *tykky* and these trees were in the early stages of a process that could cause them to bend into cloud-like sculptures.

That night, I lay on top of faux animal skins, staring up through the cabin's glass ceiling. Designed to heat up and thaw the snow, the windows showed me nothing more than the reflections from other people's rooms – not a flicker of the Northern Lights. Standing up on the bed to peer from the roof, I looked across the igloos, lit up like a wonderland at the edge of the Arctic Circle. It would take time to adjust to the near-constant darkness and I was determined, as Ludwig had suggested, to view it as something to embrace and explore.

———

'Is Santa Claus real?' Ariel asked.

It was five months earlier, in the middle of summer, and she'd chosen to watch *A Boy Called Christmas*. The film was about a young boy named Nikolas who travels in the company of a pet mouse. I stared straight ahead.

'Is he?' she asked again. I could feel her looking at me this time.

'What do you think?' I asked, deflecting like a coward.

'I haven't seen him before, so I don't think so. And the Santa at school was Sophie's dad Steve wearing a beard. I know, I saw it wasn't real. Have you seen Santa in real life?' she asked.

'No, I haven't.'

'So how do you know he's real?'

This was heavy conversation for a Sunday morning with a six-year-old and I'd been hoping she'd figure it out much later. Ruining her sister's fun was a favourite pastime and this was dreamy ammunition.

'Listen. We're going to Finland in December, so why don't you decide then after you've seen him?'

'Okay,' she said, but I could tell she was unconvinced, scanning my expression for clues. We'd once had a conversation at bedtime about the logistics of Santa delivering presents. There was a fine line to tread between keeping the magic alive and scaring the shit out of them by admitting that, while they slept, some old man could find his way into their living room even with the doors locked, the alarm activated and an anxious dachshund on alert.

We were now in the queue at Santa Claus Village, inching up the stairs to meet the man himself. An enclave of log cabins, snowmen and hundreds of Christmas trees shimmering gold, the village was surrounded by trees whose top halves had *tykky*. Uplit by coloured beams, they resembled forests of purple popcorn. As we waited, elves wandered around, their ears and shoes pulled into points.

'Are they real?' Ariel asked, as I scanned the gallery of celebrities, in particular a photo of China's president Xi Jinping with his arm on Santa's knee.

'They are indeed,' I replied, noticing that the woman behind us had lost sight of her kids. She was clenching and unclenching her fists and kept craning her neck to see the front of the queue.

'Are you okay?' I asked. 'Have your kids run off?'

'Oh, I don't have any kids,' she replied, 'I'm here to see Santa. I came all the way from Hershey, Pennsylvania.'

'Home of the Hershey Kisses,' I replied, stuck for how to respond.

'That's the one. The worst frickin' chocolate you will ever eat,' she said, counting how many people stood before her.

Xi Jinping no longer seemed so odd. But as we moved forwards, I suddenly felt the utmost admiration for this woman, who was probably fulfilling a childhood dream. Sure, she might be a howling loon, but perhaps she had made a promise to her younger self that she would visit one day. My own experience of meeting Santa had been at Binns department store in Hull in the mid-1980s. He'd had terrible halitosis and given me a plastic doll whose foot had broken off before we even reached the car park. Maybe she'd never been taken as a kid to get a crap toy and a photo, and I loved that she couldn't care less about judgement.

The girls had spent the best part of the last hour pinching each other and complaining of boredom to the point that I was almost in tears. This was meant to be a once-in-a-lifetime experience, a dream come true that would make me flush with joy at their joy, and now I was gripping one a little too firmly by the wrist and muttering threats. When it came to our turn a pair of elves in baggy red trousers called us in. I watched as the children stepped into the wooden room. Maya's mouth fell open and she quickly looked at Ariel, who exchanged the look, her mouth pursing into a nervous smile. Their eyes had never shone so brightly.

'Come in, come in,' said Santa, an ample unit who filled his armchair. With a beard that ran down to his lap, pince-nez glasses and giant felt boots covered in snow, he was enough to make me a believer again.

'Where have you come from?' he asked.

'London,' said Ariel.

'And how about you?' he asked Maya. 'Have you lost your voice?'

She shook her head, chewing her lip.

'Now, have you been good?'

'Not really,' I said.

'Oh, well. Perhaps if you *are* good, I may stop by your house next week?' he said, his mouth twitching.

They nodded as he handed over two spotted giftbags tied with bows, and waved us off.

'So, what do you think?' I asked Ariel as she ripped open her bag.

'I think he's real. You know why? Because his beard wasn't stuck on,' she said, pulling out a plush reindeer and a pair of antlers and glowing with pleasure.

Despite its festive facade, Rovaniemi had a dark and horrible history. In October 1944 it had been bombed by the Germans, almost 90 per cent of the city destroyed in one week, leaving around twenty buildings standing. Finnish architect Alvar Aalto was tasked with the postwar redesign and decided, for reasons unknown, to shape its layout like a reindeer's head. Intrigued, I arranged to meet a local historian named Marja. Jem and the kids were exploring the Arktikum science centre where she arrived wearing leggings tucked into red felt boots, her waist-length grey hair wrapped in a scarf. Originally from Helsinki, Marja had been living in Rovaniemi for almost forty years. She trudged ahead of me as I picked my knees up through the drifts.

'It is different here,' she said. 'I remember once, I had some-body from a very big city in the US come here and she told me that she had a choice of 130 concert halls every evening. But I thought, "Well, yes, it's nice but you can go only to one place at a time. If I want to attend a concert, I do it when they have a concert."'

I thought about the Finns repeatedly ranking at the top of the *World Happiness Report*, and wondered whether it was down to expectation and contentment with what was offered to them, rather than superior living standards.

Tears were rolling down my face as the wind picked up, Marja pottering along and explaining how this corner of the world had been through four or five ice ages. Convinced that we were living through a sixth, I held my breath and pulled up my snood.

'Is it true that the city is built in the shape of a reindeer?'

'Oh yes!'

'Why is that?'

'I have never read any explanations, perhaps it was in a way Aalto thought "Ha ha, it's a reindeer". But I think because there was nothing left, it was kind of a dream for an architect as he didn't have to think what the others had been doing before him.'

'Why was the city bombed?' I asked, wondering where Finland had stood during the Second World War.

Marja talked me through the Winter War, which Stalin had waged on Finland over a period of 105 days. It was a David and Goliath battle that had ended with the Moscow Peace Treaty in March 1940.

'Hitler then got an idea to use Finland to go to the Soviet Union and take what he would like. So the Germans came here.' She turned around and looked at me through snow-flecked glasses.

'Please remember that Finland was not occupied,' she said. 'Not Finland and not the United Kingdom. The Germans came here in a kind of cooperation. Eventually the Moscow Armistice signed in September 1944 demanded that Finland expel remaining soldiers. Stalin said the Finnish people need to make the Germans leave or he will send once again his Red Army to the north. During that war, the Lapland War, Rovaniemi was destroyed.'

We had arrived at a military cemetery where around 600 people were buried. Marja unwound her scarf and covered her hair again. Alone, we stood at the entrance of a cemetery protected on all sides by woods. All I could hear was my breath. For three or four minutes Marja said nothing. At any other time I would have mumbled something to lift the lull in our conversation but here I understood the Finnish aversion to small talk. It was simply not required, the solemnity of our surroundings explanation enough. Marja picked her way towards what looked like a large metal hook poking up from the ground. There were hundreds of them, evenly spaced out. I then realised they were empty flower holders. She bent down and began to scrabble around beneath one.

'Where is it? No. Where is it? Ah there,' she said, gently brushing off the snow to reveal the name of Reino Ilmari Nisko, who lay in plot 52.

'All countries have their own ways how to organise these things but this was good because people have a place where to cry. Of course, terrible work for those who collected these bodies and took care of them.'

'Wait, where did they die?' I asked, crouching over to check.

'All these soldiers died elsewhere and were brought back home. We have more than 600 of these military graveyards in Finland.' Marja pointed to a board listing the names and plots of those who had died between 1939 and 1945. 'There are 601 here and then nine unknown soldiers here.' She started to walk around the edge of the graveyard. 'And when Finland was 100 years old, on 6 December 2017 – so it was terrible – the idea was, that, I am going to cry…' she said, her voice breaking. She sniffed and took a breath. 'Beside each grave there was somebody who was the same age as the soldier. It was terrible to see how young they were,' she cried out. At that moment church bells began to sound quietly, low chimes that carried across from a small hill. It was snowing heavily now and Marja invited me to join her on a circuit.

'I know that there are cultures where people never come to graveyards and they think that there are ghosts. In Finland we feel that graveyards are easy places, people come here, they walk, they admire the names and they are often like parks or like small forests.'

We walked side by side, the quietness hanging comfortably between us. As we returned to the gates, I scanned the hundreds of names of people's loved ones, a pang of sadness for the final group of the nine unknown. I thanked Marja for bringing me here. No matter where I travelled in the world, nothing touched me more than people inviting me into the sacred spaces of their dead.

On our final morning I woke knowing something was different. It was just before 9 a.m. and I ran out of the cabin, stumbling towards the lake to witness the civil twilight, when the sun is just below the horizon. For the first time since we had arrived the sky was clean, a few smudges of cloud fading away as I watched. Half a moon burned brightly, the snow turning violet in the light. On the horizon a band of orange was blazing, softening to peach then a honey-yellow as it rose to meet the blue. I squatted in the snow. For three days I hadn't seen the sun, its energy now pumping through me, my spirit revived. It was almost worth living in total darkness to feel its return. Almost…

For the second time in a week, we left our luggage and bolted to the dining car with all the class of German tourists bagging sun loungers. It was brutal behaviour but necessary, with the *Santa Claus Express* fully booked for our return leg to Helsinki. However, we arrived to find it much quieter than expected. Departing a lot later than the outward journey, the train was at full pelt and most families had boarded and gone straight to bed. Over a final bowl of reindeer stew, we watched the snow whipping around as the girls struggled to stay awake.

On the way back to our carriage we passed through the designated dog area, where a number of breeds were lying under the seats – and on top of them. Suddenly the kids were awake again, darting between an old golden retriever and a small hound with an unfeasibly large scrotum that was spread out like an extra limb. In one crate lay Haamu – meaning 'ghost' – a white bichon frisé who got car sick whenever he travelled, compelling his owner to take the train wherever she went. A couple of rows behind was a blue-eyed Staffordshire bull terrier named Miilu who was travelling with Eerika, an occupational therapist from Rovaniemi. It reminded me of being in a vet's waiting room but without the smell of bleach and fear. Originally from Turku, Eerika had moved north for a literal change of scenery and was now travelling home with her partner for Christmas. As Miilu chewed my hand like a toy, we got chatting – dogs and children always helping to break the ice on trains. Eerika was wearing her coat like a blanket and lamented how they were supposed to be on the previous service in a private compartment. They'd missed the departure and were now relegated to the communal dog zone. I asked Eerika how she found the polar nights, and she looked amused.

'Actually, I found when I left Turku that people are friendlier, warmer and more active up in the north when it's darker. They keep themselves more busy,' she said, which mirrored what Ludwig had told me on the Nordland line.

While we talked, I could see a young man pretending not to listen, but absorbed by our conversation. He was the only one in the carriage without a dog and was patting a matted sheepdog lying at his feet. We drew into a station and Jem took the girls to the compartment. Eerika excused herself to take Miilu out and the young man leaned across.

'Uh, where are you from?' he asked, his voice so soft I strained to hear.

'London. And you?'

'Um, Myanmar. It is nice to meet you.'

Unable to hear anything, I moved into the next seat and began talking to Min, who had fled the country after the first coup. His schoolbooks lay downturned beside him. Up close I could now see soft triangles of hair on his cheeks, a few whiskers here and there on a face that was yet to feel a razor. Eighteen years old, Min was studying at a high school in a nearby town after securing a visa through an agency that worked in tandem with Myanmar to allow students to attend university in Finland. However, he had to first finish his high-school studies in the Finnish language before applying. Wearing a hoodie and clutching his iPhone, Min spoke up as the train set off.

'As you know we faced the coup. I am a CDM student, part of the Civil Disobedience Movement – it is a peaceful process. My education stopped in February 2021 when the coup started and then all the students, they don't know what to do, their education was not complete. We were waiting for university. I am still processing the coup, but I have more time to think now.'

'Why Finland?' I asked.

'I can study in university for free if I finish high school in Finland. There is only cost for living and eating. I can work in the holidays.'

Min explained that around twenty other students were spread across various towns in Finland and that none of them knew when they might see their families again. But he considered it a small price to pay when taking into account the plight of his friends in Myanmar, many of whom were in prison. He had plans to study peace and conflict studies and spent his spare time writing poetry and playing the piano.

'I do it to change my feelings,' he said. 'Sometimes it's depression, but writing poetry gives me relief. It is very real for me.'

'What do your parents do?' I asked, nervous to mention them in case I upset him.

'My parents are brokers, they are selling onions and garlics and food things. I speak to them almost every day. They feel relief that I am here. I am safe. But when the military cut off the internet, we cannot contact. Actually, it happens every day in the rural areas. They just want to destroy it all. They rape a lot. And they kill the children. Even two years old, three years old. We have to face that every day. And the educated people are all in prison.'

Min examined the back of his hand for a minute or two. 'You are a journalist, you can understand because there is no freedom for the journalists. You can be killed for writing things. And they will kill your family for writing the truth.'

As Min spoke my thoughts turned to Gaza. Just two weeks earlier Israeli forces had murdered the Palestinian poet and academic, Refaat Alareer, in an airstrike that had also killed his brother, sister and four of his nephews. Scores of Palestinian journalists had been killed in and around the Gaza Strip in the two-month period since 7 October by targeted airstrikes on their cars, homes and families, and I was struggling to understand the silence from the majority of Western journalists in the face of what constituted war crimes against their colleagues.

'Do you feel comfortable speaking the truth?' I asked.

'You can say my name is Min, because it is a common name.' Min looked out of the window to where large flakes of snow were spinning. 'This is the first time I am seeing snow,' he said. 'It is exciting. I feel cold but at the same time it is exciting, it's a mixed feeling. I can think about things politically more than I used to. And I am writing more poetry. It is good to create from the darkness.'

'You're much smarter and switched on than I was when I was eighteen.'

'Yes, that's the point, before the coup I was just a normal teenager,' he replied.

We sat in Finnish silence as Eerika and Miilu came back on board, the cold still on their jackets. The train was quiet, the dogs curled up, passengers settling in for the night. Before I got up to leave, I asked Min what he thought of the *Santa Claus Express* and he started laughing.

'Of course, it's a good train! Have you tried the trains in Myanmar? Totally different, you cannot sit still! It's just moving, it's like dancing, like this,' he said, bouncing around in his seat. 'I don't notice the movement, it is so soft and so smooth. I don't even know when the train leaves. I arrive into Tampere at 5.30 a.m. and I will be there for the whole December holiday with my best friend from Myanmar who is also studying.'

Back in our compartment, I cleaned my teeth, stripped down to my base layers and sat at the window with my diary open on my lap, writing down what Min had told me. In the glow of the nightlight I looked at the girls' sleeping heads. That one day they may be separated from us against our will, living alone, thousands of miles from home, was unbearable to imagine. Min was still a teenager, one who should have been practising piano, writing poems for pleasure, surrounded by his friends and family. Instead, he had aged overnight, pulled into political turmoil through no fault of his own, now riding the *Santa Claus Express* to spend Christmas with another teenager in the same situation. In spite of it all, he still found joy in the train journey, writing poetry – determined to find light inside the darkness. With one last look at the snow, I closed my diary and crawled into bed as the train swept on in silence.

16

THE NIGHTJET FROM VIENNA TO HAMBURG

'Maybe we can buy some chewing gum… or a lighter?' Ditta suggested as we reached the bottom of the escalator.

'*Lass das! LASS DAS!*' screamed a woman as a scuffle broke out in the doorway of the florist opposite. A man in a shabby suit scrabbled around as a woman wearing an apron shoved the door against the side of his face, where he was now stuck, one arm trapped inside, the other dropping a handful of notes on the floor.

'Holy fuck!' said Ditta as onlookers froze, unsure what was unfolding.

The man wrenched himself free and tore off towards the stairs as the shop assistant gave chase. '*Haltet ihn!*' she yelled, breaking into a Flo-Jo sprint.

Catching up, we watched the man tumble down the bottom steps, pick himself up and carry on as passers-by lunged at the wannabe Jason Bourne in loafers. Dutifully, we collected the euros he had dropped along the way and entered the florist to return them: long-stemmed roses and wet petals were strewn across the floor like a Valentine's Day gone horribly wrong. In shock, a customer picked up the buckets, recounting in German how the man had snatched money from the till.

'It's very sad. Vienna is safe, but there are many migrants who stay around the station. We can't blame them. We don't know what they have escaped.'

Vienna has a long legacy of welcoming refugees, with half the city's residents coming from a migrant background. It was a relief to hear empathy from the woman at a time when the Far Right was on an alarming ascent across Europe.

Ditta and I had arrived an hour earlier on the sleeper from Brussels. We'd struck up a friendship in 2019 when our children were colouring in rainbows together at nursery, firming it up when we'd both gone mad in lockdown. She'd recently revealed that she hadn't left the country alone since her elder son was born, which was close to a decade ago. On this horrifying news, I recruited her immediately, promising a few days' respite on sleeper trains, with museums, Michelin-starred dining – and a sex shop or two thrown in for good measure. Nightjet had finally introduced the long-awaited new fleet and as our train to Hamburg was not until 8 p.m., we were trying to stash our bags at the station. Neither credit cards nor notes were accepted for the lockers, and we'd spent the previous half-hour searching for a functioning cashpoint. Grateful to us for returning her money, Flo-Jo exchanged our notes for coins and packed us off before fetching a cloth to wipe blood off the door.

It was a little over a year since I'd last passed through the city en route to Istanbul, but it was Ditta's first visit and to her bemusement she had that week discovered her family had roots in Austria – and shoots all round the world. 'I'll tell you about it on the train,' she'd promised, darkly.

Today the sun shone happily across the rooftops as I retraced my steps from the first visit, making our first stop at the Belvedere Museum to soothe our nerves with Klimt – and some racy Egon Schiele – before walking into the centre. It was no less heavenly to see *The Kiss* for the second time and I thought back to how this was really where it all began, drawing up my dream night-train list at the Demel café. Time had flown and it was the beginning of March, the air humming with the promise of spring as we strolled through the baroque gardens, spindly branches about to bud, the faint drum of a woodpecker in the trees. The scent of sizzling wurst emanated from food trucks as we came to stand in front of a wedding cake of a building, gold ribbon wrapped around its tiers. Ditta put on her sunglasses.

'Vienna's very grand, isn't it? We could be in downtown DC, or in the past?'

The Austrian capital was the only European city where I felt physically small and mentally inferior. With a French degree under my belt, I'd read enough Racine, Molière and Sartre to feel at home around the frivolities of Paris – its Haussmannian boulevards wide, leafy and welcoming even if its people weren't. Vienna overpowered with its majesty, every other building a monument to dynasties and empires. Even H&M was housed in a historic mansion, with a spiral staircase and chandeliers lighting up the aisles for Gen Zs buying scrunchies and faux-leather leggings. Pacing in the shadows of Schubert, Strauss and Mozart, the legacy of their great minds entwined around the city, I was reminded of the enduring power of creativity. From time to time, Ditta and I would stop to inspect sculptures and statues, and I was convinced that some kind of elixir passed through Viennese waters.

'They've got so much swagger,' I said, pointing to a series of baroque sculptures on yet another splendid building which no doubt housed a Lidl or a SPAR.

'Hmm, I'm not sure,' said Ditta. 'They look like they're at an uncomfortable work event. No one's really talking to anyone. They're just standing there making sure the boss sees them before they can leave.'

We were now in front of the Leopold Museum, admiring the facade where two horse heads looked like one was photobombing the other.

'Do you ever wonder what we're creating now that people will look at in 200 years?' I asked.

'Pollution? Mass graves in Gaza?'

Taking a photo, we decided we'd had enough culture for the morning and took ourselves off for coffee and a slice of Sachertorte at the infamous Hotel Sacher. Either my memory had served me poorly or the baker was having a bad day, but the chocolate cake was drier than a piece of toast and I wished I'd taken Ditta to Demel. The venue seemed to have turned into the equivalent of the M&M's store in Leicester Square, the queue filled with Chinese women carrying Louis Vuitton shopping bags, local Viennese looking on in disdain. En route to a different district, we passed a shop with an early Easter display in the windows, brightly coloured eggs sitting on piles of shredded yellow nests.

'Oooh, I might get the kids some Easter bits,' I said, crossing towards the glass.

Ditta peered in. 'They're definitely eggs, just not the Easter kind,' she said, snorting with laughter as it dawned on me that we were looking at an array of love eggs at a sex shop.

'Definitely don't get the kids those. They'll be buzzing in the garden.'

European sex shops have a particular appeal. In the UK, no one local goes into Harmony on Oxford Street in case they get recognised while sifting through crotchless knickers and other items catering to kink. As teens we'd goad each other in pairs, coming out with chocolate willies in paper bags, giggling at the nipple clamps and chains. On the continent, no one bats an eyelid, stopping off as though popping into Tesco for milk. In the basement, Ditta tried on a pair of pink, sparkly Perspex heels to go with the dance pole fitted in her front room which left her perpetually covered in bruises. Normally five foot ten, and with carefully curled pink hair, she now towered like a burlesque star, to the enjoyment of a man with an anorak over one arm and an orange carrier bag in hand. He watched her from around a corner as I left them to it, a gurgling sound escaping his lips. To my amusement and probably that of the staff, the shop was playing 'Vienna' by Ultravox. The stench of latex gimp suits combined with eighties synth pop on a loop became too much for my delicate disposition, so I took myself upstairs and waited in the foyer for Ditta Von Teese, accompanied by a male mannequin wearing leather gym gear and a gas mask.

At the end of 2023, to the delirium of rail fans, Nightjet had finally launched its brand-new fleet of upgraded trains to increase capacity on existing routes. Built from scratch, with the sole purpose of serving as sleeper trains, the new Siemens carriages looked sharp and stylish. I'd browsed images of them on ÖBB's website, poring over the comfort-plus compartments which had extra space, pre-made beds and ensuite bathrooms.

I hadn't taken a Nightjet since my ride from Strasbourg to Vienna and felt certain that the spruced-up sleepers would appease potential passengers put off by the current state of Nightjet's knackered rolling stock. However, it was the mini-cabins that had caught my eye: single berths that resembled Japanese capsule hotels. They were designed to enhance privacy and passengers could climb inside, draw the door closed and not have to look at another human until morning. Only in the West would train operators go out of their way to indulge the traits of cold Europeans averse to social interaction. To me the beauty of night-train travel lay in the sense of community that grew out of the shared experience: hawkers waving pad thai under my nose; students sitting on my blanketed feet playing cards; the rowdiness of drunks ranting nonsense. Nonetheless, Vienna–Hamburg was the first route to get the new trains and I was curious to try the capsules. Ditta and I were now on board, staring down a long strip of two-tiered wooden lockers. Or a morgue, depending on your mood.

Brightly lit with soft grey berths and red blankets, the carriage was not designed for sitting around, chatting and drinking until the small hours. In fact, with the exception of a few pull-down seats in the corridor, it appeared as though a killjoy had thought up a layout that actively hindered any attempt to socialise. It also had the strong smell of newly opened furniture. Departing at ten past eight, the NJ 490 sailed away from the platform, thumping out of the city with impressive speed. Ditta stood back as I found our quartet of berths, which had three steps leading up to the top two berths. Above the steps was an actual set of lockers in which to store our shoes and bags. A young woman was already slotted inside one of the lower berths. She had her headphones in place and was tugging off the bottoms of her velour tracksuit.

With a quick smile out of obligation, she reached forwards and drew the door around herself and that was the last we saw of her until the morning.

'Night then,' said Ditta, quietly laughing into her jacket.

I could already see that solo women travellers might prefer such a set-up, even if it didn't appeal to me personally. And at €99 each way, the mini-cabin was cheaper than the ninety-minute flight.

The attendant arrived and turned her clipboard to me so I could show her our names.

'That's odd,' I said, 'there's a Cecily in your berth apparently.'

Ditta looked shifty.

'What?'

'That's me. That's my actual name. Cecily. Cecily Benedicta May.'

'Are you taking the piss?'

'Sshhh, don't tell anybody,' she said, hoisting herself into her berth, her biker boots dangling over the side as the top half of her face was obscured from view by the panelling.

'I'm not built for transport,' she said, getting a fit of giggles. She rolled sideways, pulling the rest of her body in and drew the door around. 'I'm going to change out of this sweaty top and put on a different sweaty top,' came her muffled voice as the attendant handed me two magnetic keycards which unlocked the cabin doors with a tap. She demonstrated that tapping the same pad again would open the lockers, the small one for my shoes and the larger one for my carry-on, which fitted inside with ease. Anything bigger would have had to spend the night in bed with me.

At the end of the train were separate loos for men and women but there was no dining car on board. This was specifically a sleeper train; not a sleeper-dinner train, but a sleeper train. Hot meals could be ordered from the attendant who was stationed at the other end, along with couscous wraps, ham sandwiches, Pringles, popcorn, peanuts and Haribo. Owing to the departure time there was no need for a dining car and ÖBB had no plans to introduce one.

The train was slowing into the first stop at St Pölten when I decided to put on pyjamas, crawling into my berth and turning around like a dog in a space which wasn't all that spacious. By the porthole window I discovered free Wi-Fi, a charging pad for my phone, a separate socket and a USB port, along with a digital panel to call the attendant for drinks and snacks. For no good reason there was also a switch to toggle the lighting between electric blue, witchy green and a brothel red, which I eschewed for darkness as I watched the platform sailing by. Snow was piled up as we swept past farms and riversides trimmed with coloured lights until there was nothing but the spatter of rain against the glass. This was not a train for window-gazing.

'How is your five-foot-ten-ness dealing with this?' I called out to Ditta.

'I'm all folded up. I fold up small. Like a greyhound.'

A hatch opened up by my elbow and her face appeared, eyes shining like a woman two ciders into a train journey.

'Sorry about that, I drank yours, I've got some lager though,' she said, lying on her back and dropping grapes into her mouth.

'You've turned this into a student flat,' I said, sticking my head through to find a bra swinging on a hook, two empty bottles of cider, Clarins face cream, an open laptop and a stuffed monkey sitting in the corner on her pillow. Named 'Safety Precaution', after his own label, the monkey came along to alleviate Ditta's travel anxieties, particularly when flying, but she'd realised she was perfectly content on sleeper trains and had no need to be soothed. The hatch was a nice touch to the mini-cabins. Only passengers travelling together could open them and chat to one another, while solo travellers could keep theirs locked. Having an opening also made me feel far less claustrophobic than I'd expected. I couldn't, for instance, handle having an MRI without tipping my head back to see the room and had worried that being enclosed would stress me.

'I've figured it out,' said Ditta, passing me a can of Stiegl. 'It's like sleeping in a bread bin.'

We were the people I usually hated when trying to sleep. From 9 p.m. passengers were expected to observe silence, but I was fascinated by Ditta's new Austrian connections and we chatted, like all good drunks, in what we thought were low voices. Out of the blue, her mother-in-law had bought her a DNA test for fun. They were intrigued by the origins of her elder son's red hair and while they found no information to explain it, it transpired that Ditta was a quarter European Jewish.

'It came back showing that I had a *lot* of what appeared initially to be first cousins – around twenty maybe? But it was weird, because none of their public family trees linked up even though they were all related to each other.'

'How is that remotely possible?'

'I sent emails to all of them in one day and this one woman replied with a big reveal. It turns out that my biological grandfather was Bertold Wiesner.'

'Why do I know that name?'

'He was an Austrian biologist who developed a fertility clinic in London with his wife, Mary Barton.'

'Wait, the creepy eugenics one for "high IQ donors?"'

'That's the one,' said Ditta, tipping the end of the Pringles down her throat. 'Except he made quite a lot of the donations himself. Probably about two-thirds. So this woman told me some of the names of the siblings and I googled them and they looked like my dad. I called my parents and told them and they got DNA tested to make sure it was him – which it was – and since then more of them have popped up. They estimate that he fathered about 600 children, but it could be as many as a thousand.'

The train pulled into Passau and we turned onto our fronts to look out of the porthole.

'We'll likely never know all of them as they burned the records… as you do with all good-practice medical clinics.'

Bewildered by Ditta's discovery, I soon snapped out of my thoughts at the sound of strange voices in the corridor. I drew

back my bin lid to find a handful of new passengers standing
around. They looked startled to see our faces, one man immediately reversing into the coffin below Ditta and drawing the door
shut. I began to wonder if the train was far more populated than
I realised, as it was impossible to know how many people were
on board without opening up each door to check. I could hear
lots of zipping and unzipping to my left, where a couple of men
were grumbling about the lack of space with good humour, and
I strained to listen. As much as I was enjoying Ditta's contor-
tionist performance, I wasn't convinced that tall men or anyone
larger than a size 14 would relish the ride. I'd sent a photo and a
video of the interior to my friend Julia who was almost six foot.
'*Thanks I hate it*,' came the reply. Followed by: '*Feel ill looking at
that*.'

Most of the new recruits were waiting for each other to stow
bags before they could settle in and in the interim one pulled
out a foldable tripod stool and sat down in the middle of the
corridor, chatting about his student years of interrailing: 'These
mini-cabins also have mini storage! You can put your bags in
your berth and then sleep outside, maybe?'

German intonation made everything funnier, and he looked
up at me laughing.

'*Guten Abend!* Have you ever seen anything like it?'

'Japan?'

'Ah *ja*, it is just like Japan?'

While his friends wrestled with their bags, the train moved
off and we compared train rides around the world, swapping
tips on trips.

'I think that you are a *Pufferküsser*?' he said, wiping his glasses
as his friends started laughing.

'Sorry, a what?'

'In German it means you are a fan of trains, a person who
kisses the buffers.'

I gathered this was not a term of endearment. 'I wouldn't go
that far.'

'Then perhaps an *Eisenbahnliebhaber*?'

Ditta was howling into her pillow. German was so literal in its translation that it was impossible to take much of it seriously. Bidding our companions goodnight, I drew the door shut and crawled back up to where Ditta was eyeing me with a smirk.

'Railway love-haver...' she murmured, before cracking open another can and slurping up the fizz.

Midnight had come and gone and I felt dreadful for the poor woman trying to sleep beneath us. I closed the hatch across Ditta and scrolled through my photos from the day, stopping on one that showed an old book lying open. Arriving into Vienna on the sleeper had graced us with far more time to explore than we'd realised and we'd managed to squeeze in a visit to the Sigmund Freud Museum, an extraordinary old house where Freud had worked for forty-seven years before fleeing the Nazis in 1938. Not only did it now display the family's private rooms, it also featured the work of his youngest daughter, Anna, a pioneer in child psychoanalysis. In a glass case, next to a copy of her book *War and Children*, was a note about what children need in times of war. It detailed how Anna and her friend Dorothy Burlingham had established wartime children's homes to house homeless and orphaned children, or those who had been brought to shelters at night by their mothers 'as safely and undisturbed by the events of the war as possible'.

The key point highlighted in the passage was how Anna and Dorothy recognised that 'the broken family bond affects the children more than war itself'. I had read it, aching with rage. It was now five months into the genocide on Palestinians in Gaza which had largely wiped out women and children. The UN had reported that Israeli bombs and targeted airstrikes had killed an estimated 12,300 children in that time, more than the number of children killed in global warfare between 2019 and 2022. Furthermore, more than 24,000 children had lost one or both parents. I'd watched the expressions of the museum visitors pacing around me, reading the notes and moving on. What use was it to preserve these observations, publish these books and nod along at information in glass cases while perpetrating similar violence?

The Israeli government and military officials had repeatedly and openly made clear their genocidal intent, and the cognitive dissonance of the Western world was beginning to melt my brain as I trawled social media seeing slaughtered Palestinian children on an hourly basis, parents running with tiny, mangled bodies, their brains hanging out of broken skulls. Like smashed grey dolls, babies were dug out of rubble, yellow onesies with elephants on one side, intestines falling out on the other. How could anyone face the day while Palestinians livestreamed their own mass murder?

My coat was hanging on a peg above my head and I reached for the lapel where a pin of the Palestine flag was permanently on display. In the morning we would arrive in Hamburg and I wanted to avoid trouble. German authorities were cracking down on any form of solidarity with Palestinians, arresting people for alleged 'antisemitism', many of whom included Jews and Holocaust survivors. Only a week earlier, at the Berlin International Film Festival, *No Other Land* had won the award for best documentary and would go on to win an Oscar. A collaboration by Palestinian filmmaker and activist Basel Adra and Israeli filmmaker and journalist Yuval Abraham, it portrayed the Israeli occupation of the West Bank and the brutality of the illegal take-over of land in Basel's home region of Masafer Yatta. During their acceptance speech the pair had called for a ceasefire in Gaza and had subsequently faced violent backlash. Israeli and German politicians decried the speech as antisemitic, and Yuval received death threats. A right-wing Israeli mob had turned up at his family's home, causing them to flee to safety in the night. Three weeks after the Oscar win, settlers attacked the Palestinian co-director, Hamdan Ballal, who was then dragged from an ambulance by Israeli soldiers and detained. I was now reading a tweet from Yuval in the darkness, heaviness in my chest.

'The appalling misuse of this word by Germans, not only to silence Palestinian critics of Israel, but also to silence Israelis like me who support a ceasefire that will end the killing in Gaza and allow the release of the Israeli hostages – empties the word antisemitism of meaning and thus endangers Jews all over the world.'

Turning onto my side, I wished that my square pillow was a little plumper, before folding my coat up and shoving it under my head. First, with guilt and shame, I undid my Palestine pin and dropped it into my handbag.

I slept on and off, waking at 7 a.m. and raising the blind to discover we were passing through the German town of Langenhagen, lakes and fields flitting by in the fuzz before dawn. My side ached from sleeping with my legs straight all night, unable to draw up one knee without banging it against the wall. With a restricted view, cramped and irritable, I hopped out of my cabin and sat on one of the pull-down seats in the corridor, watching pink light beam across the sky as though a military air display had passed overhead. With little else to do but wait for the sunrise, I nursed coffee and a couple of bread rolls and jam. The German passengers were also up, but stayed boxed-in, enough of a gap open for them to chat with the attendant who was holding a breakfast tray and looking confused.

'So, when I say we are vegan, we don't take butter. We also don't take milk,' said one.

'I have marmalade? Can you eat that?'

'Yes, I can eat marmalade, but not in my coffee.'

Twenty minutes before we were due into Hamburg, I opened my side of the hatch, releasing the stench of old cider. I gave Ditta a nudge followed by a shove, and an eye appeared from beneath a tuft of crumpled hair. She stretched, revealing Safety Precaution, who was tucked into her armpit.

'God, it's amazing waking up without hearing "Stop it! Stop it! Mama... he's doing this to me!"' she said, sitting up and pulling on her hoodie.

I didn't travel with women very often, mostly because they couldn't prise themselves away from children, work, elderly dependents or a combination of all three. But when I did travel in their company there was a different dynamic at play. Women

showed a distinct gratitude towards having time for companionship and conversation. I never found men rejoicing over this in
the same way, so infrequent was it for women to carve out a
slot for themselves. In ten years Ditta hadn't travelled by herself,
and for all her buoyancy, she was wrestling with a lot at home.
Wearing sharp red lipstick, a necklace saying 'Fuck This' and with
humour as her shield, she powered through it with the type of
resilience I only ever saw in women. By 8.40 a.m., as we drew into
Hamburg, she was pulling on her boots, ready to face another day.

It rained for the whole first day in Hamburg, providing us with
an excellent excuse to stay within the confines of the hotel,
which sat on the banks of the Alster Lake. Even when the
sun did come out, we decided to forego touring the city.
The weekend away provided a rare moment for two mothers to indulge in much-needed self-care. I'd visited Hamburg
before and neither of us could be bothered even to pretend that
we wanted to go sightseeing when the staff had laid the table
with champagne and chocolate gateaux, which we took up
to the panoramic spa on the rooftop. They'd also left a vase of
red tulips, pastries and a bag of beauty products that included
self-tanning drops.

'I might get a bit more use out of them than you,' said Ditta,
pocketing the bottle and biting into strudel.

For the first time in months I had time to read, taking breaks
in between chapters to shock myself in the iciness of the outdoor
pool, then dashing into the sauna to shock myself with the many
naked men slouched around. It was on my childhood holiday in
Cyprus that I'd first encountered the joys of German nudity
in a sauna, which contained an entire naked family – kids
included. In hindsight nudity probably wasn't allowed in Le
Meridien in Limassol, yet the family had imported their own
rules. In Hamburg the sign on the Finnish sauna was explicit,
bathing suits were absolutely *not* to be worn. The two of us

entered, feet burning on the wood, the hot scent of birch hurting my sinuses. Spreading out towels, we realised that while our train chats were revealing, we were about to get to know one another very well indeed. Ditta glanced round at the men who all appeared to have one leg up, like a troop of macaques.

'It's fine, they're all German anyway,' she said, taking a deep breath, lying on her back and wiping the sweat from her forehead. 'We won't see any of them again.'

They were all at dinner. And only one was German. The others were English and American, and they were dining with wives and partners, shooting lingering looks in our direction as we pretended we couldn't see them. For the finale of our adventure, we were sitting in Lakeside, a restaurant which held two Michelin stars, my Converse hidden beneath the skirt of the tablecloth. Over seven courses, we tasted every texture, temperature and flavour, from kimchi tempura to sweet Breton lobster in lemongrass oil. Carrots were twirled and tweezed into place, beetroot billowed with smoke, the skin of red mullet seared to wafer crisp. As a general rule I found fine-dining outrageously silly – waiters pointing at green blobs with a pinky finger – but the occasion was precisely what Ditta needed. Playful distraction, without the pomp and stuffiness. Each dish was a minuscule work of art, reminding me again of the power of creativity to alter a stranger's mood or mindset, whether that craftsmanship took the form of a sculpture, documentary or canapé.

On the return to Vienna, we'd booked an upgrade to experience the Nightjet's comfort-plus compartments, which were four times the price and ten times more comfortable. With only seven carriages in total, it was easy to spot ours as it sailed into Hamburg and came to a halt at 8 p.m. The compartment was fitted with pre-made bunk beds with fixed steps and a net to catch falling children. By the window was a table and a large seating area, along with storage for bags and coats. In ten minutes we were on the move, the repeated thud of metal coming from somewhere in the roof. There was a timid knock at the door and Ditta opened it to find the attendant carrying two small bottles of Sekt and a breakfast menu, giving me flashbacks to the Strasbourg–Vienna journey.

'God, they really want you to get pissed on this train, don't they?' said Ditta unscrewing the lid and taking a long gulp.

'Is it nice?'

'It's not shit, actually.'

'I'm getting Babycham vibes. I wasn't in the mood for it last time and I'm not sure I'm in the mood for it now.'

'Take it for the kids. Tell them it's what Mummy's teenage years tasted like.'

I caved and twisted it open, settling into my corner seat and watching the last of Hamburg's lights disappear before we were thundering south, nothing but our own reflections in the window.

'It tastes of shame,' I said, handing it to Ditta, who gladly finished it off.

There was so much space in our compartment which, in spite of the repetitive clang overhead, was soundproof and private: no one clattering up the corridor or shouting through the walls. Business travellers on the company dime would do well to book these up. It was a relief to have a private bathroom and I stepped inside to inspect the shower only to find that the previous occupant had left an abundance of blond hair in the drain and a bottle of Head & Shoulders on the shelf. At least the hair was likely clean.

'Do you need a poo?' asked Ditta, winking at me. 'If you do, I'll put my headphones on and give you some privacy,' she said, rummaging through the complimentary paper bag, which contained slippers, a flannel, an eye mask, earplugs and a tiny chocolate wafer.

'I don't think there are any secrets between us any more... Cecily,' I said, banging the door behind me.

'Fuck off!' she yelled from the other side.

I re-emerged to find her hunched over the breakfast menu.

'We have to tick boxes and stick it under the door if we want breakfast. It's very precise. Six items only. And that includes your drink. Two bread rolls is one component and the others include ham, smoked turkey breast, salami, calves liver pâté, Gouda slices, fresh cheese – and there's a gluten-free breakfast too. And a vegan one.'

'So, calves' liver then?'

'Yes. Times six.'

By 10 p.m. the train was up to speed. Curious about the onboard entertainment, I connected to the Wi-Fi and suggested we watch a show on Nightjet's Railnet TV. The first option was a film called *Poppitz*, an Austrian comedy from 2002 that told the story of a car salesman named Gerry bound for an all-inclusive holiday with his wife, and according to the blurb, his 'pubescent daughter Patrizia'.

'Next,' said Ditta.

'*Suburbia – Women on the Edge. Five women, whose biggest challenge so far has been surviving their daily hour-long luxus shopping tours burning up their husband's credit cards, are taken by complete surprise when suddenly one of them is divorced by her husband and thrown out...*'

'What the fuck is this?'

'How about *Dark Waters? The body of a 17-year-old girl is pulled out of Lake Mattsee...* '

'No! I'd rather drown myself in a lake than watch any of that.'

None would stream and the Wi-Fi soon stopped working, so we gave up, taking to bed with our books. It had been sitting on my shelf at home for years but as I left for our trip the title had jumped out at me and I was now reading *Nocturnes*, a collection of short stories by Kazuo Ishiguro. The final story, 'Cellists', opened with the narrator, a musician, explaining that he and his group were playing the *Godfather* theme for the third time, and my mind wandered back to the previous year's train to Palermo with Ariel. That journey had marked a turning point in our relationship. Whenever nervous friends were expecting babies, I told them that having children was like building your own best mate, and our train ride had firmed up that belief. We'd ridden along together watching the ocean and enjoying our picnic in bed as pals. Herman and his son Assar on the train from Berlin to Stockholm had struck me as having a similar relationship, and I understood better than ever after this weekend with Ditta that sleeper trains intensified relationships. The close proximity; the sound of the other sleeping; the need to tolerate, adapt and function in a state of symbiosis all played into a deeper understanding of the other. In two nights on board a train I'd learned more about her than I had in four years. Suitably sleepy from the sway, I slotted my phone into the wireless charging pouch and wedged in earplugs, taking the advice of the pillow upon which was written: *Dream now. Enjoy tomorrow.*

Over the previous couple of years, I could have counted on one hand how often I'd slept through the night on a train. For all its crystal and glamour, even the *Venice Simplon-Orient-Express* had slung me around for hours. The new Nightjet, however, cradled me like a baby. It was a little before 7 a.m. and I had slept a record stretch of more than eight hours without waking once. Turning around I reached out and nudged up the blind to find we were pulling out of Passau. I slipped out of the door and stood in the corridor to watch as the train turned at the Dreiflüsseeck, the confluence of three rivers: the Danube, the Ilz and the Inn. Austria to my left and Germany to my right, I listened to the eerie sound of the wheels passing across the bridge, the sun winking through skeletal trees. Spotting me hovering around, the attendant brought breakfast and I tiptoed back into the compartment and took a seat by the window, watching mist hang off the Neuburg forest like cobwebs, deer scattered in the foreground. The Inn river raced to catch up, its waters green and inviting in the softness of the morning light. Ditta was breathing deeply and I left her in peace. The train was due to arrive around 9.20 and she could certainly do with the lie-in before returning to her boys.

As national parks swept by and mountains rippled on the horizon, I made a ham and cheese sandwich with my six items and opened my diary. Through a combination of luck and good timing I'd managed to cross off all the sleeper trains I'd hoped to ride. Except for one. It was just so far across the world, and it wasn't one to experience alone. I needed a group of friends to accompany me, but that was a tall order. Accepting defeat, I closed the diary, sat back and sipped my coffee as the train carried on to Vienna.

THE ANDEAN EXPLORER

It was never too early for a pisco sour, especially when standing at the tail end of a train clattering through the Peruvian Andes. Besides, the froth was simply an egg in a different form. Practically breakfast. I whistled at the cocktail's strength and tartness and turned to lean over the railings of the observation car. The sun was already on high, toasting the top of my head as I watched the track narrowing into the distance. Unbothered by the train's loud and old-fashioned clacking, black cattle munched the remains of harvested wheat, the smell of smoke and farmland strong in the air. Behind me an electric guitar picked up pace. The live band's cajón drumbeat brought passengers to their feet and I looked over my shoulder to where a group of Ecuadorian friends in fedoras were jutting out hips, belted ponchos flaring out over white jeans. It wasn't even 9.30 a.m. and the party was in full swing, passengers dancing to 'La Bamba' and slopping wine around their seats – a far cry from the desolate Nightjet.

It was the end of June and I was on board the *Hiram Bingham*, one of Peru's two Belmond trains. Belmond was marking twenty-five years in Peru and the company had invited a small group of journalists and dignitaries to enjoy a week of celebrations. I couldn't quite believe my luck. It was my first time in South America and I was finally going to ride my dream train – but not for a couple of days. Half an hour earlier the blue and gold carriages had pulled out of Poroy station in the south-eastern district of Cusco and over the next three hours we would descend into the Urubamba valley – the Sacred Valley of the

Incas – before arriving at the town of Aguas Calientes, at the foothills of Machu Picchu. This train service had been running for more than twenty years and the *Hiram Bingham* was the only luxury train along this route, a 47-mile journey that was impossible by road. It was named after an American – the first Western explorer to come upon Machu Picchu in 1911, with the help of Indigenous farmers – and I couldn't think of a more stylish way to travel to reach the beating heart of Inca civilisation. A woman crossed the tracks behind us. She was holding the hand of a little girl in a tracksuit who waved through the cloud of dust and I wondered what local residents thought of this festive train rattling along through villages of half-finished houses with rebars poking through the roofs.

Eucalyptus trees towered along the tracks as we started to follow the curves of the Kachimayu river, which was no bigger than a creek, bubbling in the light. Imported from Australia by the thousands in the early 1900s, eucalyptus provided the oily wood needed to build railway sleepers, but the trees spread monstrous roots that stunted native vegetation, which was why they stood in isolation. Their branches were also too straight for Peruvian birds to nest in, rendering them an all-round hostile presence to nature, albeit one that was needed for construction. A fellow passenger tapped me on the shoulder as we took a corner, the brakes beginning to wail. He winced, waiting for the piercing noise to stop before asking if I could send him videos of the disappearing track. Hugo was a Peruvian journalist from Lima, also on board for the first time. He gestured to my empty goblet and asked how I was feeling.

At almost 3,400 metres above sea level, a handful of passengers were experiencing altitude sickness. A few years ago I'd been gripped by vice-like headaches on the Qinghai–Tibet railway to Lhasa, so knew I was prone to suffering. I'd skipped the previous night's gala at the hotel, following the advice to hydrate, avoid alcohol and rest. With an oxygen tank for company and a plate of risotto on my lap, I'd hugged a hot water bottle and watched *Miss Simpatia* – *Miss Congeniality* in Spanish – while the others had rubbed shoulders with the real Miss Peru. Or at least tried. Natalie Vértiz was at least six foot, towering over most of the men in her heels. Meanwhile, Edson, the hotel concierge, had brought coca tea to ease the symptoms and produced a homemade spray from his pocket that his grandmother had always used. The vial was stuffed with coca and eucalyptus leaves and infused with rosemary and cedar. Spraying it into my cupped hands, Edson had asked me to inhale twice, the vapours hurting my nasal cavities. On the third occasion, he told me to rub my hands over my head and throw my headache into a corner of the room. Sceptical, but not one to argue with Indigenous grandmothers, I'd done as I was told and in fifteen minutes the headache had gone. I'd slept soundly, waking to find our WhatsApp group blowing up with reports of projectile vomiting, along with calls for nurses, oxygen and ibuprofen. For reassurance, the resident doctor was now on board with his leather bag, tucking into steak tartare canapés and having a grand old time, bopping to the beats.

Announcing its presence with an insistent horn, the *Hiram Bingham* entered a town whose walls were painted in blocks of lime, orange and mustard. It ran so tightly to roadside butchers that I could see stacks of feathered eggs, and yellow chicken feet splayed in the air as though they each wore tiny pairs of Marigolds. Piled up in the shade were red and blue sacks of potatoes, and I'd just caught sight of a couple flirting on a corner when we departed, leaving me to imagine the outcome.

'I'm fine now,' I told Hugo, watching a trio of moto-taxis trying not to hit each other. They reminded me of Indian auto-rickshaws, only bigger. 'Mild headache, nothing major, but I might swap the cocktails for coca tea.'

'Coca tea is okay,' said Hugo, 'but muña tea is better, it is more relaxing. I drink it every morning.' He rubbed his fingers together. 'It's a soft Andean mint and it gives a slow feeling of wellness, not the sudden shock from coca tea, like an electrified person. At least we are descending now into the valley, you should feel better. Machu Picchu is lower, around 2,400 metres or something.'

In between the train's fog-horn warnings to farmers, kids and livestock tempted to cross the tracks, I asked Hugo about the Peruvian production of coca leaves which were regarded as sacred by the Incas, burned in rituals and used to heal. Coca was still brewed in tea, chewed to kill hunger, and used as a stimulant for labourers as they walked for miles. However, government officials estimated that almost 90 per cent of Peru's coca leaves were illegally used for cocaine. In the 1980s Hugo's father had worked as a police officer combatting small-time drug dealers, mainly armed farmers who supplied Pablo Escobar's Medellín cartel.

'We produce more leaves than Colombia and export them as coca paste,' said Hugo, 'but the Colombians have all the laboratories for processing the paste, we don't have that many. We have little airports in the jungle, but they're very well hidden. It's so vast, it's hard for satellites to pick them up.'

I asked Hugo if he ever thought they could win the war on the drugs trade and he laughed. 'Not in my lifetime. If the consumer is still there, in Europe and the US, the producer will be there.'

From what I could tell, a single ski season in Verbier was enough to keep the trade alive.

On the descent into water-rich landscape, I watched the scenery come to life – green, swaying and blooming. The Kachimayu river had widened, gathered pace and softened to a shade of olive, adopting the guise of the Huarocondo, owing to the Inca tradition of renaming each section as it flowed through different regions. After a brief stop at the town of Ollantaytambo, where new passengers came aboard, we returned to our seats for lunch, passing through carriages where wine glasses trembled on white linen. In keeping with the 1920s parlour-car décor – Art Deco lamps and polished wood panelling – I'd expected a stuffy meal and stingy portions, but found instead a variety of wooden and ceramic bowls laid out for sharing: soft pork belly with tucupi, Andean potatoes with aji chilli, quinoa salad, and choclo con queso – corn purée scattered with cubes of cheese – all of which was sourced from the surrounding Sacred Valley and speckled with teeny flowers. During lunch, clusters of bright yellow

Spanish broom thrust up towards the window, followed by pads of prickly pear, the fruit trimming the edges like spiky boiled eggs. Around us, the hillsides were cut into *andenes*, agricultural terraces that the Incas built to create microclimates. From the lowest to the highest, the difference in temperature could vary by up to 10°C, allowing the Incas to experiment with seeds and grain, birthing hybrid varieties of crops – one reason why Peru produces more than 3,000 varieties of potato.

Their puddings half-finished and wine refilled, passengers were reading quietly, glancing across at the glaciers still sparkling on Mount Nevado Verónica, while others were eyeing a Brazilian influencer perfecting her pout as a minion adjusted her hair. Behind me a table of Italians were having a volatile conversation about their prime minister's neo-fascism, when Alexandra sat down across from me.

'God, everyone's so suave and elegant,' she said, looking around. 'You just know they're not English.'

I had warmed quickly to Alexandra: a thirty-something from London with green eyes and bad hair. She was wearing an oversized Oxford shirt and cycling shorts and untied her hair as she eyed the Italians.

'Does it look terrible?' she asked, running her hand through. 'I know, it's basically a mullet.'

She wasn't wrong but I didn't know her well enough to agree.

Alexandra had been vomiting the previous night and was now on medication for altitude sickness, as was Bella, another member of our journalist group who was prancing around in a pair of tight black trousers and a poncho. Bella was chatting to Collin, a photographer from New York, and Diego, a jovial Peruvian in a pink T-shirt and beanie. Bella was doing her best to engage Diana, a novelist also from London, who appeared more comfortable behind a book than joining our conversations which had so far covered everything from Gaza and Alexandra's time working for Harvey Weinstein, to open marriages and constipation. It was a hazard of travelling in close proximity and at high altitudes where brains went haywire and pisco sours flowed freely.

A post-lunch lull settled and I wandered back to the observation car, in awe of the staff who managed to hold aloft trays of glasses without spilling a drop as the train increasingly wound round bends and tilted to the side, passing through ever-narrowing canyons and tunnels. Through gaps in the jungle I saw that the sky was bluer, the clouds like fluff. Spanish moss tickled the roof of the train, and I wondered if there were snakes dangling between the creepers. The Urubamba river thrashed below, roaring over fallen trees. As I scanned the slopes, I was reminded again of the singular charm of train travel that allowed me to invade the privacy of other people's lives: a mother drying tiny vests on a balcony, a child on a makeshift swing, a labourer whispering to his donkey. Catholic shrines appeared on boulders alongside flowers in old cooking-oil bottles, and I felt a surge of compassion for the soul who had left them with a note I wanted so badly to read. On a final curve, three porters crossed the tracks behind us, carrying backpacks for Inca Trail trekkers, and I realised we were approaching our destination. Tubular cantuta flowers brushed past the railings, like fiery bells ringing out our arrival, and with one last screech of brakes we pulled into Aguas Calientes in the Urubamba valley.

A bus corkscrewed uphill and on the ascent I could see how the Incas had kept Machu Picchu, their magical citadel, hidden from Spanish invaders. Creepers swung down the cliffs, trees grew horizontally, and clouds obscured the valley.

'I don't think I'm going to come in,' said Alexandra, picking at a shimmery nail.

'What? Why not?'

'I'm not mega up for ancient civilisation chat. I'm more of a here-and-now nature girl.'

'You've flown fifteen hours from London via Madrid, two hours from Lima, thrown up, taken a train, taken a bus and now you're going to hang around outside one of the greatest Unesco

World Heritage Sites because you can't be arsed to listen to the guide?'

Alexandra looked at me. 'The medication's given me explosive diarrhoea. I just didn't feel the need to announce it. But now that you've probed.'

After twenty minutes we arrived at a shaded plateau on the eastern cordillera of the Andes and merged with a small crowd jostling at the entrance, as Alexandra bolted up the steps of the Sanctuary Lodge hotel, barging guests out of the way. The medication had had the opposite effect on Bella who was bloated, eating handfuls of dried fruit and asking around for laxatives. With limits on the number of visitors permitted to enter Machu Picchu each day, we waited outside, long enough for Alexandra to return with a thumbs-up.

Inside, we edged along in single file, and I held my breath. Stone walls closed in, cool to touch, and I stepped out of the shadows to a sight I knew so well from photos: the Lost City of the Incas. With goosebumps, I looked out across the manicured terraces, like grass staircases leading down to a sea of cedar and *queuña* treetops. Rock steps ran up to small stone temples. Covered in tropical forest, the jagged mountains surrounding the sanctuary looked terrifying, the kind that trigger mad thoughts of how it might feel to run off the edge, slip down the side or get lost at night.

'Take a mental picture of where you are,' said Bella, striding along the path and fanning out her green manicure.

'Or just a... regular picture,' said Alexandra, pulling a quizzical face and taking out her phone.

A question mark hovered over the citadel. The Incas had left no documentation about its creation and even the name Machu Picchu meant nothing more mystical than 'old mountain' in Quechua, a language that was spoken but never written down by the Incas. According to our guide, the story of its origin and purpose was always unfolding and it was largely accepted that the emperor Pachacuteq had built the temple-city around 1450 in an attempt to expand the empire. Archaeologists estimated that

Machu Picchu had been home to a population of around 500 royals, philosophers, astronomers and climatologists, and given its location – linking the Andes and the Amazon jungle – it had probably been used as a base for political and religious control. While the guide was chatting, I noticed a pair of what looked like fat chinchillas freeze on the wall above. They'd been nuzzling one another, clearly annoyed that their foreplay had been interrupted by a busload of loud tourists.

'Those are viscachas,' said Diego, 'they look a bit more like rabbits than chinchillas.'

Alexandra wasn't wrong and I soon remembered that my own capacity for listening to guides was severely limited. I waited for the one teacher's pet to fire off enough questions that I could break off and explore by myself. Collin had vanished at the start, so Diego and I wandered around the temples together, spellbound. At least I was; Diego was here for the fifth time and took me in and out as though introducing me to an old friend, showing me how the Incas had designed their doorways and windows in trapezoidal shapes to withstand earthquakes. I placed my hand against the stones which were impeccably aligned, no indication of cement or grout holding them in place. Diego took out a credit card and pressed it against the space.

'It is amazing,' he said, 'it is so perfectly interlaced that not even a piece of paper or card will fit in between.'

Alexandra appeared, fresh from cooing over the cute quartet of llamas that were kneeling on the lawns. She gave me a vacant look that I'd come to recognise as her way of gauging how much I'd relish a salty comment.

'I love how the Incas built Machu Picchu, creating microclimates for hybrid grains and the Spanish were like "Hi, we're here to civilise you,"' she said, shaking out her mullet.

The sun was dropping and I watched as shadows lengthened like spectres. Hundreds of years ago the Incas paid homage here to the power of Pachamama, their Mother Earth. Worshipped as the one who blesses her people with food, shelter and fertility, Pachamama is believed to inhabit the mountains, bringing the rains and rustling the leaves. I don't believe in god or deities of any kind, but at that moment, in the silence, a powerful presence hovered in the chill, shadows and wind. The distant hoot from a train drifted up from the valley and I took one last look at the panorama, cloud floating in, before I began the descent.

Back in Cusco, I had a free afternoon before the final big railway adventure, and Diego had promised to show me where to buy coffee, chocolate and hats for the girls. We strolled downhill from the hotel, passing elderly women bottle-feeding baby alpacas decorated with pompoms, and demanding money for photos. Aware of the thinness of the air, I took the cobbles slowly, petting dogs wearing fringed ponchos, and stopping to sniff leather handbags. The former capital of the Inca empire, Cusco at the time had more importance than Machu Picchu and more significance architecturally, but now its streets and squares were shaped by numerous baroque churches and palaces that Spanish colonisers had built on top of Inca temples. Not next to them, but literally on top – demolishing the culture and artistry of the Incas with a deliberate malice that foreshadowed contemporary destruction in the Middle East. Enjoying the theatre and noise of shoppers haggling for alpaca blankets, cardigans and gloves, I learned from a young Quechuan woman selling patterned woollen hats that each line of design symbolised a specific element of the Andes, the spirit of Pachamama ever present.

'The red zigzag represents the mountains,' she said, in a delightful singing voice. 'The red is important: it is the colour of Inca resistance. The black is for earth and the curves are the rivers. And these colours... the pink is from cochineal, the orange is from lime salt and the yellow from cauliflowers.'

'*Cauliflowers?*'

'*Q'olle* flowers,' Diego corrected, 'it's a small tree with little flowers from the Sacred Valley.'

Weighed down by bags containing alpaca blankets, knitted alpacas, llama keyrings, pencils, coffee beans and seventeen slabs of chocolate, I waited for Diego to dither over a white fedora.

'There are so many Pride flags everywhere,' I said, noticing that they hung from almost every balcony and window. He shook his head, smiling.

'Cusco – it is one of the most LGBTQ-friendly cities in South America,' he said. 'But these are not Pride flags. This is the Inca flag. The rainbow symbolises that we come from the earth and return to the earth.'

Bella spotted us and crossed the street to join us. She'd been to have a nail repaired and was looking perplexed.

'Are you okay?' I asked.

'This guy in a wheelchair just called me a "fucking coloniser",' she said.

I bent over laughing. 'Why? What happened?'

'I was standing in the wrong queue apparently.' She put her hand on my arm. 'I did move when he told me to.'

In all my time witnessing fights where race had come into play – and there had been many – I had never heard anyone being called a coloniser and it signalled to me a seismic shift in how the subjugated were no longer willing to hide their feelings.

That evening at the hotel I tipped the entire pot of salt crystals into a hot bath, cleared out the mini bar of complimentary chocolate and packed everything that wasn't nailed down before opening Instagram, which I'd avoided for a week. The top post was from the Palestinian poet Mosab Abu Toha. He'd put up a photograph of a burned-out car with a detailed explanation of an investigation into the murder of five-year-old Hind Rajab and her family. Her disappearance had gripped the world for twelve days after she was last heard on the phone to the Palestinian Red Crescent Society, pleading with them to rescue her from where she was trapped in a car under Israeli tank fire that had already killed her family. Her remains were later discovered along with the bodies of the two paramedics dispatched to save her. The investigation concluded that the tank had shot 335 machine-gun bullets at the car, and a military bulldozer had then run over it. At the time of her death she was the same age as Ariel, her face uncannily similar. I sent a screenshot to Alexandra and sat down on my bed and wept.

It was now eight months into the genocide and the events had not so much tilted the world's axis as spun it off its hinge. Describing the Nazis in his Oscar-winning film *The Zone of Interest*, filmmaker Jonathan Glazer said in an Academy interview that 'genocide becomes ambient to their life', which aptly described the apathy in the West. What was happening in Gaza brought me to my knees on a near-daily basis. Back at home, I'd be tucking the children into bed, the breath squeezing out of my chest as I kissed their warm hands, grieving for the parents who no longer had children to put to bed and the children sleeping on their parents' graves. Even being in Peru, riding on luxury trains and sleeping in fancy hotels filled me with guilt. It felt wrong to talk about anything else while humans destroyed other humans, bombing hospitals and orphanages, burning libraries, blowing up schools and sniping toddlers, while Western leaders aided and abetted one massacre after the next, funded by our taxes. Gaza had made its way into everyone's lives, ending friendships, threatening jobs and dividing families, but it had also created something beautiful through resistance. New friendships were blossoming as allies found each other, risking jobs and reputations to throw themselves into the fight for Palestinian freedom. Alexandra was one such ally. She had recently become estranged from a parent who condemned her stance against Israel's illegal occupation of Palestinian territories, and we'd propped each other up, discussing writing as resistance, the impact of poetry and the importance of creating at a time of destruction. I didn't know her well enough to agree she had a mullet, but when she knocked on my hotel room door in her pyjamas, I knew her well enough to shift up in bed, where we each held alpaca-shaped hot water bottles with bells round their necks and talked until we slept.

The big morning had finally arrived and I was struggling to contain my excitement as we approached the platform at Cusco's Wanchaq station. Eighteen carriages extended along the track, but I didn't have to walk far, spotting 'Ñucchu' at the top and clambering aboard with Collin, whose compartment was one along from mine. Named after a native red flower, my carriage was, however, not native to Peru. In their previous life, these carriages had formed the Great South Pacific Express, a short-lived tourist train in Australia. After incurring horrendous losses, the service had ceased to exist and in 2016 the carriages were shipped to Peru and reincarnated, becoming the country's first and only sleeper train. The highest luxury train in the world, the *Andean Explorer* had jumped to the top of my railway bucket list: I'd stared at images of the carriages snaking through long grass at dawn, yearning to find myself on board one day, sipping tea and watching the sun rise over Lake Titicaca.

Until now. To my delight, our carriage was attached to the bar car and observation deck, and as the train rumbled out of the station, we picked our way up the corridor, listening to the familiar wail and squeak of the wheels settling in. On one side warped pieces of corrugated iron separated shacks from the tracks, and on the other a busy highway ran parallel as the train thumped out of the city, clouds of red dust in its wake.

Over two nights we would ascend into the Andean highlands, stabling at the city of Puno for a day trip to the islands of Uros and Taquile on Lake Titicaca, before ending the adventure in the old colonial-era capital of Arequipa. Our group had diminished: Hugo and Diego had returned to Lima, and Diana to London. It was now just Bella, Alexandra and Collin, along with around thirty-five other passengers to seek out and befriend – or avoid like the plague. Collin was a train novice: no more than the odd Amtrak under his belt. He stepped onto the observation deck, which was twice the size of the *Hiram Bingham*'s, a circle of cushioned seats in the middle, the shadows from wrought-iron railings marking the wooden floor with floral curls and hearts. From the tail I watched him taking in the bright, blanketed sofas, ceramic bowls of snacks, the bartender shaking a cocktail. He closed his eyes, the smile on his lips giving me a burst of satisfaction. Seeing a newbie appreciate a sleeper train was a joy in itself. It was like watching someone as they heard a beautiful piece of music for the first time, the recognition on their faces of all that a train could bring.

'This is insane,' he said. 'I can't believe we get to sleep on this. And you do this all the time.'

'Not this level of luxury.'

'For sure, but this is still so cool and you get to see everything.' Collin looked down as the train ran tightly to vendors, so close we could count the sacks of pink and purple potatoes, the ground carpeted with green beans drying in the sun.

'Pisco sour?' I suggested.

'Yes!'

'Boy from Ipanema' by Nancy Wilson played in the bar as Collin and I collected drinks and sought out the dining car, looking for the others. The carpeted compartments each contained a long banquette that folded down at night to make twin bunks. They also had an ensuite bathroom, along with a table and footstools, with blinds on either side for peripheral views of the scenery. But this was not the kind of train where you locked yourself away. The communal areas were homely, the shelves stacked with boxes of dominoes, playing cards and chess, encouraging passengers to mingle and make friends.

Under the sound of Andean flute music playing overhead, I noticed the train's determined *chook-chook-chook-chook* as we began a gradual ascent, our old friend the Urubamba river once again at our side. I ducked down to see the train had already shed the city like a skin and was galloping south-east through the district of Oropesa. It was almost lunchtime and I sat down, scouring the menu, which featured mixed quinoa, lupine beans and ceviche in tiger milk. So far Peruvian food struck me as fresh and full of natural flavours. With the exception of a little frippery and fun with flowers and powdered grains, it was mostly unfussy. Peru was one big laboratory, its people relishing the earth, watering it with love and reaping all its rewards from Pachamama.

'Everything's so clean and fresh,' said Bella, arriving at the same time as a tray of corvina ceviche, a buttery white fish marinated in lime. She steadied herself as the train went into a bend, then slid into a seat beside me. She smelled like freshly chopped wood: I asked what perfume she was wearing to which she responded by thrusting her neck in my face.

'Jo Malone?'

'Ugh, basic,' she said, looking repulsed. 'It's Santal 33 by Le Labo. Anyway, as I was saying, I feel really awake and healthy. Peruvians must be in such good shape.'

Collin speared a cube of ceviche then dipped it in chilli, pulling a face of appreciation as the tableware clinked and rattled. 'This is why in America people are all just fat and out of shape,' he said.

'I thought everyone in New York is fit and into wellness?' said Bella, looking shocked.

'Health and wellness in the US is so confusing,' said Collin. 'I think there are so many different schools of thought about what's a healthy lifestyle. You have Weight Watchers and you have all these other programmes that came up in the nineties and 2000s... that people still do...'

'Like Nutrisystem,' said a woman sitting across the aisle and taking a sip of her wine. I'd noticed her pretending not to listen, guessing she was American, and was worried she was going to tear Collin in half.

'Nutrisystem! Oh my god,' said Collin. 'It's a Ponzi scheme.'

'It's like a lot of money,' said the woman. 'And they'll send you crap food. So it will be like a tiny cinnamon bun, but it's just one little cinnamon bun and you eat that for breakfast. And then you eat one other little crappy entrée, and it's like $400 a month and you're basically just eating crap food.'

'And you don't know where it comes from,' said Collin. 'I think that's the point. The Western way, the way we interact with the land, the way we farm land, has been the same for generations, and it's not healthy for the soil. People are so disconnected from what their food means and that connection with the earth. They don't have a connection to the things that they're putting in their bodies and how it affects how they are as a person. Then there's all these different schools of thought, like "Oh you're overweight, try this programme" or "You want to lose weight, try this programme". I mean, you can eat a tablet and get skinny.'

'Oh, everyone is doing that Ozempic,' said Bella.

'What's Ozempic?' I asked.

'It's a drug designed for type 2 diabetes,' said the woman, 'but it's increasingly been used for weight loss.'

'This writer, whose name I can't remember, wrote a really honest and open article about how she uses Ozempic,' said Bella. 'But I didn't agree with it as I don't think it should be normalised. I think it should be used only when you're extremely over-weight. She's like you and me. She wants to lose five or ten kg and so she takes this drug.'

I blanched at the assumption and sucked in the top one of my stomach rolls.

'I think altitude sickness is the new Ozempic,' said Alexandra. 'I've lost so much weight since I've been out here.'

'That's because you've been yacking your guts out and not eating,' I said, releasing my stomach roll and biting into a skewer of tenderloin.

'I know, I look amazing. Do you think Miss Peru uses Ozempic?' said Alexandra, looking up her handle @msperu on Instagram.

Before we'd left Cusco, we'd bumped into Miss Peru in the hotel and chatted to her and her husband Yaco about ayahuasca ceremonies, where participants drink a powerful plant-based brew with hallucinogenic effects. He had a personal shaman who came to their home to perform a private ceremony and he explained the importance of being surrounded by loved ones so that you could cry on them once the drug and purging kicked in. Natalie had told us that she would never take ayahuasca, but that she prayed to Santa de Huanca, the lord of miracles. Natalie had repeated '*huanca*' at least five times until we'd had to stop her, crying with laughter, and explaining our rudeness as she wondered what was happening.

'Hang on,' I said, googling Natalie. 'She's not even the current Miss Peru! She was Miss Peru in 2011.'

'Wait, 2011?' said Collin, in disbelief. 'When did she set up her Instagram?'

'2012.'

'So, she's just sat on the handle for thirteen years? That is awesome.'

'The current Miss Peru must be so pissed off,' said Alexandra, feverishly scrolling.

'Your skin's amazing,' said Bella, suddenly. She was peering at me so closely I could smell her perfume again. Bella was a curious character. Half French and from Fulham, she switched in and out of fluent Spanish with lightning speed, observing everything like the hawks circling the valley beside us. She was fully lasered from the neck down, had zero sense of personal space and no filter, describing in skin-crawling detail how the doctor had manually cured her constipation. This went some way to explaining why she fitted in so well with strangers on trains and I applauded her for it.

After lunch we made an hour-long stop at Raqch'i to see the Inca temple of Wiracocha and a series of *collcas* (granary houses) which had been used to store dehydrated corn, potatoes and meat – including llama, alpaca and guinea pig – for up to two years at a time. Known as *cuy* (kwee), for the noise they made, guinea pigs were still fried, roasted or grilled on sticks and eaten with hot sauce. Wiracocha was a nice, short burst of Inca history, followed by a market stop where the village residents could flog their wares. Picking up two hand-painted ceramic mugs for the girls and a box of muña tea, I noticed a number of families were on board the train – with teenage children and twenty-somethings – which was unusual but exciting to see. For the most part these trains attracted retirees spending their kids' inheritance. I also clocked a group of Indian friends who had taken up half the train. From Missouri, they told me that they took an annual journey as a group of eighteen and were thoroughly enjoying Peru, with the exception of the food which was far too bland for their palates. My grandma had a tendency to find Western food tasteless, threatening in restaurants to pack pieces of meat that she could take home and refry with ginger and garlic. It turned out that the group had already spoken to the chefs on board and asked if there was cumin and turmeric in the galley and I immediately texted my dad who replied with a string of emojis crying with laughter.

Early July in the Andes felt much like being in the desert. During hours of daylight it was hot enough for sun cream and T-shirts, but the moment the sun had taken leave the air turned icy, temperatures plummeting to single figures. Zipped up in fleeces and leather jackets, we were huddled around the observation deck watching the front of the train barrel past villages, black smoke piping from the engine as it strained uphill. From the perfect angle, we could see its long body slinking like a snake around the Urubamba, the clouds turning yellow, their shadows shading the slopes. For the first time, I noticed that stems grew from between the spikes of agave plants, tall and twisted like candelabra guarding Catholic graveyards. Wheat wigwams stood tied in the foreground near families playing football and cattle swished their tails. In the twilight, La Raya mountain range looked soft, as though dusted with cocoa, the lights from townships like fireflies in the folds. Leaning over the railing, I watched a single halo of pink cloud hovering in the empty sky, a yellow strip of light sitting on silhouetted ridges. The tracks gleamed with the brightness of bars of silver against the darkness, the last of the light reflecting off streams as though little fires burned around the ground.

During dinner the compartments were made up, and I decided to turn in after a pair of ibuprofen for pudding. We had an early start and en route to Puno we'd ascended to almost 3,800 metres. A headache creeping up my neck, I opened my door to find the space had been transformed into a low-lit cosy room with a heavy duvet in place, slippers by the bed and my things folded, wrapped and hung up. After a hot shower, I lay under the duvet listening to footsteps going back and forth in the corridor, then feeling the train slowing I turned to lift up the blind. After dark, on board these trains, attention was focused within the walls of the carriages, and it was easy to forget sometimes that the world was still turning outside. We were in Juliaca, rolling through a level crossing as pedestrians and cyclists waited below the window, feet poised to pedal off once we'd passed. Locking eyes, we waved to one another as I sat up and took in what was a busy city, restaurants full, the streets heaving. Eighteen months earlier, Juliaca had been the centre of political upheaval, anti-government protesters revolting against President Dina Boluarte and it was hard to believe that I was now passing through the site of such recent bloodshed. As I lay on my front, staring at groups smoking beneath neon hoardings, street-food carts and markets just an arm's reach from my berth, the lottery of birth had never felt starker.

'You wanted to bring a fucking suitcase!'

Startled by the rude awakening, I checked my phone with one eye closed. It was just before 5 a.m. and I inched up the blind to find a violet sky, a scattering of stars still visible. The golden lights of a city were shimmering on water and I looked down to see a number of tracks. The train had stabled overnight at Puno station, allowing us uninterrupted sleep – until now – and I could feel the carriages rocking as passengers disembarked to watch the sunrise. There was always one 'character' on board these trains and, as awful as their presence was, they usually served as a catalyst for friendships as other passengers bonded over a shared disgust. Unluckily for me and Collin, she was in between our compartments and was now shouting at her children, the most morose teens I'd ever seen, or perhaps her husband, who wore a permanent expression of having just received bad news.

The woman had altitude sickness and wouldn't stop describing it to anyone who would listen – even those who wouldn't – moaning about everything from the cold to the heat to the way her husband took photographs. I sat up, looking for my trainers. Borrowing one of the kids' new alpaca blankets, I wrapped it around my shoulders and stepped into the corridor, wondering if Collin was still inside his compartment. He was on assignment and the sunrise was a highlight of the journey. The sky was rapidly changing and I knocked gingerly on his door.

'Collin…'

Not wanting to behave like my parents on holiday, but fearing I'd passed the point of no return, I tried again.

'Collin…' I knocked harder this time. 'Collin, I'm heading out in my pyjamas so you could probably do the same, don't worry about getting ready.'

The door flew open next to me. 'You're really loud!' shouted the woman, her blue hair hanging in limp curls.

'Oh, gosh, sorry,' I said, not sorry at all, but also not in the mood for high-altitude aggression. Abandoning my attempt to rouse Collin, I hopped off board, shivering as I walked the length of the platform towards a supernatural light. Whispering and muttering, stamping their feet to stay warm, the other passengers were sipping cups of coca tea, their breath clouding as they waited for the sun to come up over Lake Titicaca. The highest navigable lake in the world, its waters mirrored the sky, a deep orange band expanding on the horizon.

'Where's Collin?' asked Bella, adjusting her glasses.

'I have absolutely no idea,' I said, warming my hands on a cup of muña tea. The propeller of a little wooden boat buzzed in the distance and a pair of Andean ruddy ducks swam by, quacking in protest at our presence; otherwise it was silent. My legs ached and my breathing was laboured but the sight soon distracted me from my ailments. The colours intensified, pulsating until a nuclear blaze of light exploded on the lake. It took a few minutes to soften and settle, the water turning back to normal as the day arrived, along with Collin who was now walking up the platform as the rest of us climbed back on board for breakfast.

Like a cruise ship, the train was parked for the day at Puno, from where we took a ferry across the lake to visit the Uros and Taquile islands, which were inhabited by Indigenous communities. Around three miles away, the series of floating Uros were built from totora reeds that were dried, compacted and layered up to three metres deep. A wooden platform was built on top, which was also covered in reeds, and it felt much like sitting in a farmyard as we listened to the guide explain the method of construction. Six families lived on the particular island we were visiting and I enquired as to where the children were, learning that they were at school on a separate island. We were permitted to nose around inside their homes in exchange for buying bracelets, rugs and other bits and bobs for payment in US dollars; and once again I felt conflicted about the way in which we were interacting with Indigenous communities. This train was full of wealthy tourists providing income to the Uros people; at the same time, I wasn't sure I'd take kindly to a bunch of strangers crawling around my bedroom and wondering where I peed.

Back on the boat, a short ride took us to the much larger island of Taquile, which had a community of around 2,200 people, most of whom were weavers. As Collin and I walked up the sand we passed two Dutch friends who were walking the opposite way from the performance on the beach.

'It's too commercial,' said one, waving her hands. 'I don't like it. I'm going to sit up by the restaurant.'

It wasn't the best time of year to be selling woven gloves, hats and shawls, all of which were laid out around the restaurant area, and while the other passengers browsed, I went down to the shore with Collin. The sun was searing, the clear waters lapping creamy sand. I crouched down and waved a hand in, only to find it cold as ice. Together Collin and I clambered around the rocks, picking our way through huge bushes of pink geranium towards a small hill. Hauling myself up, I pulled off the spiderwebs that stuck to my arms like chewing gum, hoping not to meet the makers then panicked as scree escaped beneath my shoes. At the top I sat down on a boulder and looked around, taking a deep but ragged breath. An empty bottle of Jägermeister lay on its side, its owner knowing a good vantage point when they saw one. Like a Finn, I found no reason to chat to Collin, the view articulating all that needed to be said. A breeze trembled over the lake, sending ripples across the green and blue. It could have been a Greek island, but as I looked ahead to where the crags of the Bolivian Andes met my eyeline, I was reminded that we were sitting on top of the world.

With forty minutes for tea until departure, I was pacing the platform, checking my phone. I'd arranged another railway rendezvous and was now convinced it was not going to take place. A couple of years earlier I'd come across a book called *Fifty Miles Wide* by a British-Turkish writer named Julian Sayarer, who had cycled across Israel and Palestine detailing his encounters. We'd never met but had struck up a friendship online owing to our shared passion for Palestinian freedom. Our chats had intensified over the previous months and a few days earlier Julian had clocked that I was in South America after seeing a social media post. He was researching his next book, following the route of Che Guevara's *The Motorcycle Diaries*, and had reached La Paz the same day I arrived in Cusco. He'd decided that it was an opportune moment to try and meet and had ridden for a night and a day, covering around 130 miles to cross over the border, arriving in Puno the night before. Now, neither of us had any data or Wi-Fi to call the other and he was on foot, hunting out the train which was parked in a private yard, hidden from the road. Only fifteen minutes remained until departure, and my heart was sinking when I saw a figure, dark hair sticking out from under a turquoise beanie. Waving wildly, Julian jogged into the gates and we hugged tightly. His nose was bright red, sunburned from riding hundreds of miles at high altitude.

'Well, this is on brand isn't it,' he said, 'me turning up on a bike and you on a train.'

'In Peru!'

'How are you getting on with your journeys? Much left?' he asked, lighting up as he noticed the Palestine pin on my fleece.

'I think I'm more or less done,' I said, realising with a pang of sadness for the first time that my sleeper-train adventures had reached their crescendo on board this beauty. 'You?'

'Oh, I've got months left,' he said, 'heading from here to Cusco and Machu Picchu. Then out of the Andes, down into the deserts and the Pacific at Lima... then onto boats into the Amazon and Colombia.'

'And how has it been so far?'

'Good, been meeting a lot of Palestinians long displaced to Latin America.'

In the short time remaining, we managed to fit in a cup of tea and a pair of tepid empanadas before the train wailed in warning and we hugged goodbye, much to the confusion of the other passengers who were watching the encounter with curiosity. As the steps were drawn up, I made my way down to the observation car and leaned over the railings, as Julian walked alongside the moving train, waving us off, like a scene from the 1950s. Alexandra appeared at my side as the train clanked out of the gates and across a busy junction, crawling up a main road where a market was set up by the tracks. There were clothing stalls, vegetable stalls and mothers holding babies in their laps, cross-legged, metres from the rails.

'Who was that?' she asked.

'Another ally,' I said, watching his beanie disappear into the crowd, as she threw an arm around my shoulders.

That evening, after dinner, the train parked by Lake Saracocha where we were stabling again for the night. It was tucked into the slopes, not a soul for miles. Led by a guide, a group of us climbed the grassy pathway, the wind cutting. In the absence of light pollution, the sky glittered with millions of stars, the Milky Way a spray of silver mist. This hideout in the mountains felt like a secret, one that only a journey by rail could reveal. I looked down to where the train stretched out like a python. Through the windows, I could see Marga and Johann, a fun-loving Filipino couple who were celebrating their silver wedding anniversary. I could see the piano bar where the Missouri group were enjoying a singalong, sipping Scotch. From one carriage to the next, the scenes were joyful. Within the sleeper train renaissance, luxury trains were seeing a resurgence of their own. The Accor Group had announced the launch of La Dolce Vita Orient Express, which included a number of itineraries around Italy. Belmond had announced the *Britannic Explorer*, the first luxury sleeper in England and Wales, which would no doubt see a surge in tourists from America, Japan and China wandering about the Cotswolds. Even the Middle East was gearing up for its first five-star train service, with the launch of Saudi Arabia's *Dream of the Desert*. Everyone I had spoken to on board the *Andean Explorer* had travelled on luxury sleepers before and once they'd had a taste for the romance of opulent railways, they only wanted more.

Popping in a pair of earplugs, I slept soundly for a second night and woke to witness a final sunrise sending rainbow rays across the lake before we began the descent towards Arequipa. After breakfast I had a quiet hour alone in my compartment, getting stuck back into my latest read, *Aunt Julia and the Scriptwriter* by Mario Vargas Llosa. I'd started it on arrival in Cusco and had forgotten how funny it was, reflecting many of the relationship chats we'd had on board. Perhaps it was the short-lived adventure that allowed for the baring of souls, safe in the knowledge that the train was the keeper of our confessions. I made it no further than a couple of chapters, as I could hear shrieks of laughter. Always afraid to miss out, I put down the book to see what was going on and at that moment caught sight of the corner of my diary sticking out from underneath a blanket. I opened it onto the page of my bucket list, lines through every train but one. With a feeling of deep satisfaction, I drew a line across the *Andean Explorer* and closed the diary. My journeys were complete.

The majority of passengers were lounging around the bar car, giggling about Blue Hair who had come out of her compartment to scream at everyone for being loud as they'd made their way back to bed the previous evening. At breakfast she'd retold the tale to an unsuspecting bystander, calling everyone 'assholes' then immediately suffered another bout of altitude sickness. To Marga's horror she had repeatedly confused Johann for the onboard doctor, despite the fact that the doctor was Peruvian, not Filipino, and at least a foot shorter. She was last seen hobbling through the piano car with an entourage carrying breathing apparatus.

'Maybe if she saved her oxygen by not yelling she would feel okay,' said Marga, laughing behind her scarf and showing me photos of their children, as the other passengers followed each other on social media, a firm group of friends cemented in the final hour of the ride. I couldn't have wished for a better group. One last pisco sour in hand, I moved to the observation deck with Collin, who was writing a letter and staring into the distance. As the train thundered around meadows, we spotted delicate vicuña bounding through the dry grass, followed by swathes of yellowing wilderness. On the descent, we curled into a wide arc and the majesty of El Misti rose into view, one of the country's most violent volcanoes, its dormant tip scooped out. A trail of smoke drifted above and as we turned to watch, the mood became sombre. The train thudded onto flat ground, clanking past homes and gardens, the noise of Arequipa's traffic and roadside music rising around us. I looked back, knowing that something had left us. It was still in the mountains, rippling across the lakes and rustling the eucalyptus leaves. With a lingering glance at the twist of El Misti's smoke, I bade a silent farewell to the spirit of Pachamama.

THE NIGHT TRAIN TO PARIS

Warm, in my little nest, I lay still, relishing the sway. There was a reason why babies in utero slept for most of the day as their mothers moved around. It was also why rocking chairs felt soothing, and why sleeper trains lulled me to a state of calm. Rocking releases endorphins and for a few minutes after I'd woken my thoughts were clear, free from worry as I listened to the wheels softly thud.

It was now February, seven months since my big journey in Peru and I was returning to London after a couple of days in Venice, having travelled there once again on *The Good Night Train*. Since the inaugural journey from Brussels to Berlin, European Sleeper had successfully extended the route to Dresden and Prague and this month they'd launched a new winter service to Venice via Innsbruck and Bolzano. The carriages were still a pick-and-mix of rented rolling stock from the 1950s, but now there was a dining car attached and passengers had crowded in, drinking and steaming up the windows. Owing to last-minute Italian bureaucracy at the border we'd had to change trains at Innsbruck and Verona, arriving into Venice only a couple of hours behind schedule as the sunset fired up the lagoon. Few on board had minded. They were there for the train and the craic, the destination somewhat of an afterthought.

For almost three years I'd been falling asleep in one city and waking in another and each morning had felt like Christmas; the anticipation of nudging up the blind or pulling back curtains to discover something new – somewhere new. At times daylight flooded the compartment. Occasionally the night was still holding on, reluctant to take leave, a sliver of moon and a shard of sunlight sharing the stage together. But what was always present was a moment of wonder. Shuffling down the berth in my sleeping bag, I pushed up the blind to find a milky blue sky crisscrossed with pink contrails. It was a little before 8 a.m. and the train was entering the commune of Melun, on the south-eastern outskirts of Paris. The silver body of the Seine flowed behind leafless woods, lined up like a row of stencils, birds' nests knotted into bare branches. Tight to the river, the train allowed me to indulge once more in a sunrise that was burning like a bonfire, an obscure cloud appearing like smoke at the tip. It looked cold outside and I could almost smell the moss and morning dew. Bands of wood, water and forest mist swirled between the train and the horizon, and I stared into the heart of the growing light as though drawing on its warmth.

Fishing out my socks from the bedclothes, I sat on the edge of the berth thinking back to moments of solitude over the previous three years, when I'd sat quietly at a window staring into the ink-black lakes in Finland, the shadows of the Andes, the misty clifftops in Aberdeen. I understood now why I found night trains so alluring: they helped me to move through darkness with protection. That space, both geographical and temporal, felt safe to navigate from within the confines of a cosy compartment. Secure under the softness of blankets, my presence was concealed from those looking back at me. Sleeper trains enabled me to work my way through the night, discovering for myself that peace lay in the darkness.

I pulled on my shoes and stepped into the corridor. Only one other passenger was awake as I went in search of the kiosk serving coffee. He was standing at the window, gazing out across the water and I watched his chest rise as he breathed in the sight, a small smile on his face, one I knew too well. Back in my compartment, I drew the door shut and got back into my berth, moving towards the window and watching the sunrise reflecting in the river, the trees upside down. In the warmth of many sleeper berths, I'd risen to dawn breaking all over the world, watching commuters shovelling driveways, lights flickering on in bedrooms and farmers trudging across fields to feed their flocks. Each moment had felt like an honour, a stroke of luck to catch the movements others would never see. Pulling the covers around my shoulders, I flicked back through my Rolodex of memories and came to rest on Elena on the *Dacia*, Susan on the *Silver Meteor* and Ender on the *Doğu Express*. Their lives revolved around these night trains, which they relied upon for work and study; while I stepped on, rummaged around their world for a night, then stepped off. And yet, that short time on board was enough for me to remember the scent of Elena's jumper and her buoyant morning greeting; the generosity of Ender's spirit; and Susan's soft Southern drawl as she'd held my arm and thanked me for making her time on the platform more fun.

When I'd first clocked the rumble of sleeper trains returning to the tracks, I'd wondered how long the trend would last, but it was much more than nostalgia bringing passengers back onto the rails at night. So many were passionate about climate change, and for them there was no going back to old habits and short-haul flights. They and countless others were geared up for the fight to keep night trains alive. After four years of fundraising effort, the French start-up Midnight Trains had given up on its dreams to launch a 'hotel on wheels' and admitted defeat, but Interrail had experienced another record year of sales in 2023, Nightjet's new fleet was thriving, and European Sleeper was proposing another new route, to Barcelona this time. Outside Europe there was now a direct sleeper from Bangkok to Vientiane, a high-speed sleeper from Hong Kong to Beijing and Shanghai, and towards the end of 2024 Amtrak had launched the *Floridian*, a two-night ride between Miami and Chicago via Savannah, DC and Pittsburgh. September 2025 would mark 200 years since George Stephenson's locomotive pulled the world's first passenger train on a public line, between Stockton and Darlington, and I felt the engineer would have been astonished to see the expansion of his pioneering work.

We approached Paris, and I stared into the water, recalling the bread bin to Hamburg, the suite on *The Royal Scotsman* and the reclining seats on the Nordland line to Bodø. But what I remembered most clearly wasn't the nifty tech, the polished wood panelling or the softness of the covers. It was the people sitting alongside: Ditta with her cider and Safety Precaution; my mum sketching the deer; Marc deep in meditation. These trains had swept me up darkening coastlines, pulled me over brightening borders and drawn me through towns at twilight, but what they'd given me was the gift of slowness and time. Time with my family, time to firm up friendships and valuable time by myself. They'd allowed me to enter realms of darkness, guiding me through and showing me beauty where my fears once lay. No one can predict the future of travel, but one thing was certain: night trains embodied the essence of railways, and they would continue to ignite the flames of romance for as long as they were here.

Acknowledgements

In 2010, when I stepped off the eightieth train in India and my flip-flop snapped from exhaustion, I vowed never again to embark upon anything of that scale, madness and intensity. Little did I know that it was only the beginning and the next fifteen years of my life would be given over to three further books about the magic of life on the rails. Writing is a private endeavour, solitary and sometimes lonely, but my observations and opinions are just a small part of the machinery that births a book.

None of this would be possible without David Godwin, my agent extraordinaire, or Michael Fishwick, whose fear of flying and love of sleepers allowed me to twist his arm into taking on yet another book about trains. Being part of the Bloomsbury family continues to be a delight and I'm indebted to Jasmine Horsey for excellent edits, generosity with praise and support, and to Lauren Whybrow, Kate Johnson, Gurdip Ahluwalia, Anna Massardi and Akua Boateng for looking after the book so lovingly. Special thanks to Charlotte Phillips and Jing Zhang for the cover and illustrations – I couldn't have wished more for a design of such elegance.

My heartfelt thanks go to Ahmet Erdem Tozoğlu, Deniz Mert iÇÖZ, Vedat Türk, Ferhat Karabulut, Erik Sveberg Dietrichs, Ericka Phillips, Todd Harris, Taía Harris, Alfio Puglisi and Urmila Dongre for welcoming me into their homes, restaurants and bars, walking me around their cities, fact-checking my pages and trusting me with their stories. The team at Kazerne Dossin were extraordinarily helpful in providing access to archival sources around the 20th Convoy as were Nico Wouters and Dr Laurence

Schram, and I thank Simon Gronowski in particular for tirelessly giving his testimony. Professor Russell Goulbourne, Rajendra B. Aklekar, Gareth Dennis, Jon Worth, Koen Berghuis, Diana Novaceanu, Chris Guichot de Fortis and Jamie Lafferty offered their expertise which ranged from editing the entire manuscript, interpreting, and inserting facts about loos, to swapping head-lamps for brake lights, correcting distances and balking at eating haggis in summer: these edits were priceless.

While solo travel suits some, I know that this book would be nothing had I not shared compartments, kebabs and confessions with Jamie Fullerton, Ramin Farahani, Rekha Rajesh, Adrian D'Enrico, Jeremy Bassetti, Alexa Withers, Diego Cánovas, Alexandra Perreira, Collin Hughes and Benedicta Bywater – all power to your Perspex heels, lady.

Writing a book isn't easy, not least when the world is on fire and we're watching Palestinians live stream their own genocide for 20 months. There were days when I couldn't type, couldn't eat, couldn't sleep, throwing my notes aside in a state of despair. But a handful of people kept me going, reminding me of the need to hope, to write and resist. Thank you Chimene Suleyman, Faiza Khan, Caroline Eden, Humaa Jamil, Professor Sunny Singh, Sam Missingham, William Dalrymple, Julian Sayarer, Matthew Teller, Taran Khan, Mishaal Khan, Julia Buckley, Adam Benzine, Edward Price and my parents, for memes, gifs, hugs, humour, wisdom and advice. And of course, to Marc Sethi for your big laughs, beautiful photos and love.

To my darling girls, I've kicked you out of the office four times while writing this, but one day I hope you will forgive my absences and inability to plait your hair on demand, and that you'll see how I write from a place of love, in the hope of leaving behind the world for you in a better way than I found it. You're already such curious little travellers with much empathy and understanding and I put that down to your dad. Jem, the last five years would not have been possible without your calm, generous spirit and eternal faith in me. Thank you.

A NOTE ON THE AUTHOR

MONISHA RAJESH is a British journalist whose writing has appeared in *Time* magazine, the *New York Times* and *Vanity Fair*. Her first book, *Around India in 80 Trains*, was named one of the *Independent*'s best books on India. Her second book, *Around the World in 80 Trains*, won the *National Geographic Traveller* Book of the Year and was shortlisted for the Stanford Dolman Travel Book of the Year. In 2023, Rajesh was named in *Condé Nast Traveller*'s Women Who Travel Power List, alongside Eva Longoria, Padma Lakshmi and others. She lives in London.

A Note on the Type

The text of this book is set in Bembo, which was first used in 1495 by the Venetian printer Aldus Manutius for Cardinal Bembo's *De Aetna*. The original types were cut for Manutius by Francesco Griffo. Bembo was one of the types used by Claude Garamond (1480–1561) as a model for his Romain de l'Université, and so it was a forerunner of what became the standard European type for the following two centuries. Its modern form follows the original types and was designed for Monotype in 1929.

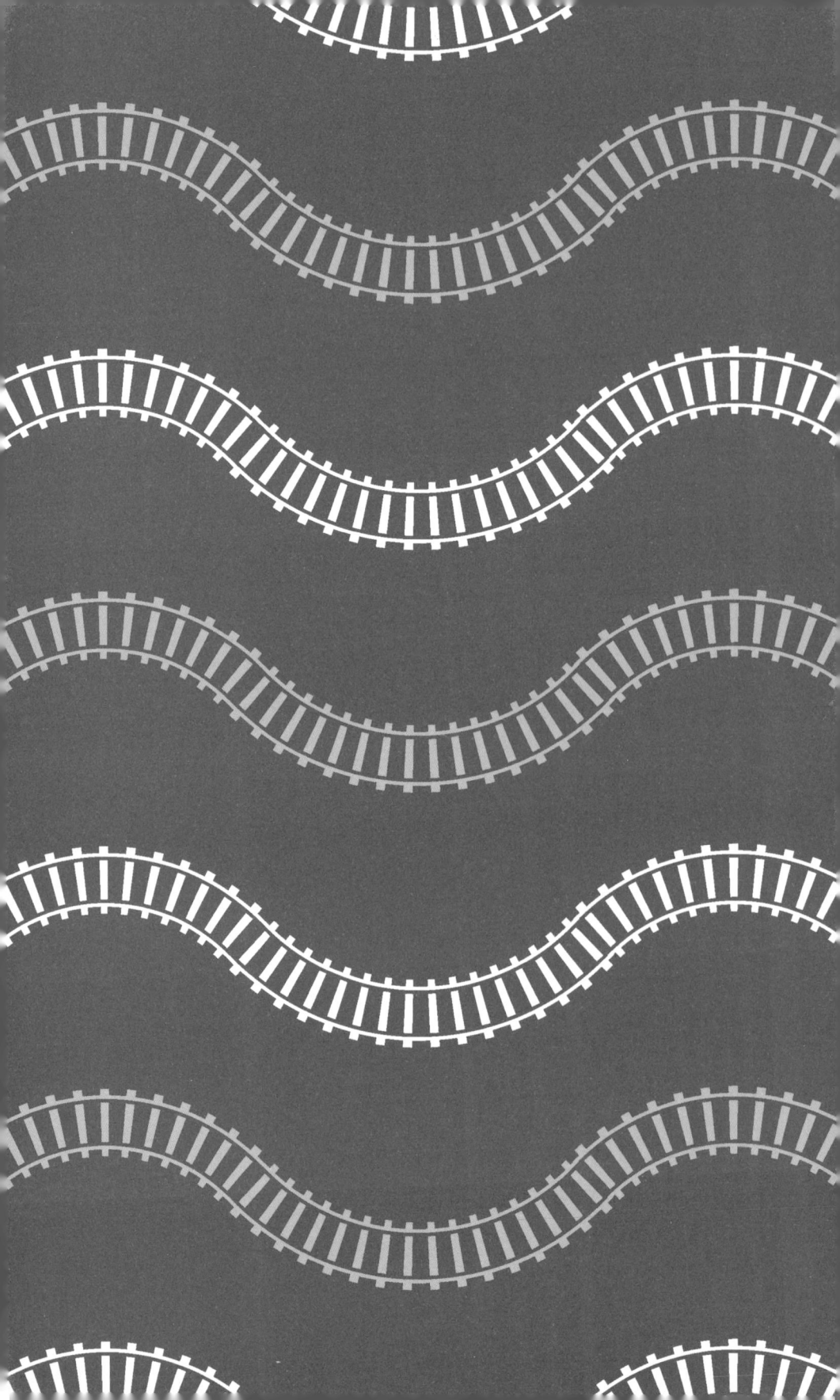